THE WORLD OF WILLIAM

ii

By the same author

Love and Drollery
Jest Upon Jest
The Demaundes Joyous
Kings, Lords and Wicked Libellers
The Caricatures of George Cruikshank
Juggernaut
Cruikshank 200
Lovers, Rakes and Rogues

The World
of
William
Hone

A new look at the Romantic age
in words and pictures of the day

Compiled, introduced and annotated
by
JOHN WARDROPER

Shelfmark Books
London

iv

British Library Cataloguing-in-Publication Data
A catalogue record for this book is
available from the British Library

ISBN 0-9526093-2-0 — paperback
ISBN 0-9526093-1-2 — hardback

Shelfmark Books, 60 St Paul's Road, London N1 2QW

Set in Palatino
And printed in Great Britain by Biddles Ltd, Guildford

CONTENTS

vi

ILLUSTRATIONS

'I have been a lover of the world and its pleasures,
a curious observer of men and manners,
an insatiable reader in search of truth,
an anxious inquirer after happiness'

Sketch of William Hone, done by Edwin Landseer in 1818
just after Hone's dramatic acquittal on blasphemy charges

The fact that Landseer, then a precocious 15-year-old, was
a pupil of Benjamin Robert Haydon will account for his
meeting Hone, for Haydon was acquainted with reform-
minded figures such as William Hazlitt and Leigh Hunt.

Present whereabouts of the drawing unknown
Photograph courtesy of the National Portrait Gallery, London

William Hone, an uncommon man

THE CREATOR of this book is William Hone. He published many things, but the most substantial were three unfading treasuries of high and low learning, humour, poetry, art and warmhearted reporting: *The Every-Day Book*, *The Table Book*, *The Year Book*. Here for the first time, and in an accessible format, is a selection from what Hone's public enjoyed during a few years of the turbulent, romantic and reforming age a little before the reign of Queen Victoria.

A short account of Hone's life will give some idea of his times and especially of the publishing world in which he produced these works. Born in 1780, Hone was in the course of more than forty working years a clerk, bookseller, book auctioneer, printer, radical pamphleteer, satirist, journalist, innovative publisher, poet and bankrupt. He fought for reform. He believed in social and economic progress, but also delighted in old customs and unspoilt rural scenes, and grieved at their passing. In his early years he was an atheist, having become at sixteen, he said, 'a believer in all unbelief' (partly in reaction against his father, a 'sinner saved'), but late in life himself became devout.

Three of his early memories are clues to the making of this complex, humorous, troubled man.

As a boy he would chat with a cobbler whose shop was near his home in the Holborn district of London, 'an honest old man who patched my shoes and my mind'. Young William won 'so much of his good-will and confidence' that he lent the boy some fragments of early printing, from William Caxton's *Polychronicon* (1482) and Richard Pynson's *Shepherd's Kalendar* (1506), which he kept in a drawer with tools of his trade. In those days cobblers were notable among artisans as literate men, thinkers, often radicals. 'This blackletter lore, with its woodcuts,' says Hone, 'created in me a desire to be acquainted with our old authors, and a love for engravings.'[1]   (*For source-notes, see p 315*)

He also soon discovered the fields and green lanes which then, in the 1780s and '90s, began not far north of Holborn. He used to ramble out and 'frolic in the newmown hay or explore the wonders of the hedges and listen to the songs of the birds'.[2] Years later, as he saw new streets thrusting into the fields on every side of London, he bemoaned the loss, as a number of passages in the present book show.

His earliest political memory was of the day when, just turned nine, he was bowling his hoop in the street and a boy he knew told him excitedly, 'There's a revolution in France!'[3] That revolution of 1789 stirred up in Britain the sharpest outcry yet heard for reform of its own unjust, corrupt political system. Hone began fighting for that cause in his teens by joining the leading radical association, the London Corresponding Society; but soon this and other reform movements were pushed underground by William Pitt's repression of everything he saw as sedition.

Having left school at thirteen, Hone clerked in lawyers' offices, longing to escape — 'fit only for literature', he said. His education came from every book he could get his hands on. In 1800 he married, and with the help of his wife's mother set himself up as a bookseller, a role which in those days often extended to some publishing. In 1801 he is recorded as becoming the partner of a master printer, Kidd Wake: a significant name, for Wake had just finished doing five years hard labour for shouting 'No George! No war!' at George III's carriage during a radical demonstration in 1795. It is probably from Wake that Hone acquired the printing skills that were to serve him well.

Soon he began a bookselling/publishing partnership with another radical, John Bone, who as secretary of the London Corresponding Society had been seized on a treason warrant and held in jail, untried, for three years. The two later took over the business of an older radical, J S Jordan, notable as the publisher in 1791/2 of Thomas Paine's *Rights of Man*, a work whose democratic daring kept it on the banned list for most of Hone's life. The partners, however, had other material to work on, such as the scandal of George III's favourite son, the spendthrift Duke of York, commander-in-chief against Napoleon, who financed his costly mistress by the sale of commissions.

Established in Fleet Street, in the midst of all sorts of publishing, Hone was well placed to exchange unservile ideas with journalists and others. One was George Cruikshank, an artist twelve years his junior, who was etching caricatures for a satirical monthly, *The Scourge*, and for various other outlets. Hone knew Cruikshank as early as 1811: in the corner of a caricature of that date (exposing a phoney evangelist), the nineteen-year-old Cruikshank introduces a group of friends: himself, his brother, Hone and the *Scourge* publisher. It was to be a friendship, and professional relationship, of many years.

Early days:
George Cruikshank,
just 19, puts himself
(holding sketchpad)
and friends into a
corner of one of his
caricatures, 'Interior
View of the House of
God', in 1811.
On left, W N Jones,
publisher of *The
Scourge*. Hone is
behind George, talking
to George's brother
Robert, also an artist.

Soon after the defeat of Napoleon, Hone launched out on his own as a publisher. When the government no longer had the war as an excuse for stifling all attempts at reform, it seemed a time for a lively new polemical scene to open. In his first two and a half years he issued 'upwards of one hundred and thirty pieces, chiefly of my own production'.[4] Many of these were what he called political squibs: pamphlets, illustrated broadsides and caricature prints. He abhorred Britain's role in establishing the reactionary Holy Alliance on the continent. The first things he employed Cruikshank to do for him were caricatures on this theme. One shows the vastly fat Louis XVIII, France's restored Bourbon, climbing the slippery pole, supported by Wellington's sword, John Bull's money and the monarchs of the Holy Alliance. Another, 'The Royal Shambles', shows John Bull forced to march in a Holy Alliance parade over the bodies of crushed republicans, with Louis riding on a 'divine right' cannon, monks rejoicing and protestants suffering brutal torments and decapitations.

At home, the target was the Prince Regent and his unloved Tory ministers. It must be noted that although the editors of newspapers or the authors of pamphlets risked jail if they *wrote* too frankly about a corrupt parliament or the dissipated, adulterous, bloated, unprincipled spendthrift who was performing the functions of majesty on behalf of his mad father, caricatures were by long custom above, or beneath, prosecution. Hone created a series of attacks on the regent's uncaring luxury in the midst of distress — sixpenny broadsides with comical Cruikshank images of a regent not potent and royal, 'the First Gentleman of Europe', but infantile and ridiculous. And the regent was pained by ridicule.

In 1817 the government thought it saw a chance to silence Hone. He published three unillustrated twopenny pamphlets satirizing ministerial corruption. The regent and his ministers and a vast array of sinecurists and understrappers were alarmed in this postwar period by agitation for reform, but they could no longer always count on juries to find disaffected writings seditious. Hone's pamphlets, however, seemed a sure target for prosecution, for they were parodies of the Church of England catechism, litany and creed. The attorney-general prosecuted him for the high crime of blasphemy, and hypocritically declared that there was 'nothing of a political tendency' in such passages as this (Tory MPs speaking): 'Our Lord who art in the Treasury, whatsoever be thy name, thy power be prolonged... Give us our usual sops and forgive us our occasional absences on divisions... Turn us not out of our places, but keep us in the House of Commons, the land of pensions and plenty; and deliver us from the people.'[5]

An event of Hone's boyhood helped to preserve him from a long jail term. At the age of eleven, already a browser for old books, he came upon 'an old printed leaf which seemed to be part of an energetic defence of some man'. He took it from bookshop to bookshop until he found one that had the book from which it came — a report of the trial in 1651 of John Lilburne, leader of the Levellers, for publishing pamphlets denouncing Oliver Cromwell's monarchic power. Hone saved up his pennies, bought the book for two shillings and sixpence (such bargains were possible then), and read the transcript of Lilburne eloquently defending himself, lawyerless, over many hours. 'Since the Pilgrim's Progress no book had so riveted me,' Hone recalled. 'I felt all Lilburne's indignant feelings, admired his undaunted spirit, rejoiced at his acquittal, and detested Cromwell as a tyrant.'[6] When Hone went on trial at the London Guildhall, after having been held for a long spell in King's Bench Prison, Lilburne was his model. Many parallels can be found between Lilburne's trial and Hone's — especially in his appeals to the jurors as independent defenders of a lone man persecuted by lordly power.

He did not find his most persuasive arguments in lawbooks but in a collection of lampoons and prints (Cruikshank helped to provide them) which had parodied scripture but had never been prosecuted — because, as Hone said, they were 'on the right side'. One was even by a member of the cabinet, the witty George Canning. 'If I am con-victed,' Hone told the judge, 'he ought to follow me to my cell.'

The jury acquitted him on the first charge. The lord chief justice, furious, himself took over. Again it was Not Guilty. By now Hone was exhausted, having spoken in his defence for nearly thirteen hours, but the prosecution persisted. As the third day opened he almost col-lapsed, but he roused his spirits, kept on his feet another seven hours and won a final acquittal. Those were 'three remarkable days', he said, 'that will never be blotted from my calendar'.

The verdicts were greeted by cheering crowds as a blow for press freedom. News of his triumph swept through the country. He gained distant friends. A printer at Bungay, Suffolk, John Childs, sent him a turkey (it was just before Christmas), and sent one every Christmas thereafter. Childs said he would not let his children forget Hone's victory, 'for on every Christmas day I give them the history of your prosecutions, and give the toast, "Mr Hone and his jury" — which I and my sons drink with all the noise we can make'.[7]

Such was the mood of many people in those pre-reform days. But the ordeal had so disordered Hone's health that for a time he was almost silenced. He tried bookselling and auctioneering again. With a letter of recommendation from William Godwin he got a ticket for the British Museum library and began researching for a History of Paro-dy; but a year after the trials he wrote to Childs, 'I have been, and am, ill — dying but not dead. Blood at the head, apoplectic affection — cupping — bleeding — blistering — lowering — a fortnight at Bath, &c — vexation at home and habitual melancholy which increases upon me... The Trials have given me a physical shake which has com-pelled me to abandon what I entered upon with alacrity and spirit, the sales by auction of libraries, &c...'[8]

He did however publish a full report of his trials, as well as an early William Hazlitt collection, *Political Essays*. And in 1819 examples of deadly injustice twice stirred him into action.

Near the shop he now occupied at No 45 Ludgate Hill, men and women were frequently hanged outside Newgate jail for passing (knowingly or innocently) forged £1 notes. In the course of twenty years, more than 300 had been hanged, but the Bank of England had done nothing to change the note's easily imitable copperplate design. Hone and Cruikshank invented a 'Bank Note not to be imitated', in which elements of the real note were transformed into shackles, skulls, a noose and a row of hanged people. It was a big seller.

In August 1819 came news of a murderous attack by sabre-wielding cavalry on a peaceful mass meeting of reformers at Manchester — the event still remembered as the Peterloo Massacre. The regent announced his 'great satisfaction' at this action to preserve 'public tranquillity'. His ministers enacted yet more laws to stifle reformers and their writings. Then Hone demonstrated, with an innovatory twenty-four-page shilling pamphlet, *The Political House that Jack Built*, that the press could still print things that gagging laws could not silence.

In verses by Hone and images by Cruikshank, it declared that the printing press would prevail 'in spite of new acts'; labelled a line-up of a courtier, guardsman, clergyman, tax-gatherer and lawyer as THE VERMIN, plunderers of 'the Wealth that lay in the House that Jack Built'; called the Home Secretary 'a driv'ller, a bigot, a knave without shame'; said that WATERLOO-MAN aimed to crush REFORM, 'the Watchword, the talisman word', with his sword; and depicted the regent bulging out of a grotesque uniform, with a dangling corkscrew among his array of medals, and with peacock feathers comically replacing the usual feathers of the heir to the throne.

This is THE MAN
    All shaven and shorn,
All cover'd with Orders
    and all folorn;
THE DANDY OF SIXTY,
    who bows with a grace
And has *taste* in wigs, collars,
    cuirasses and lace;
Who to tricksters and fools
    leaves the State and its treasure
And when Britain's in tears
    sails about at his pleasure;
Who spurn'd from his presence
    the friends of his youth,
And now has not one
    who will tell him the truth...

Hone and Cruikshank at work together, Hone writing with a quill
pen, Cruikshank drawing on a boxwood block. Cruikshank drew
this as a frontispiece for Hone's collected edition of his pamphlets (*Facetiae*, 1827) containing 120 Cruikshank cuts. Hone
added an 'auld lang syne' caption from Burns:
'We twa hae paidl't.'

Before, during and after his trials Hone had been denounced from
pulpits and in ministerial journals as a blasphemer and infidel; but the
fame of his victory over his prosecutors far outweighed such abuse
among the growing force of people who longed for change, deplored
the regent and were alarmed by his government. In six weeks the
pamphlet sold forty thousand copies, and it went on to sell many
thousands more. The regent wanted to prosecute this wounding
nursery-rhyme parody, but the Lord Chancellor talked him out of that
'for fear of the consequences' — that is, another defeat.

The huge printings were possible because Cruikshank's illustrations were not etched on copperplate, which begins to wear out after a
thousand impressions, but were engraved on end-grain blocks of
dense wear-resistant boxwood. Furthermore, wood-engraved illustrations were cheaper to make, and also cheaper to print, being set in the
same page as the metal type of the text, whereas copperplate illustrations have to be printed on a separate press. Hone was making use
of advances in the wood-engraver's art (it was only a generation after
the pioneering Thomas Bewick), and was proud of his achievement.
'By showing what engraving on wood could effect in a popular way,

and exciting a taste for art in the more humble ranks of life,' he wrote, 'they created a new era in the history of publication. They are the parents of the present cheap literature.'[9] And they helped to lead before long to his *Every-Day Book* and its successors.

Several causes can be found for Hone's evolution from political to non-political publisher. He was pained by Tory vilification (this afflicted others near him by mere association: his brother, a barrister, was so much boycotted, even though politically conservative, that he emigrated to Australia). Hone refers several times to the blackening of his name. For example, in 1822 he writes a little scene in which a woman comes into his shop at No 45 Ludgate Hill and asks for *The Political House that Jack Built* and other pamphlets. She is surprised to learn that the man behind the counter is Hone himself. 'Why, indeed, sir, I did not suppose I should *see* you — and I did not expect — (*embarrassed*) — That is, I thought — I expected — I — I —'

'Allow me, madam, to conclude: you expected I had horns and hoofs and a forked tail, and spouted fire?'[10]

He was, besides, still feeling after-effects from the 'physical shake' of 1817. He had fits of depression and hallucinatory attacks. One of these he recalled later in *The Every-Day Book*: :

> In 1823 the editor of this work, being mentally disordered from too close application, left home in the afternoon to consult a medical friend and obtain relief under his extreme depression. In Fleet-street, on the opposite side of the way to where he was walking, he saw a pair of legs devoid of body, which he was persuaded were his own legs, though not at all like them. A few days afterwards when worse in health, he went to the same friend … and on his way saw himself on precisely the same spot as he imagined he had seen his legs, but with this difference, that the person was entire, and thoroughly a likeness as to feature, form and dress. The appearance seemed as real as his own existence.[11]

Perhaps a psychiatrist will speculate that Hone was a divided man, torn between the longstanding active radical and the lover of literature, learning and ancient ways.

Certainly his devotion to books made him wish to publish work less ephemeral than satirical pamphlets and caricatures. His projected History of Parody (never achieved) would have been a sort of bridge between the two worlds. After the success, and good earnings, of *The Political House that Jack Built* he resumed work on this project in the British Museum, 'to be quiet,' he said, 'and out of the way of politics'. After the regent became George IV in January 1820, Hone was pulled back into politics for a time by the drama of the sinful George's attempt to divorce his sinful Queen Caroline. With Cruikshank as artist, he created half a dozen more satires, potent but unprosecuted, again selling in tens of thousands.

In the same year, though, his quiet research produced something quite different, though still controversial. He published an *Apocryphal New Testament* (for which he was attacked by a clergyman in the high-Tory *Quarterly Review* as 'a wretch, as contemptible as he is wicked ... a poor illiterate creature'). And in 1823 came *Ancient Mysteries Described*, a pioneering account of the medieval mystery plays, together with other rare material — on festivals of fools, boy bishops, Christ's Descent into Hell, Christmas carols, pageants. One chapter was about 'the Giants in Guildhall', the statues known as Gog and Magog. He commissioned Cruikshank to etch them, but when he failed to deliver on time, Hone dispatched a four-page letter ('To be read *directly* without fail'). A few sentences give a lively glimpse of Hone the publisher:

> I am seated on thorns... Now my good fellow if the plate could have been managed this week it would have placed me beyond apprehension — but as it is, what is to be done? ...I say seize the moment as it flies... If you *can* do them, pray, I entreat you, be at them *instantly*, for I assure you there will not be time to colour them otherwise. Besides I want your *touch* with them... Go and look at them & do not leave a curl on the toenail or a single hair undefined ... for we shall both be laughed at for want of antiquarian feeling if there be inaccuracy in any point... Do you understand me? Done well and done quickly... [12]

Cruikshank did etch the plate, not omitting the giants' toenails. His doing so under pressure shows, by the way, his regard for Hone, for Cruikshank had to be handled with care. A few months later Hone writes to an author anxious for some overdue work from Cruikshank, 'As I am privy to his wishes and purposes and know him better almost than he does himself, my sincere advice is that you do not *hurry* him... You must let him have his own way or you will not have his style. The very attempt to *draw* his talent out causes it to recede.' [13]

Hone well knew the younger man's wayward side. While the two were collaborating on the satires, Cruikshank was 'seeing life', as the phrase was, and his sprees got in the way of work. The Hones tried to manage and cosset him (one of the Hone girls said he was 'the only one our mother ever had a bed made up for'), but it was not easy. Early in 1821 Hone writes to John Childs that he cannot get on with his next pamphlets — these would be *The Right Divine of Kings to Govern Wrong*, with two Cruikshank designs, and *The Political Showman*, with twenty-four — unless 'my friend Cruikshank will forswear late hours, blue ruin [gin] and dollies'. Cruikshank, in a 'demoniac' state, has been answering Hone's complaints with 'You be d----d' and

'Go to hell', telling him to 'Go and teach my granny to suck eggs,' blowing smoke over Hone and his books, invading Mrs Hone's bed-room to shave himself before going out on the town, and perhaps worst of all, revealing that he is 'by no means friendly to Reform!' [14]

Hone was perhaps helped in coping with such vagaries by being himself wilful, a man of quirks, 'a queer fellow'. He discusses his own character in a letter to Francis Place, a reformer and utilitarian, in which he teases Place for beginning letters to friends with an abrupt surname ('Hone', not 'Dear Hone'):

> Dear Place — Yes! ...Plain *Place* is too much like 'plain Place' *himself* to be the language of William Hone... *I must do things in* MY OWN *way,* and *one* of my ways is to be in *some* things like other people, and *this* is one of them. I dare to say that *I* am, on a few points, as prominently *out* of the way as *you* are in the commencement of a letter — and *between us* (you know it's secret to everybody else) we are two *queer* fellows. However, *this* I do know ... *if I cannot do a thing* IN MY OWN WAY *I never can do it at all.* I do not *aim* to do things differently from other people, and yet they *are* different... I never metaphysicized about myself to inquire *how* all this is...
>
> All this comes of not being able to get over plain 'Place' — and I think I hear *him* saying, 'Why, *what* is the fool about? Did you ever *hear* such a fool? He's drunk!' No, I am *not* drunk! ...I tell you *what*, Mr Place, I've had nothing but broth and gruel and slops since last Sunday fortnight, shut up in my bedroom...[15]

When Hone launched *The Every-Day Book* in January 1825, with weekly deadlines more urgent than a book's, he did call upon Cruik-shank, but used in all only eleven of his illustrations — the last that Cruikshank did for him. His chief illustrator was Samuel Williams, a versatile artist who engraved his own designs. At that time other literary journals rarely had any illustrations; *The Every-Day Book* had 311 over two years. Again Hone was 'showing what engraving on wood could effect', this time in a style soon widely adopted for book illustration, which had its heyday in the decades that followed.

His editorial scheme was innovatory too: to make the days, months, seasons of the passing year give a structure to the content. He announced his weekly as 'An Everlasting Calendar of Popular Amusements, Sports, Pastimes, Ceremonies, Manners, Customs and Events Incident to Each of the Three Hundred and Sixty-five Days in Past and Present Times ... including accounts of the weather, rules for health and conduct, remarkable and important anecdotes, facts and notices in chronology, antiquities, topography, biography, natural history, art, science and general literature; derived from the most authentic sources and valuable original communications ... for daily use and diversion'. News and current politics were out: papers and journals that carried them had to pay a heavy tax designed to price them out of the hands of troublesome humble people.

Before the first issue, Hone wrote to friends for material. Some topics to come are foretold in a lively plea, 'Xmas day 1824', to John Childs at Bungay: 'Any *new* bellman's verses or carols this year? Any *old* ones? Anything else in *my* way, that nobody at Bungay cares about? No old ballads? No old customs to tell me of and to describe? Nothing? No old Father Christmas? No mummings? No plough days? no mayings? or aleings or soulings? Nothing? Nothing? Ah *John!*' (Soulings were door-to-door pleas for donations on All Souls' Eve.)[16]

Each week Hone gave his readers sixteen double-column octavo pages, about 12,000 words plus illustrations, for threepence. Though he had to compete with a number of general-interest journals, his sales began well. He wrote urgently, 14 January 1825, to Augustus Applegath, on whose new steampowered presses the journal was being printed: 'I find myself without a single N° of the *first* number, turning away people every minute! and cutting the throat of the work I have given all my attention to, the instant it is born! ... Since I took *this* paper & pen in hand the post has brought orders from the country for upwards of 1,000 of N° 1 and for between 5 & 600 of N° 2.'[17]

Good sales were essential, as his illustrations were costly: for artist plus engraver, often £4 each (320 threepences), sometimes more, whereas typesetting a page cost about five shillings (only 20 three-pences). To enlarge his revenue, every four weeks Hone reissued four numbers bound together for a shilling; then the complete year as a thick volume for fourteen shillings. He knew the book's lasting worth and gave it not only a general index but also five others listing, for example, the   saints and the flowers (with their botanical names) associated with the passing days.

Each week was a heavy task for one man. He dipped into old books and magazines, quoted from new ones, solicited contributions from readers round the country, and served constantly as his own feature writer. London past and present was one of his chief topics (he had lived there from the age of three). He wrote too about his rare rural excursions, but lamented that they generally extended little further than what was 'allowed to a tethered dumb animal'. 'If now and then ... I exceed this boundary, it is only for a few miles into one of the four counties [bordering London], to a woodland height, a green dell, or beside a still flowing water, to enjoy the features of nature in lone-liness and quiet — the sight of "every green thing" in a glorious noontide; the twilight; and the coming and going of the stars.'[18] Many times he deplored the encroachments and spoliation he saw, a theme which made him still a protester, in a journal free of party politics.

Always a lover of poetry, he printed hundreds of pieces, from Chaucer onwards. Many are by poets of his own day: Blake, Wordsworth, Coleridge, Byron, Crabbe, Keats, Shelley and John Clare (one of his readers and contributors). And somehow during the stressful years 1825–27 he produced eighty-five verse pieces of his own.

In his dealings with contributors he shows the talent of a features editor before his time. Here is how he wrote in October 1825 to Robert Childs, brother of John, when trying to get information about a Mrs Hannah Want who had died in her 106th year:

> So! — you send me an 'Account sent to the Newspapers'! — *you*! This won't do — I must have more… Was she remarkable for nothing but living beyond her time? Acquaint me with her temper & her usual diet. Did she rise early? & if early, how early? How long did she sleep? How was her appetite? her eyesight? her memory? Was she of any religious persuasion? and what? Bigoted or tolerant? Had she any mind? & how much? distinguishing the qualities thereof… Was she temperate in drinking? & how temperate? drinking no, or little, spirits or wine or beer? or water only? &c &c. Talkative or taciturn? But a few *anecdotes* respecting her would be very acceptable. These are the *materials* of article writing. [19]

The pursuit of material was a pleasure as well as a labour. At the end of the year he told his readers: 'In gathering for others, I have in no small degree been teaching myself.' At the start of the second year he made a general appeal: 'It will be gratifying to everyone who peruses this work, and highly so to the editor, if he is obliged by letters from readers acquainted with customs in their own vicinity similar to those that are informed of in other counties, and particularly if they will take the trouble to describe them in every particular. By this means the *Every-Day Book* will become what it is designed to be made — *a storehouse of past and present manners and customs.*' [20]

One reader who became a contributor was Charles Lamb, best known for the essays he wrote, as 'Elia', for the *London Magazine* in the 1820s. He had known Hone's shop on Ludgate Hill, and Hone himself, for some time, for Lamb passed the shop on his daily walk to and from work at East India House in the City. Kind support from Lamb moved Hone to dedicate the first annual volume of *The Every-Day Book* to him:

> Your letter to me within the first two months from the commencement of the present work, approving my notice of St Chad's Well [pages 159–61], and your afterwards daring to publish me your 'friend' … I shall never forget. Nor can I forget your and Miss Lamb's sympathy and kindness when glooms outmastered me; and that your pen spontaneously sparkled in the book when my mind was in clouds and darkness. These 'trifles', as each of you would call them, are benefits scored upon my heart.

Lamb's 'daring' to call Hone his friend (for some worthy people still deplored the 'blasphemer') was in the form of a verse tribute in the *London Magazine*. Four of Lamb's six quatrains:

> I like you, and your book, ingenuous Hone!
>   In whose capacious, all-embracing leaves
> The very marrow of tradition's shown,
>   And much that history — much that fiction — weaves.
>
> By every sort of taste your work is graced.
>   Vast stores of modern anecdote we find
> With good old story quaintly interlaced —
>   The theme as various as the reader's mind...
>
> Rags, relics, witches, ghosts, fiends, crowd your page;
>   Our fathers' mummeries we well-pleased behold;
> And proudly conscious of a purer age
>   Forgive some fopperies in the times of old...
>
> Dan Phoebus loves your book — trust me, friend Hone —
>   The title only errs, he bids me say:
> For while such art — wit — reading there are shown
>   He swears, 'tis not a work of *every day.*

Hone reprinted this in *The Every-Day Book* in July 1825, followed by his own verse reply, a self-revealing open letter. Some extracts:

> In feeling like a stricken deer, I've been
>   Self-put-out from the herd, friend Lamb; for I
> Imagined all the sympathies between
>   Mankind and me had ceased, till your full cry
> Of kindness reach'd and roused me as I lay
>   'Musing on divers things foreknown': it bid
> Me know, in you, a friend; with a fine gay
>   Sincerity, before all men it chid,
> Or rather, by not chiding, seem'd to chide
>   Me for long absence from you...
>
> Few people understand me: still, I am
>   Warmly affection'd to each human being,
> Loving the right, for right's sake; and, friend Lamb,
>   Trying to see things as they are...
>
> No schools of science open'd to my youth;
>   No learned halls, no academic bowers;
> No one had I to point my way to truth,
>   Instruct my ign'rance or direct my powers.
> Yet I, though all unlearned, p'rhaps may aid
>   The march of knowledge in our 'purer age',
> And without seeming, may perchance persuade

9.50

> The young to think — to virtue, some engage.
> So have I hoped, and with this end in view
> My little *Every-Day Book* I design'd.
> Praise of the work, and of its author too,
> From you, friend Lamb, is more than good and kind...[21]

The friendship ripened. In the summer of 1826 Hone accepted an invitation to make use of Lamb's house, Colebrooke Cottage, Islington (it still stands) while Lamb was in the country. And Lamb began contributing articles, probably gratis.

When Hone followed *The Every-Day Book* in 1827 with *The Table Book* ('a kind of literary kaleidoscope', he called it), Lamb turned his fondness for old plays to Hone's service by giving him weekly extracts from the large collection that David Garrick left to the British Museum library. Announcing his plan, Lamb gives an affectionate picture of the early days of what is now a rather different library: 'Imagine the luxury to one like me, who above every other form of poetry have ever preferred the dramatic, of sitting in the princely apartments, for such they are, of poor condemned Montagu House [the mansion that first housed the British Museum], which I predict will not speedily be followed by a handsomer, and culling at will the flower of some thousand dramas. It is like having the range of a nobleman's library, with the librarian to your friend. Nothing can exceed the courteousness and attentions of the gentleman who has the chief direction of the reading-rooms here; and you have scarce to ask for a volume before it is laid before you.'[22] For Hone he was 'Your humble Abstractor'.

Later on, Lamb wrote to the poet Robert Southey, 'Those Every-Day and Table Books will be a treasure a hundred years hence; but they have failed to make Hone's fortune.' Hone had begun *The Every-Day Book* 'under the hope of retrieving my affairs'. But that hope soon faded. Within a few months the task began to take its toll. Again he was plagued with melancholy. He decided he must have fresh air and exercise, so gathered up his books and papers and left his wife and children 'for a room in the back of Pentonville' in sight of the fields of Islington — 'and being unfit for society, spent the summer in a solitary manner, overwhelmed with hypochondria, working out my book, sheet by sheet, and taking fitful and lonely walks ... till the weather drove me back to Ludgate Hill'.[23]

He found that bills were unpaid and writs were flying. Like many publishers, Hone was undercapitalized; but it was only later that he learned, besides, that a man called Percy, employed to deal with the business side, had been milking his cash. As one of Hone's daughters put it, 'That man sat daily at our table for years, took his six pounds every Saturday, and when he had cleared out all the ready cash, left my father starving at his work on the Every-Day Book within the rules of King's Bench Prison.'[24] 'Within the rules' means he was lodged in an approved house near the prison in Southwark 'Mr Poole's, Tobacconist, No 2 Great Suffolk Street'. From there he wrote to John Childs:

My family is thrust out from Ludgate Hill... From the moment I found my affairs irretrievable ... I worked like a horse to put the Every-Day Book beyond the reach of destruction by transferring it to Messrs Hunt & Clarke in trust for my creditors... All was removed into their warehouse in a few hours ... and I was transferred hither, after writing a N° in the lock-up house; since when I have got out last week's, arranged the index to make the first volume an immediately productive asset, & have just got the proofs from the printers... But my family are in great distress. My wife and six of the children ... sleep in one room of my father's house.[25] [The Hunt of Hunt & Clarke, a small new publishing partnership, was a nephew of the author Leigh Hunt; the Clarke was Charles Cowden Clarke, one of John Keats's earliest friends. Within three years they too were to go broke.]

Somehow Hone managed to keep the weekly issues coming out to produce revenue. Accounts he produced for his creditors of his outlays from January 1825 give some interesting glimpses of Hone the editor at work. To provide fifteen months' illustrations, he said, had cost more than £660, including £150 for expenses —

Fees to parish clerks, sextons and porters; gifts to showmen [at Bartholomew Fair]; civility money to persons exhibited; gratuities for information and permission to sketch; ... stage hire and other travelling expenses every week, to Islington, Canonbury, Hagbush Lane, Hornsey, Highgate, Tottenham, West Wickham and Greenwich, and to Bullock's Museum, Cross's Menagerie, Bartholomew Fair, Charlton and other fairs, and different places in town and country, frequently accompanied by artists and always bearing their charges; besides sums paid for the loan of books, prints and drawings, &c &c.[26]

Before long, as some articles in *The Every-Day Book* show, he was granted enough freedom to make excursions in pursuit of material, and then in 1827 to produce *The Table Book*. But he had had to pledge his collection of hundreds of books, pamphlets and prints, many dating from the 17th century, as security for loans. When he could not pay, he had to sell them at auction. It was his painful task to prepare the catalogue. Among them were the books and prints used for his defence at his 1817 trials, plus many collected for the project 'nearest my heart', the History of Parody. Many things went far too cheaply, *The Times* noted. 'Among the books were a large collection of tracts by and concerning John Lilburne from 1639 to 1656, which sold for five guineas... The original engraved woodblocks ... of *The Political House*,

The Man in the Moon, *The Queen's Matrimonial Ladder*, *Non Mi Ricordo*, *Form of Prayer for the Queen*, *Political Showman* and *Right Divine* [and other pamphlets of 1819–21], in all seventy-eight blocks, sold for £6 15s.' (Where are they now? They might fetch thousands.) The sale, one of his daughters said, 'cost him a wrench of feeling which few persons can realize'. And still he was not clear of debt.

The villainous Mr Percy inflicted yet another sorrow. For years, Hone and Cruikshank had helped each other with short-term loans. At the time of *The Every-Day Book* Cruikshank lent generously, sometimes £50 at a time, more than a workman earned in a year. In 1827, when Hone could not repay, Cruikshank broke with him, perhaps refusing to believe that a man with successful publications had no money. The two did not speak again until Hone was on his deathbed.

The Table Book survived only a year. In 1828 Hone had to settle for bankruptcy to escape from the prison. Here it is fitting to hear from Mrs Hone, née Sarah Johnson, mother of twelve children, and unsung colleague through all Hone's tribulations. In sketches of her by Cruikshank she is a plump smiling woman. She certainly needed equanimity. Here she is writing to her mother after the bankruptcy:

> Our happiness or misery depend, I consider, much if not wholly upon ourselves, more especially in married life, and the sacrifice made in one way must be balanc'd in another. There is no one in the world without some trouble... Upon the whole I am sure there are few happier in the world than I am, for tho' he shows it oddly at times, I know my husband loves me and there is nothing that his industry can get me, but I have it...[27]

Hone sold his rights in *The Every-Day Book*, *Table Book* and other work — with the stereotype plates from which they could be printed again and again. Soon they were acquired by an astute Cheapside publisher and printseller, Thomas Tegg. Hone moved with Sarah and their younger children to the hamlet of Newington Green, amid fields beyond Islington. In a house formerly occupied by a man he must have admired, Dr Richard 'Civil Liberty' Price, a scholar, outspoken dissenter and reform advocate, he worked for other publishers. The country scene helped to cheer him. In May 1829 he sent an invitation to a musical friend, Charles Behnes:

> Dear Charley, come hither on Sunday, and see
> My wife and the children, the garden and me.
> Don't fail to come early — you'll sniff the fresh breeze —
> After 6 in the morning, as soon as you please.
> We've brown bread and mutton, at 1, for our feeding —
> We've fruit trees in blossom, & rabbits a-breeding...[28]

By year's end, though, they were back in town. Well-intentioned friends made donations to establish the family in the Grasshopper Coffee House and Hotel ('Good Beds and Early Breakfasts') in Gracechurch-street, on a busy route leading up from London Bridge. Mrs Hone and two elder daughters ran the place while Hone worked on a new project: a sixty-four-page monthly magazine, *The Year Book*. This time he was not the proprietor, but for a fee of £400 provided the text and illustrations for a year's issues. The publisher was Thomas Tegg.

It did not go happily. After a year Tegg complained, 'The expense far exceeds the amᵗ stated by you in the estimate'; he had lost 'several Hundred Pounds'. And he ordered, 'Please *not* to put any more churches, they are not liked by the readers.'[29] (Hone did overdo them: ten engravings of churches, plus other religious images.) A bit later Tegg offered some praise: 'The last part of the Year Book (unlike most last parts) is the best of the whole work. The pictorial parts are exceedingly well done.'[30] But Hone broke with him, evidently after a dispute over payment. The disaccord between the prosperous Tegg, who had a fine villa on the road to Highgate, and his needy editor no doubt helped to inspire some remarks about British 'Mammon-worship' in Hone's preface to the collected volume of *The Year Book*: '...the enormous heaps of wealth accumulated by unblest means ... the sudden and fierce outbreakings of the hungry and ignorant ... private gentlemen "live like lords", tradesmen and farmers like gentlemen...' Tegg was soon selling thousands of copies of all the reissued Hone volumes, and reaping 'a rich harvest', according to one of the Hone girls. Hone's lack of the wealth-accumulating spirit meant that a man with capital enjoyed the benefit of his long labours.

At the Grasshopper, one daughter broke down from overwork, another left. At the end of 1832 Hone wrote to one of his learned friends, Francis Douce, that he was labouring 'from morn to night in the bar and coffee room ... hard and appalling work', with no time for literature. 'I take it I am a doomed man'.[31]

It is not clear how he made his escape. The next notable event is his conversion in 1834, at the age of fifty-four, to the Congregational church, 'after much communication personally and in writing' with a noted preacher, Thomas Binney, of the church's Weigh-House Chapel in the City of London. For years he had resisted adopting a particular church's doctrine. In 1824 the position he had reached was, 'My religion is the religion of the New Testament ... a pure principle, a mental illumination'.[32] Looking back years later, he wrote, 'I both wished and dreaded to be religious.'[33]

The conversion freed him from conflict. It certainly kept him as distant as ever from the Anglican establishment: just the year before, Binney had caused great controversy by saying 'The established church is a great national evil... It destroys more souls than it saves.' For a few years Hone worked as sub-editor of *The Patriot*, a dissenting weekly. But his health declined; he had 'paralytic attacks' — minor strokes. He retired to the quiet village of Tottenham. 'Our dwelling,' he wrote to a daughter, playing on the village's name, 'is a little *tot* of a house. The room I write in is where my books are and is our living room — it is about 7 feet wide by 10 feet long ... and looks down *our garden* which is about 14 feet wide and fifty feet long, with some kale and broccoli plants in it.'[34]

In the autumn of 1842 Hone knew he was near death. He asked George Cruikshank to come to see him, and they ended their fifteen-year rupture. Another touching scene soon followed. Cruikshank had recently illustrated the first books of a rising young author, Charles Dickens. Now Hone asked Cruikshank to persuade Dickens to visit him. As Dickens wrote, 'having read no books but mine of late, he wanted to see and shake hands with me before (as George said) "he went".'[35] Cruikshank and Dickens journeyed out together. Hone 'was greatly delighted to see them,' one of Hone's daughters recalled, and Mrs Hone recorded, 'He held George's hand the whole time.'

Hone died, aged sixty-two, a month later. Dickens drove Cruikshank to the funeral on a 'muddy, foggy, wet, dark, cold' November day. Dickens, as was his way, makes a droll scene of it: 'George has enormous whiskers which straggle all down his throat in such weather, and stick out in front of him like a partially unravelled bird's-nest.' Cruikshank was 'in a state between jollity (he is always very jolly with me) and the deepest gravity (going to a funeral, you know)', and Dickens had to laugh at his erratic philosophical remarks.[36] It may be that Cruikshank was talking at random to cover his sorrow over his old friend. At the funeral, the Hone family were weeping; and so was Cruikshank.

The Hones were almost destitute. Dickens generously joined with Cruikshank and others in soliciting aid for them from the Royal Literary Fund and in public appeals. In a letter seeking a contribution, Dickens pays this tribute: 'He was not a common man.'

That would have made a worthy inscription on Hone's gravestone in Abney Park Cemetery, Stoke Newington. In fact the stone records little more than place and date of his birth and death, and the deaths of his wife and others. In 1842 the cemetery was far beyond the edge of town. Now London extends many miles beyond it (a sight that would amaze and grieve him). And yet he lies in a setting he could approve, for the cemetery, now almost disused, has become a wild and variegated woodland where people of his turn of mind can wander along green lanes and muse over half-hidden gravestones.

ABOUT THIS SELECTION

From the start of *The Every-Day Book* to the close of *The Year Book*, Hone gave his readers about 2,500,000 words, close-set in double columns. I have passed over hundreds of items of antiquarian, historical, topographical and botanical lore, and have favoured what is somewhat obscured among them, the pieces that show us the life of his time or within living memory. One pleasure of the rediscovery is to find that topics that seem modern stirred Hone 170 years ago. He is an ecologist and environmentalist, a century before those words arose.

ARRANGEMENT: Items are often contenders for more than one of the eight sections. Fairs are for both work and fun; many customs arise from work; the boundary between London and country is changing in Hone's own time. But I hope the sections prove helpful.

EDITING: *Nothing is rewritten*, but I have done some cutting, often of phrases, sometimes much more. Hone, I think, would have trimmed a good deal if he had not been under deadline pressure, often while dogged by illness and creditors. Every cut (except when at the start of an item) is indicated thus: … Spelling and punctuation are modernized. I provide introductory paragraphs and helpful annotations.

ILLUSTRATIONS: All the engravings (save three in the introduction, and one in page 180 not from Hone) are in their original size. For 39 of them I have gratefully used a source that often shows their finer touches better than in Hone's printed volumes: a pair of albums in the Victoria & Albert Museum's department of prints and drawings (Nos 93.A.103 and 104) containing original proofs, mainly from the blocks of Hone's best artist/engraver, Samuel Williams. Perhaps the albums were compiled by him. The museum bought them from the London bookdealer Quaritch in 1890 for £5 5s: an excellent buy.

ACKNOWLEDGMENTS

I am grateful first of all, as always, to the British Library, that supreme resource for authors. For help of various kinds I wish to thank the Guildhall Library, London; the Bodleian Library, Oxford; archivists or local-history specialists of Bromley, Camden, Greenwich, Hampstead; Bradford, Newcastle upon Tyne, Nottingham; Cornwall, Staffordshire, Wiltshire; Jesus College and Queen's College, Oxford; and the Irish Traditional Music Archive, Dublin.

Illustrations from proofs in pages 27, 32, 67, 99, 102, 104, 112, 116, 119, 120, 122, 124, 135, 142, 144, 145, 147, 155, 163, 191, 194, 198–99, 202–03, 205–07, 209, 220, 224, 234, 243, 247, 253, 265, 283, 288, 307 are by courtesy of the Board of Trustees of the Victoria & Albert Museum. Illustrations from *The Year Book* in pages 133, 212, 242, 310 are by permission of the British Library; in pages 130 and 292, of the Libraries Department, London Borough of Islington.

Fancies, fairs
and frolics

'Very deaf, indeed'

Selected by Hone from Thomas Hood's *Whims and Oddities*, 1826, with this comment: 'There is one design, so excellent a specimen of Mr Hood's clear conception and decisive execution, that merely in further illustration of his talent it is here introduced.' And see pages 68–70.

Jack, Sal and the men in chains

I HAVE HAD another holiday — a Whitsuntide holiday at Greenwich [May 1825]. It is true that I did not take a run down the hill, but I saw many do it who appeared to me happier and healthier for the exercise and the fragrant breezes from the fine May trees...

I soon got to the observatory... The old pensioners who ply there to ferry the eye up and down and across the river with their telescopes were ready... I took my stand, and in less than ten minutes was conveyed to Barking church, Epping Forest, the men in chains, the London docks, St Paul's Cathedral and Westminster Abbey. From the seat around the tree I watched the early comers... In every instance save one, the sight first demanded was 'the men in chains'. These are the bodies of pirates suspended on gibbets by the riverside to warn sailors against crimes on the high seas.

An ablebodied sailor, with a new hat on his Saracen-looking head, carrying a handkerchief full of apples in his left hand, with a bottle neck sticking out of his jacket for a nosegay, dragged his female companion up the hill with all the might of his right arm and shoulder, and the moment he was at the top assented to the proposal of a telescope-keeper for his 'good lady' to have a view of the men in chains. She wanted to 'see something else first'.

'Don't be a fool,' said Jack, 'see *them* first. It's the best sight.' No; not she; all Jack's arguments were unavailing. 'Well! What is it you'd like better, you fool you?'

'Why, I wants to see our house in the court, with the flowerpots, and if I don't see that I won't see nothing. What's the men in chains to *that*? Give us an apple.' She took one out of the bundle, and beginning to eat it, gave instructions for the direction of the instrument towards Limehouse church, while Jack drew forth the bottle and refreshed himself. Long she looked, and squabbled, and almost gave up the hope of finding 'our house'; but on a sudden she screamed out, 'Here, Jack! Here it is, pots and all! And there's our bedpost. I left the window up o' purpose as I might see it!'

Jack himself took an observation. 'D'ye see it, Jack?'

'Yes.'

'D'ye see the pots?'

'Yes.'

'And the bedpost?'

'Ay, and here Sal, here, here's the cat looking out o' the window.'

'Come away, let's look again,' and then she looked, and squalled, 'Lord! What a sweet place it is!' And then she assented to seeing the men in chains, giving Jack the first look; and they looked 'all down the river' and saw 'Tom's ship' and wished Tom was with them.

The breakings forth of nature and kindheartedness, and especially the love of 'home, sweet home' in Jack's 'good lady', drew forth Jack's delight, and he kissed her till the apples rolled out of the bundle, and then he pulled her down the hill.

From the moment they came up they looked at nobody nor saw anything but themselves and what they paid for looking at through the telescope. They were themselves a sight; and though the woman was far from —

Whatever fair high fancy forms, or lavish hearts could wish —

yet she was all that to Jack; and all that she seemed to love or care for were 'our house', and the flowerpots, and the bedpost, and Jack.

The gibbeted pirates were removed two years later on the orders of the Duke of Clarence, Lord High Admiral (later William IV) — 'the last men in chains in the vicinage of the metropolis', Hone says.

A drap a' yel at Avingham

A fair at Avingham (now Ovingham), on the Tyne west of Newcastle, is described by John Jackson, who was born there in 1801, was apprenticed to the wood-engraver Thomas Bewick, and had begun a notable wood-engraving career in London when he wrote this in 1826. He tells of a time 'when I first drew halfpence from my breeches pockets'.

AVINGHAM FAIR is on the 26th of April and 26th of October... In the morning a procession moves from the principal alehouse for the purpose of *riding the fair*, as they call it, headed by the two Northumberland pipers, called *the Duke of Northumberland's pipers*, in a light blue dress, a large cloak of the same colour with white cape, a silver half-moon on one arm as a cognizance, and white band and binding to the hat. Each is mounted on a rosinante, borrowed without consent from some whisky smuggler or cadger, reconciled to the liberty by long custom...

The pipers, followed by the duke's agent, bailiff, constable and a numerous body of farmers, principally the duke's tenantry, proceed first through the fair ... and then, the duke being lord of the manor, they walk the boundary of all that is or has been common or waste land. That task completed, they return to the alehouse with the pipers playing before them, where they partake freely of store of punch at the duke's expense...

Avingham Fair, like others, is attended by many a gaberlunzie with different kinds of amusement for children; ...and above all, for the amusement of the pig-drivers and gadsmen, Punch and Toby (so called by them) and a number of those gentlemen who vomit fire...

At my last visit I was much amused with one who seemed to have been just arrived from the sister kingdom [Ireland]. He was surround- ed by ploughboys and their doxies, their cheeks as red as their topknots. He had a large pan suspended from his neck and, as the girls observed, a 'skimmering' white apron and bib, and he bellowed as loud as he could,

> 'Hearse a' yer rale dandy candy,
> 'Made ap wa' sugar an' brandy
> 'An' tha rale hoile a' mint.
> 'It's cood far young ar old,
> 'Cough ar cold —

'A shortness a' breath ar a pain at tha stomach. It's cood far hany camplaint whatsamever. Ah, fait'! an yil try it! Noo, leddies, hif ye try it, an' yer sure ta buy it...'

The October fair is more numerously attended by those who go for pleasure... 'Hearst' [harvest] is just ended, and they have then most money, which with the 'leddies' is generally expended in dress... After baking a sufficient number of barley bannocks for the following day, and the milk set up, they throw off their linsey-woolsey petticoats and 'hale-made bed-goons' for a gown, a good specimen of their taste, in the two warmest colours, a red flower or stripe upon a yellow ground, and as much of a third colour round the waist as would make them vie with Iris... The style of dancing is the same as in Scotland, country dances, reels, jigs and hornpipes...

The following day is called by the inhabitants 'Gwonny Jokesane's day'. Why so is not known; all they know is that it is and has been so called since the recollection of the oldest alive... When a sufficient number have assembled they elect what they are pleased to call a mayor, whom they mount upon a platform which is borne along by four men, headed by the musician that attended the preceding evening, and followed by a number of bailiffs with white 'wans' and all the men, wives, maids and white-headed urchins in the village...

They proceed first to the minister's house and strike up a dance in front. His worship 'the mayor', as a privileged person, sometimes evinces a little impatience, and if the minister has not made his appearance, demands to speak to him. On his advancing, 'his wor- ship' begins thus, 'A yes! [oyez] Twa times a yes! An' three times a yes! If ony man, or ony man's man, lairds, loons, lubburdoons, dogs, skelpers, gabbrigate swingers, shall commit a parliament as a twar- liament, we in the township o' Avingham shall hea his legs an' heed tied to tha cagwheel till he say yence, twice, thrice, Prosper the fair o' Avingham an' Gwonny Jokesane's day.'

This harangue, however ridiculous, is always followed with cheering, in which their good-tempered pastor freely joins with his hat above his head, and stepping forward, shakes 'his worship' by the hand ... trusting he will not leave the manse till he takes 'a drap a' yel, a' his ain brewin'... The ale being handed round in plenty, and being found to be good — 'an' what is na guid that the minister hes?' — they engage themselves for some time, 'while news much older than their ale goes round'. The musicians meanwhile play such airs as 'The Reel Rawe', 'The Bonny Bit', 'Laddie, Wylam Away', &c... [*These seem not to survive. Wylam is near Ovingham.*] The dance goes round ... until silence is called, when 'his worship' gives as a toast,

> Health, wealth, milk and meal.
> The de'il tak ye a' thot disent wish him weal —
> Hip! hip! huzza!

Raising 'his worship' shoulder-height again, they proceed round the village, repeating their gambols in front of every respectable house, where they meet with a similar reception. After this, footracing commences, for hats, handkerchiefs and, as Charles Mathews [comedian] calls them, she-shirts [smocks]... Races run and prizes distributed, they return to the last and gayest of their mirthful scenes...

> Wi' merry sangs, an' friendly cracks,
> I wat they didna weary;
> An' unco tales, an' funny jokes —
> Their sports were cheap an' cheery...
> Syne, wi' a social glass o' strunt
> They parted aff careerin',
>   Fu' blythe that night.   *Burns*

'Money if you please!' for the puppets

Hone does a review of a roving puppet show, a fantoccini, in August 1825. It is in Pentonville, Islington, near his friend the artist George Cruikshank's home, and Hone gets Cruikshank to illustrate it.

ITS COMING was announced by a man playing the pan-pipes, or 'mouth organ', which he accompanied by beating the long drum. After him followed the theatre, consisting of a square framework about ten feet high ... carried by a man within the frame. The theatrical properties were in a box strapped on the inside near the bottom.

The musician was preceded by a foreign-looking personage — the manager. As soon as he had fixed on a station he deemed eligible, the trio stopped, the theatre was on its legs in a minute... The band of two instruments was set in motion by its performer ... the carrier of the theatre assuming the important office of money-collector.

'Come, ladies and gentlemen,' he said, 'we can't begin without you encourage us. Please to remember what you are going to see!' Boys came running in from the fields, women with children got good places, windows were thrown up and well filled, the drummer beat and blew away lustily, the audience increased every minute, a collection was made, and the green curtain at length drew up...

Scene 1. A jolly-looking puppet performed the tricks of a tumbler and posture-master with a hoop.

Scene 2. The money-taker called out, 'This is the representation of a skeleton.' The music played solemnly and the puppet skeleton came slowly through a trap-door in the floor of the stage. Its under jaw chattered against the upper, it threw its arms up mournfully till it was fairly above ground, and then commenced a 'grave' dance. On a sudden its head dropped off, the limbs separated from the trunk in a moment, and the head moved about the floor, chattering, till it resumed its place together with the limbs and in an instant danced as before... At last it sank into a sitting posture and remained still. Then it held down its skull, elevated its arms, let them fall on the ground several times dolorously; fell to pieces again; again the head moved about the stage and chattered; again it resumed its place, the limbs reunited and the figure danced till the head fell off with a gasp. The limbs flew still further apart; all was quiet; the head made one move only towards the body, fell sideways, and the whole redescended to a dirge-like tune...

Scene 3. The scene was delayed for the collector to come round again with his hat. 'You can't expect us to show you all for what you've given. Money if you please! Money, we want your money!' As soon as he had extracted the last extractable halfpenny the curtain drew up and — enter a clown without a head, who danced till his head came from between his shoulders to the wonder of the children, and, almost to their alarm, was elevated on a neck the full length of his body, which it thrust out ever and anon ... presenting greater contortions than the human figure could possibly represent...

Scene 4. Another delay of the curtain for another collection. 'We have four and twenty scenes,' said the collector, 'and if you aren't liberal we can't show 'em all — we must go.' This extorted something more, and one person ... sent out a shilling with a request that 'all' might be exhibited. The showman promised, the curtain drew up and another puppet-tumbler appeared with a pole, which being

Cruikshank's sketch of the fantoccini, 'patronised by the royal family'

placed laterally on the back of two baby-house chairs, he balanced
himself upon it, stood heels upwards upon it, took the chairs up by
it, balanced them on each end of it, and down fell the curtain.

Scene 5. A puppet sailor danced a hornpipe.

Scene 6. A puppet Indian juggler threw balls.

Scene 7… The collector said, 'This is the representation of Billy Waters,
Esq,' and a puppet Billy Waters appeared with a wooden leg and
danced to the sound of his fiddle for a minute or two, when the
curtain dropped and the manager and performers went off with
their theatre, leaving the remaining seventeen scenes, if they had
them, unrepresented…

Hone is not much impressed: 'Our old acquaintance Punch will survive all
this.' Billy Waters, a black man with a wooden leg, was a much-loved
street performer in the 1820s, dancing to his fiddle.

Prizefights and uproar in Mayfair

London's great May Fair, held in the district north of Piccadilly which came to be known as Mayfair, flourished until the 1760s, when the spread of fashionable streets squeezed it out. Hone reprints this from *The Gentleman's Magazine* of March 1816:

FIFTY YEARS have passed away since this place of amusement was at its height of attraction. The spot where the fair was held still retains the name of Mayfair, and exists in much the same state as at the above period: for instance, Shepherd's market and houses surrounding it on the north and east sides, with White Horse-street, Shepherd's-court, Sun-court, Market-court. Westwards an open space extending to Tyburn-lane (now Park-lane), since built upon in Chapel-street, Shepherd's-street, Market-street, Hertford-street, &c. Southwards, the noted ducking-pond, house and gardens, since built upon... [A few of these names have changed.]

The market-house consisted of two storeys. First storey [ground floor], a long and cross aisle for butchers' shops; externally, other shops connected with culinary purposes. Second storey used as a theatre at fair-time for dramatic performances... The butchers gave place to toy-men and gingerbread-bakers... In the areas encompassing the market building were booths for jugglers, prizefighters both at cudgels and backsword, boxing-matches and wild beasts. The sports not under cover were mountebanks, fire-eaters, ass-racing, sausage-tables, dice-tables, up-and-downs, merry-go-rounds, bull-baiting, grinning for a hat, running for a shift, hasty-pudding eaters, eel-divers and an infinite variety of other similar pastimes...

Before a large commodious house, with a good disposure of walks, arbours and alcoves, was an area with an extensive basin of water, otherwise 'ducking-pond', for the recreation of lovers of that *polite* and *humane* sport. Persons who came with their dogs paid a trifling fee for admission... Others who visited the place as mere spectators paid a double fee. A duck was put into the pond by the master of the hunt. The several dogs were then let loose to seize the bird. For a long time they made the attempt in vain, for when they came near ... she dived under the water and eluded their remorseless fangs. Herein consisted the *extreme felicity* of the interesting scene. At length some dog more expert than the rest caught the feathered prize and bore it away amidst the loudest acclamations to its most fortunate and envied master. This diversion was held in such high repute about the reign of Charles II that he and many of his prime nobility did not disdain to be present, and partake with their dogs of the elegant entertainment...

Ti-tiddy ti-ti, tiddy diddy dol-lol

Here too was Tiddy-Doll. This celebrated vendor of gingerbread ... was always hailed as the king of itinerant tradesmen. He was a constant attendant in the crowd on Lord Mayor's day... He affected to dress like a person of rank: white goldlaced suit of clothes, laced ruffed shirt, laced hat and feather, white silk stockings, with the addition of a fine white apron. Among his harangues to gain customers, take this as a specimen:

Mary, Mary, where are you *now*, Mary! I live, when at home, at the second house in Little Ball-street, two steps under ground, with a wiscum, riscum and a why-not. Walk in, ladies and gentlemen. My shop is on the second floor backwards, with a brass knocker at the door. Here is your nice gingerbread. It will melt in your mouth like a red-hot brickbat and rumble in your inside like Punch and his wheelbarrow.

He always finished his address by singing this fag-end of some popular ballad: *Ti-tiddy ti-ti, ti-tiddy ti-ti, ti-tiddy ti-ti, tiddy diddy dol-lol, ti-tiddy ti-tiddy ti-ti, tiddy tiddy dol*. Hence arose his nickname of Tiddy-

Doll. In Hogarth's print of the execution of the Idle Apprentice at Tyburn [published 1747], Tiddy-Doll is seen holding up a gingerbread cake with his left hand ... and addressing the mob in his usual way — 'Mary, Mary, &c'... For many years (and perhaps at present) allusions were made to his name, as thus: 'You are so fine' (to a person dressed out of character) 'you look like Tiddy-Doll.' 'You are as tawdry as Tiddy-Doll.' 'You are quite Tiddy-Doll,' &c.

Soon after the late Lord Coventry occupied [in 1764] the house, corner of Engine-street [now Brick-street], Piccadilly ... he being annoyed with the unceasing uproar, day and night, during the fair the whole month of May, procured, I know not by what means, the entire abolition of this festival of misrule and disorder.

Ballad scholars who would like to identify the Tiddy Doll tune will find it in the 1825 *Every-Day Book*.

The baiting of Nero and Wallace

Cruelty to animals was in the news. In 1822 the MP Richard Martin achieved the first animal-welfare legislation, 'to prevent the cruel and improper treatment of cattle', and in 1824 he helped to found what became the Royal Society for the Prevention of Cruelty to Animals. So when the owner of a touring menagerie, George Wombwell (1778–1850), devised a show in 1825 in which dogs would bait a lion, many newspapers carried critical reports. Hone quotes them at length. A much-reduced summary:

FOR SEVERAL MONTHS the country has been amused with notices that a fight between a lion and dogs was intended [says *The Morning Herald*], and time and place were more than once appointed. This had the desired effect, making the lion an object of great attraction in the provincial towns, and a golden harvest was secured by showing him at two shillings a head. The next move was to get up such a fight as would draw all the world from London, as well as from the villages, to fill places marked at one and two guineas each...

The magnitude of the stake of £5,000 said to be at issue was so far out of any reasonable calculation that the whole was looked upon as a fabrication... But the proprietor of the concern was too good a judge to let the flats [his dupes] altogether escape him...

George Wombwell, the proprietor, as the leader of a collection of wild beasts, may be excused for his proficiency in trickery, which is the essence and spirit of his calling. But we think him accountable as a man for his excessive cruelty in exposing a poor animal that he has reared himself and made so attached that it plays with him and fondles him like a spaniel, that has never been taught to know its own powers or the force of its savage nature, to the attacks of dogs trained to blood and bred for fighting. The lion [Nero], now five years old, was whelped in Edinburgh, and has been brought up with so much softness that it appears as inoffensive as a kitten, and suffers the attendants of the menagerie to ride upon its back or to sleep in its cage…

Wombwell announced in his posting-bills at Birmingham, Coventry, Manchester and all the neighbouring towns that the battle was to be for £5,000, but communicated by way of secret that in reality it was but £300 a side, which he asserted was made good with the owner of the dogs… The dogs, to be sure, were open to the inspection of the curious, and a roughcoated, gamekeeping, butcherlike, honest ruffianly person from the north announced himself as their ostensible friend on the occasion; but by whom employed he was unwilling to declare.

A Quaker gentleman named Hoare hands a letter to Wombwell urging him to call off the show. A short extract:

> Allow me to ask thee how thou wilt endure to see the noble animal thou hast so long protected, and which has been in part the means of supplying thee with the means of life, mangled and bleeding before thee? …Whatever thou mayest gain by this disgraceful exhibition will, I fear, prove like a canker-worm among the rest of thy substance… Remember that He who gave life did not give it to be the sport of cruel man, and that He will assuredly call man to account for his conduct toward his dumb creatures. Remember, also, that cowards are always cruel, but the brave love mercy…

The Morning Chronicle *reports Wombwell's response*:

He looked at his preparations, he looked at his lion, and he cast a glance forward to his profits, and then shook his head.

July 1825: a cage is set up on a stage in a Warwick factory yard. About 250 people attend, paying up to two guineas. Three dogs at a time are loosed on the lion. He beats them off with his paws. The Times *reports*:

After about five minutes' fighting the fallow-coloured dog was taken away, lame and apparently much distressed, and the remaining two continued the combat alone, the lion still only working with his paws, as though seeking to rid himself of a torture the nature of which he did not well understand. In two or three minutes more the second dog, Tiger, being dreadfully maimed, crawled out of the cage, and the brown dog, Turk, the lightest of the three but of admirable courage, went on fighting by himself.

A most extraordinary scene then ensued. The dog, left entirely alone with an animal of twenty times its weight, continued the battle with unabated fury, and though bleeding all over from the effect of the lion's claws, seized and pinned him by the nose at least half a

'The dogs would not give him a moment's respite, and all three set on him again, while the poor animal, howling with pain, threw his great paws awkwardly upon them as they came.' — *Morning Herald*

dozen times; when at length, releasing himself with a desperate effort, the lion flung his whole weight upon the dog and held him lying between his fore paws for more than a minute, during which time he could have bitten his head off a hundred times over, but did not make the slightest effort to hurt him. Poor Turk was then taken away by the keepers, grievously mangled but still alive... Wombwell went into the cage instantly, and alone, carrying a pan of water, with which he first sluiced the animal and then offered him some to drink...

The second combat presented only a repetition of the barbarities committed in the first...

This is not the end of it. Wombwell has another lion. Hone reports:

Determined not to forgo a shilling which could be obtained by the exposure of an animal to torture, Wombwell in the same week submitted another of his lions to be baited. *The Times*, in giving an account of this renewed brutality, after a forcible expression of its 'disgust and indignation at the cruelty of the spectacle and the supineness of the magistracy', proceeds thus:

He matched his Wallace, a fine lion cubbed in Scotland, against six of the best dogs that could be found. Wallace's temper is the very opposite of that of the gentle Nero. It is but seldom that he lets even his feeders approach him... He showed himself a forest lion, and fought like one. He clapped his paw upon poor Ball, took Tinker in his teeth and deliberately walked round the stage with him as a cat would with a mouse... He at length dropped Tinker, and that poor animal crawled off the stage as well as he could. The lion then seized Ball by the mouth and played exactly the same game with him... Ball would have been almost devoured, but his second got hold of him through the bars and hauled him away...

Two more dogs are vanquished. Then Samuel Wedgbury, 'well known in London for his breed of dogs', sends in Billy and Tiger — with misgivings, 'casting a most piteous look upon the wounded dogs around him'.

Wallace seized Billy by the loins, and when shaking him — Tiger having run away — Wedgbury cried out, 'There, you see how you've gammoned me to have the best dog in England killed.' Billy, however, escaped with his life. He was dragged through the railing after having received a mark in the loins which ... will probably render him unfit for any future contest...Several well-dressed women viewed the contest from the upper apartment of the factory.

[Hone comments] *Women!*

Outrage over Wombwell's stunts helped to bring the banning, ten years later, of the baiting of animals, and cockfights too. Wombwell continued to prosper. His grave in Highgate Cemetery is dignified with a grand memorial to 'George Wombwell, Menagerist', topped by a lifesize marble figure of Nero. (*More on Wombwell, page 52*)

Popping corks and rude disorder

Most trades traditionally took holidays on Easter Monday and Tuesday.
For thousands of Londoners the riotous day out was at Greenwich fair.

THE CHIEF ATTRACTION to this spot is the park, wherein stands the Royal Observatory on a hill, adown which it is the delight of boys and girls to pull each other till they are wearied. Frequently of late this place has been a scene of rude disorder. But it is still visited by thousands and tens of thousands...The lowest join in the hill sports; others regale in the public houses; and many are mere spectators of what may be called the humours of the day...

At the very dawn of day working-men and their wives, 'prentices and their sweethearts, blackguards and bullies, make their way to this fair. Pickpockets and their female companions go later. The greater part of the sojourners are on foot, but the vehicles for conveyance are innumerable. The regular and irregular stages are, of course, full inside and outside. Hackney-coaches are equally well filled; gigs carry three, not including the driver; and there are countless private chaise-carts, public pony-chaises and open accommodations. Intermingled with these, town-carts, usually employed in carrying goods, are now fitted up with boards for seats...

Now and then passes, like 'some huge admiral', a full-sized coal-wagon, laden with coalheavers and their wives, and shadowed by spreading boughs from every tree that spreads a bough. These solace themselves with draughts of beer from a barrel aboard, and derive amusement from criticizing walkers and passengers in vehicles passing their own... The six-mile journey of one of these machines is sometimes prolonged from 'dewy morn' till noon. It stops to let its occupants see all that is to be seen on its passage, such as what are called the gooseberry fairs by the wayside, where heats are run by half-killed horses or spare and patient donkeys.

Here are the bewitching sound to many a boy's ears of 'A halfpenny ride O! A halfpenny ride O!' ...There are numberless invitations to take 'a shy for a halfpenny' at a 'bacca box full o' ha'pence' standing on a stick stuck upright in the earth at a reasonable distance for experienced throwers to hit ... but which is a mine of wealth to the costermonger proprietor from the number of unskilled adventurers.

Greenwich fair, of itself, is nothing; the congregated throngs are everything... Group after group succeeds till evening. Before then the more prudent visitors have retired to some of the numerous houses in the vicinage of the park whereon is written, 'Boiling Water Here' or 'Tea and Coffee', and where they take such refreshment as these places and their own bundles afford...

At nightfall, Life in London, as it is called, is found at Greenwich. Every room in every public-house is fully occupied by drinkers, smokers, singers and dancers, and the 'balls' are kept up during the greater part of the night. The way to town is now an indescribable scene... Of all sights the most miserable is that of the poor broken-down horse, who having been urged three times to and from Greenwich, with a load thither of pleasure-seekers at sixpence a head, is now unable to return for the fourth time with a full load back, though whipped ... by a reasoning driver who declares, 'The hoss did it last fair, and why shouldn't he do it again?'

The open windows of every house for refreshment on the road, and clouds of tobacco-smoke therefrom, declare the full stowage of each apartment, while jinglings of the bells and calls louder and louder yet speak wants and wishes to waiters... Now from the wayside booths fly out corks that let forth pop and ginger-beer, and little particoloured lamps give something of a joyous air to appearances that fatigue and disgust. Overwearied children cry before they have walked to the halfway house; women with infants in their arms pull along their tipsy well-beloveds; others endeavour to wrangle or drag them out of drinking-rooms; and until long after midnight the Greenwich road does not cease to disgorge incongruities only to be rivalled by the figures and exhibitions in Dutch and Flemish prints.

Greenwich fair was abolished in 1857.

Whitsun Ales

At Islington
A fair they hold
Where cakes and ale
Are to be sold.

At Highgate and
At Holloway
The like is kept
Here every day;

At Tot'nam Court
And Kentish Town
And all those places
Up and down.

From *Poor Robin's Almanack*, 1676

A day in the life of Bartholomew Fair

THIS IS the only fair now held within the City of London... The proclamation is read at the gate leading into Cloth Fair [Smithfield] by the lord mayor's attorney, and repeated after him by a sheriff's officer in the presence of the lord mayor and sheriffs... The procession afterwards proceeds round Smithfield and returns to the Mansion House, where, in the afternoon, the gentlemen of his lordship's household dine together at the swordbearer's table...

On September 5, 1825, Hone spends all day at the fair, making notes as he goes. First he surveys pavement vendors in the streets off Smithfield, selling 'oysters, fruit, inferior kinds of cheap toys, gingerbread, small wicker baskets' and one with 'discontinued woodcut pamphlets [chapbooks] at a halfpenny each in great quantities' and 'large folio bible prints at a halfpenny each'. All round Smithfield itself are covered stalls.

These covered stalls ... belonged to dealers in gingerbread, toys, hardware, garters, pocketbooks, trinkets and articles of all prices from

a halfpenny to a half sovereign. The gingerbread stalls were conspicu-
ously fine... The largest stalls were the toy-sellers'. Some of these had
a frontage of five-and-twenty feet, and many of eighteen. The usual
frontage of the stalls was eight, ten or twelve feet. They were six feet
six inches or seven feet high in front ... and all formed of canvas
tightly stretched across light poles and railing...

The sheep-pens occupying the area of Smithfield, heretofore the
great public cookery at fair times ... were not, as of old, decked out
and denominated, as they were within recollection, with boughs and
inscriptions tempting hungry errand-boys, sweeps, scavengers, dustmen, drovers and bullock-hankers to the 'princely pleasures' within
the Brighton Pavilion, the Royal Eating Room, Fair Rosamond's
Bower, the New London Tavern and the Imperial Hotel ... but there
was sound, and smell, and sight, from sausages almost as large as
thumbs, fried in miniature dripping-pans by old women, over fires in
saucepans; and there were oysters, which were called 'fine and fat'
because their shells were as large as tea-saucers.

Cloths were spread on tables or planks, with plates, knives and
forks, pepper and salt, and above all those alluring condiments to persons of the rank described, mustard and vinegar. Here they came in
crowds. Each selecting his table-d'hôte dined handsomely for threepence and sumptuously for fourpence.

The purveyors seemed aware of the growing demand for cleanli-
ness of appearance, and whatever might be the quality of the viands,
they were served up in a more decent way than many of the con-
sumers were evidently accustomed to...

I shall now describe or mention every show in the fair. It may be
more interesting to read some years hence than now... Our posterity
may cultivate the 'wisdom of looking backward' in some degree, as
we do the higher wisdom of 'looking forward'...

SHOW 1

The inscription outside, painted in black letters at little more than an
inch in height on a piece of white linen, was as follows:

Murder of Mr Weare, and Probert's cottage
— The Execution of William Probert
A View to be seen here of the Visit of Queen Sheba to
King Solomon on the Throne
Daniel in the Den of Lions — Saint Paul's
Conversion — The Tower of Babel
The Greenland Whale-Fishery — The Battle of Waterloo
A View of the City of Dublin — Coronation of George IV

This was what is commonly, but erroneously, called a puppet-show. It consisted of scenes rudely painted, successively let down by strings pulled by the showman, and was viewed through eyeglasses of magnifying power... 'Only a penny — only a penny!' cried the showman. I paid my penny and saw the first and the meanest show in the fair.

Weare, Probert: victim and killer in a sensational murder

SHOW 2

'Only a penny — only a penny! Walk up, pray walk up.' So called out a man with a loud voice, on an elevated stage, while a long drum and hurdy-gurdy played away... The showcloths described —

> MISS HIPSON, *the Middlesex Wonder, the Largest Child in the Kingdom, when young the Handsomest Child in the World*
>
> *The Persian Giant — The Fair Circassian with Silver Hair*
>
> *The Female Dwarf, Two Feet Eleven Inches high*
>
> *Two Wild Indians from the Malay Islands in the East*

— and other wonders... I was permitted by the proprietor of the show, Nicholas Maughan of Ipswich, Suffolk, to go 'behind the curtain'... Miss Hipson, only twelve years of age, is remarkably gigantic, or rather corpulent, for her age; pretty, well-behaved, and well-informed. She weighed sixteen stone [224 lb, 101 kg] a few months before and has since increased in size. She has ten brothers and sisters, nowise remarkable in appearance. Her father, who is dead, was a bargeman at Brentford. The name of the 'little lady' is Lydia Walpole. She was born at Addiscombe, near Yarmouth, and is sociable, agreeable and intelligent. The Fair Circassian is of pleasing countenance and manners. The Persian Giant is a goodnatured, tall, stately negro. The two Malays could not speak English, except, however, three words, 'Drop o' rum', which they repeated with great glee...

SHOW 3

The inscription outside was Ball's Theatre. Here I saw a man who balanced chairs on his chin; and holding a knife in his mouth, balanced a sword on the edge of the knife. He then put a pewter plate on the hilt of the sword horizontally, and so balanced the sword with the plate on the edge of the knife as before, the plate having previously received a rotary motion, which it communicated to the sword...

These feats were accompanied by the grimaces of a clown, and succeeded by children tumbling and a female who danced a hornpipe. A 'learned horse' found out a lady in the company who wished to be married; a gentleman who preferred a quart of beer to going to church to hear a good sermon; a lady who liked to lie abed in the morning;

and made other discoveries, which he was requested to undertake by his master in language not only 'offensive to ears polite' but to common decency...

SHOW 4

Atkins's Menagerie

This inscription was in lamps on one of the largest shows in the fair. The display of showcloths representing some of the animals ... reached about forty feet in height... The admission was sixpence. As a curiosity, and because it is a singularly descriptive list, the printed bill of the show is subjoined:

MORE WONDERS IN
ATKINS'S ROYAL MENAGERIE
Under the Patronage of HIS MAJESTY

Wonderful Phenomenon in Nature!

The singular and hitherto deemed impossible occurrence of a LION and TIGER cohabiting and producing young has actually taken place in this menagerie, at Windsor. The tigress, on Wednesday, the 27th of October last, produced *three fine cubs*. One of them strongly resembles the tigress; the other two are of a lighter colour, but striped. Mr Atkins had the honour, through the kind intervention of the Marquis of Conyngham [husband of George IV's mistress], of exhibiting the *lion-tigers* to his majesty on the first of November, 1824, at the Royal Lodge, Windsor Great Park, when his majesty was pleased to observe they were the greatest curiosity of the beast creation he ever witnessed.

The royal striped *Bengal Tigress* has again whelped three fine cubs (April 22), two males and one female. The males are white, but striped; the female resembles the tigress... She fondles them with all the care of an attentive mother...

That colossal animal, the wonderful performing
ELEPHANT,

upwards of ten feet high! Five tons weight!! His consumption of hay, corn, straw, carrots, water, etc, exceeds 800lbs [360 kg] daily... His trunk serves him instead of hands and arms... He alone drags machines which six horses cannot move. To his prodigious strength he adds courage, prudence and an exact obedience. He remembers favours as long as injuries...

Atkins's list goes on: a lion and lioness with four cubs, a male Bengal tiger, the onagra (onager), two zebras, a Nepal bison only 24 inches high, a panther, a pair of rattle-tail porcupines, a hyena, an elegant leopard, a laughing hyena, the spotted cavy (guineapig), a pair of jackals, a pair of sledge dogs 'brought over by Captain Parry from one of the northern expeditions', a pair of raccoons, the 'oggouta' from Java, a pair of wild cats, an anteater, a pair of 'those extraordinary and rare birds, pelicans', a gigantic emu, a pair of rapacious condors, 'the largest birds of flight when fully grown', the great horned owl of Bohemia, several species of gold and silver pheasants 'of the most splendid plumage', yellowcrested cockatoo, scarlet and buff macaws.

The people 'tumbled up' in crowds, to the sound of clarinets, trombones and a long drum, played by eight performers in scarlet beefeater coats ... while a stentorian showman called out, 'Don't be deceived! The great performing elephant! The only lion and tigress in one den that are to be seen at the fair, or the proprietor will forfeit a thousand guineas! Walk in! walk in!'

I paid my sixpence... The elephant, with his head through the bars of his cage, whisked his proboscis diligently in search of eatables from the spectators, who supplied him with fruit or biscuits, or handed him halfpence which he uniformly conveyed by his trunk to a retailer of gingerbread, and got the money's-worth in return. Then he unbolted the door to let in his keeper, and bolted it after him; took up a sixpence with his trunk, lifted the lid of a little box fixed against the wall and deposited it within it, and some time afterwards relifted the lid and taking out the sixpence with a single motion, returned it to the keeper. He knelt down when told, fired off a blunderbuss, took off the keeper's hat and afterwards replaced it on his head with as fitting propriety as the man's own hand could have done. In short, he was perfectly docile, and performed various feats that justified the reputation of his species for high understanding.

The keeper ... answered the questions of the company with readiness and civility. His conduct was rewarded by a good parcel of halfpence when his hat went round with a hope that 'the ladies and gentlemen would not forget the keeper before he showed the lion and the tigress'. The latter was a beautiful young animal, with two playful cubs about the size of bulldogs, but without the least fierceness. When the man entered the den they frolicked and climbed about him like kittens. He took them up in his arms, bolted them in a back apartment, and after playing with the tigress a little, threw back a partition which separated her den from the lion's, and then took the lion by the beard.

This was a noble animal. He was couching, and being inclined to take his rest, only answered the keeper's command to rise by extending his whole length and playfully putting up one of his magnificent paws, as a cat does when in good humour. The man then took a short whip, and after a smart lash or two on his back the lion rose with a yawn and fixed his eye on his keeper with a look that seemed to say, 'Well, I suppose I must humour you.'

The man then sat down at the back of the den with his back against the partition, and after some ordering and coaxing the tigress sat on his right hand and the lion on his left... He threw his arms round their necks, played with their noses and laid their heads in his lap. He arose and the animals with him. The lion stood in a fine majestic position, but the tigress reared, and putting one foot over his shoulder and patting him with the other as if she had been frolicking with one of her cubs, he was obliged to check her playfulness.

Then by coaxing and pushing him about, he caused the lion to sit down, and while in that position opened the animal's ponderous jaws with his hands and thrust his face down into the lion's throat, wherein he shouted, and there held his head nearly a minute.

After this he held up a common hoop for the tigress to leap through, and she did it frequently. The lion seemed more difficult to move to this sport. He did not appear to be excited by command or entreaty. At last, however, he went through the hoop, and having been once roused, repeated the action several times. The hoop was scarcely two feet in diameter.

The exhibition of these two animals concluded by the lion lying down on his side, when the keeper stretched himself to his whole length upon him, and then calling to the tigress, she jumped upon the man, extended herself with her paws upon his shoulders, placed her face sideways upon his, and the whole three lay quiescent till the keeper suddenly slipped himself off the lion's side, with the tigress on him, and the trio gambolled and rolled about on the floor of the den like playful children on the floor of a nursery...

This sixpenny show would have furnished a dozen sixpenny shows, at least, to a 'Bartlemy Fair' twenty years ago.

SHOW 5

This was a mare with seven feet... The following is a copy of the printed bill:

To Sportsmen and Naturalists

Now exhibiting, one of the greatest living natural curiosities in the world, namely, a thoroughbred chestnut MARE with seven legs! Four years of age, perfectly sound, free from blemish, and shod on six of her feet. She is very fleet in her paces, being descended from that famous horse Julius Caesar, out of a thoroughbred race mare descended from Eclipse, and

is remarkably docile and temperate. She is the property of Mr
T. Checketts of Belgrave Hall, Leicestershire...

This mare was well worth seeing. Each of her hind legs, besides its
natural and well-formed foot, had another growing out from the
fetlock joint. One of these additions was nearly the size of the natural
foot. The third and least grew from the same joint of the foreleg...

SHOW 6
Richardson's Theatre

The outside of this show was in height upwards of thirty feet and
occupied one hundred feet in width. The platform on the outside
was ... lined with green baize and festooned with deeply-fringed
crimson curtains, except at two places where the money-takers sat ...
roomy projections fitted up like gothic shrine-work, with columns and
pinnacles. There were fifteen hundred variegated illumination-lamps
disposed over various parts of this platform, some ... in the shape of
chandeliers and lustres, and others in wreaths and festoons.

A band of ten performers in scarlet dresses similar to those worn by
beefeaters continually played on clarinets, violins, trombones and the
long drum, while the performers paraded in their gayest 'properties'
before the gazing multitude...

The following bill of the play was obtained at the doors:

*** Change of Performance each Day

RICHARDSON'S
THEATRE.

This Day will be Performed an entire New Melo-Drama, Called, the

WANDERING
OUTLAW,

Or, The Hour of Retribution.

Gustavus, Elector of Saxony, *Mr Wright*
Orsina, Baron of Holstein, *Mr Cooper*
Ulric and Albert, Vassals to Orsina, *Messrs Grove and Moore*
St Clair, the Wandering Outlaw, *Mr Smith*
Rinalda, the Accusing Spirit, *Mr Darling*
Monks, Vassals, Hunters, &c.
Rosabella, Wife to the Outlaw, *Mrs Smith*
Nuns and Ladies

The Piece concludes with the Death of Orsina
and the Appearance of the

ACCUSING SPIRIT

The Entertainments to conclude with a New Comic Harlequinade,
with New Scenery, Tricks, Dresses and Decorations, called

HARLEQUIN
FAUSTUS!

OR, THE

Devil Will Have His Own

Luciferno, *Mr Thomas*.
Dæmon Amozor, afterwards Pantaloon, *Mr Wilkinson*.
Dæmon Ziokos, afterwards Clown, *Mr Hayward*.
Violoncello Player, *Mr Hartem*. Baker, *Mr Thompson*.
Landlord, *Mr Wilkins*. Fisherman, *Mr Rae*.
Doctor Faustus, afterwards Harlequin, *Mr Salter*.
Adelada, afterwards Columbine, *Miss Wilmot*.
Attendant Dæmons, Sprites, Fairies, Ballad Singers,
Flower Girls, &c, &c.

The Pantomime will finish with

A SPLENDID PANORAMA,

Painted by the First Artists.

BOXES 2s.   PIT 1s.   GALLERY 6d.

The theatre was about one hundred feet long and thirty feet wide, hung all round with green baize and crimson festoons. 'Ginger beer, apples, nuts and a bill of the play' were cried... The seats were rows of planks, rising gradually from the ground ... without any distinction of 'boxes, pit or gallery'... There was a painted proscenium like that in a regular theatre, with a green curtain, and the king's arms above ... and five violin players in military dresses... There were at least a thousand persons present...

[*Hone gives a laconic account of the drama. A few glimpses:*] A forest scene and a cottage ... a castle ... an old church and a marketplace ... a prison, and a ghost appeared to the tune of the evening hymn... The castle ... the performance was here enlivened by a murder... Rocks, with a cascade, and there was a procession to an unexecuted execution, for a ghost appeared and saved the Wandering Outlaw from a fierce-looking headsman, and the piece ended.

Then a plump little woman sang 'He loves and he rides away', and the curtain drew up to Harlequin Faustus, wherein, after Columbine and a clown, the most flaming character was the devil, with a red face and hands, in a red Spanish mantle and vest, red 'continuations', stockings and shoes ditto … a red Spanish hat and plume above, and a red brass bugle horn… These performances were, in a quarter of an hour, repeated to another equally intelligent and brilliant audience.

The playbill survives in the British Library, with an instruction from Hone to his printer on it: '*Display this in the column as much as possible like the life itself.*' John Richardson was the leading manager of a touring theatre.

SHOW 7

ONLY A PENNY
There never was such times, indeed!

NERO

The largest Lion in the Fair, for a Hundred Guineas!

These inscriptions, with figured showcloths, were in front of a really good exhibition of a fine lion with leopards and various other beasts of the forest… One of the leopards was carried by his keeper a-pick-a-back. Such a show for 'only a penny' was astonishing. [*This is a different Nero from Wombwell's: see Show 22.*]

SHOW 8

SAMWELL'S COMPANY

Another penny show, 'The Wonderful Children on the Tight Rope, and Dancing Horse, Only a Penny!' I paid my penny to the money-taker, a slender 'fine lady' with three feathers in a 'jewelled turban' and a dress of blue and white muslin and silver… The 'fat, contented, easy' proprietor was arrayed in corresponding magnificence… Obesity had disqualified him for activity…

He superintended the dancing of a young female on the tightrope. Then he announced, 'A little boy will dance a hornpipe on the rope,' and he ordered his 'band' inside to play. This was obeyed without difficulty, for it merely consisted of one man who blew a hornpipe tune on a Pan's-pipe… The little boy danced on the tightrope…

'The little boy will stand on his head on the rope,' said the manager, and the little boy stood on his head accordingly. Then another female danced on the slack wire, and after her came a horse, not a dancing horse but a 'learned' horse…

44

SHOW 9

Large placards were pasted at the side with these words:

CLARKE'S FROM ASTLEY'S
Lighted with Real Gas, In and Outside.

...The interior was very large, and lighted by only a single hoop about two feet six inches in diameter, with little jets of gas about an inch and a half apart... A light bay horse was mounted by a female in trousers, with a pink gown fully frilled, flounced and ribboned, with the shoulders in large puffs. While the horse circled the ring at full speed she danced upon him, and skipped with a hoop like a skipping-rope. She performed other dextrous feats, and concluded by dancing on the saddle with a flag in each hand while the horse flew round the ring with great velocity.

These and subsequent performances were enlivened by tunes from a clarinet and horn, and jokes from a clown, who when she had concluded said to an attendant, 'Now, John, take the horse off, and whatever you do, rub him down well with a cabbage.' Then a man rode and danced on another horse, a very fine animal, and leapt from him three times ... alighting on the horse's back while he was going round. This rider was remarkably dextrous.

In conclusion, the clown got up and rode with many antic tricks, till, on the sudden, an apparently drunken fellow rushed from the audience into the ring and began to pull the clown from the horse. The manager interfered and the people cried 'Turn him out!', but the man persisted, and the clown, getting off, offered to help him up, and threw him over the horse's back to the ground.

At length the intruder was seated, with his face to the tail, although he gradually assumed a proper position; and riding as a man thoroughly intoxicated would ride, fell off. He then threw off his hat and greatcoat, and threw off his waistcoat, and then an under-waistcoat, and a third, and a fourth, and more than a dozen waist-coats. Upon taking off the last, his trousers fell down and he appeared in his shirt; whereupon he crouched, and drawing his shirt off in a twinkling, appeared in a handsome fancy dress, leaped into the saddle of the horse, rode standing with great grace, received great applause, made his bow... [*Astley's, a noted circus, specialized in trick riders.*]

SHOW 10

The Indian Woman — *Chinese Lady and Dwarf,* &c. A clown outside cried, 'Be assured they're alive — only one penny each.' The crowd was great... I did not go in.

SHOW 11

On the outside was inscribed:

To be seen alive!
The Prodigies of Nature!

The Wild Indian Woman and Child,
with her Nurse from her own Country

The Silver-haired Lady and Dwarf

Only a Penny

The showmaster made a speech: 'Ladies and gentlemen, before I show you the wonderful prodigies of nature, let me introduce you to the wonderful works of art,' and then he drew a curtain where some waxwork figures stood.

'This,' said he, 'ladies and gentlemen, is the famous Mother Shipton; and here is the unfortunate Jane Shore, the beautiful mistress of King Edward the Second [he means Edward IV]. Next to her is his majesty King George the Fourth of most glorious memory [he means George III]; and this is Queen Elizabeth in all her glory. Then here you have the Princess Amelia, the daughter of his late majesty, who is dead. This is Mary Queen of Scots, who had her head cut off; and this is O'Bryen, the famous Irish giant. This man here is Thornton, who was tried for the murder of Mary Ashford; and this is the exact resemblance of Othello, the moor of Venice, who was a jealous husband, and depend upon it, every man who is jealous of his wife will be as black as that negro.

'Now, ladies and gentlemen, the two next are a wonderful couple, John and Margaret Scott, natives of Dunkeld in Scotland. They lived about ninety years ago. John Scott was a hundred and five years old when he died, and Margaret lived to be a hundred and twelve; and what is more remarkable, there is not a soul living can say he ever heard them quarrel.'

Here he closed the curtain, and while undrawing another continued thus: 'Having shown you the dead, I have now to exhibit to you two of the most extraordinary wonders of the living. This,' said he, 'is the widow of a New Zealand chief, and this is the little old woman of Bagdad. She is thirty inches high, twenty-two years of age, and a native of Boston in Lincolnshire.'

Each of these living subjects was quite as wonderful as the waxen ones. The exhibition, which lasted about five minutes, was ended by courteous thanks for the 'approbation of the ladies and gentlemen present', and an evident desire to hurry them off lest they might be more curious than his own curiosities.

SHOW 12

'*Only a penny*' was the price of admission to '*The Black Wild Indian Woman — The White Indian Youth — and the Welsh Dwarf — All Alive!*' There was this further announcement —

> *The Young American will Perform after the Manner of the French Jugglers at Vauxhall Gardens, with Balls, Rings, Daggers, &c...*

The 'white Indian youth' was an Eskimo; and the exhibitor assured the visitors upon his veracity that 'the black wild Indian woman' was 'a court lady of the island of Madagascar'. The exhibitor himself was 'the young American', an intelligent and clever youth in a loose striped jacket or frock tied round the middle. He commenced his performance by throwing up three balls which he kept constantly in the air, as he afterwards did four and then five, with great dexterity, using his hands, shoulders and elbows apparently with equal ease. He afterwards threw up three rings, each about four inches in diameter, and then four... To end his performance he produced three knives which, by throwing up and down, he contrived to preserve in the air all together. These feats reminded me of the Anglo-Saxon gleeman who 'threw three balls and three knives alternately in the air, and caught them, one by one, as they fell, returning them again in regular rotation' [quoting Joseph Strutt's *Sports and Pastimes of the People of England*]. The young American's dress and knives were very similar to the gleeman's as Strutt has figured them from a manuscript in the Cotton collection [British Library]. This youth's was one of the best exhibitions in the fair, perhaps the very best...

SHOW 13

The inscriptions and paintings on the outside of this show were:

> *The White Negro who was rescued from her Black Parents by the bravery of a British Officer, the only White Negro Girl Alive — The Great Giantess and Dwarf — Six Curiosities Alive! Only a Penny to see them All Alive!*

...One side of the place was covered by a criminal attempt to represent a treadmill, in oil colours, and the operators at work upon it, superintended by jailers, &c. On the other side were live monkeys in cages, an old bear in a jacket and sundry other animals.

Underneath the wheels of the machine [caravan] other living creatures were moving about, and these turned out to be the poor neglected children of the showman and his wife. The miserable condition of these infants, who were puddling in the mud while their parents outside were turning a bit of music and squalling and bawling with all their might, '*Walk in — only a penny*' ... raised a gloom in the mind.

I was in a reverie concerning these beings when the curtain was withdrawn, and there stood ... 'the tall lady' and 'the white negro, the greatest curiosity ever seen — the first that has been exhibited since the reign of George the Second. Look at her head and hair, ladies and gentlemen, and feel it. There's no deception, it's like ropes of wool...'

The girl herself, who had the flat nose, thick lips and peculiarly shaped skull of the negro, stooped to have her hair examined, and being close to her, I felt it... Of a dirtyish flaxen hue, it hung in ropes of a clothy texture... Her skin was the colour of a European's.

Afterwards stepped forth a little personage about three feet high in a military dress, with topboots, who strutted his tiny legs and held his head aloft with not less importance than the proudest general officer could assume upon his promotion to the rank of field marshal. Mr Samuel Williams, whose versatile and able pencil has frequently enriched this work, visited the fair after me and was equally struck by his appearance. He favours me with the subjoined engraving of this little man...

SHOW 14

BROWN'S GRAND TROOP, FROM PARIS

The performance began by a clown going round and whipping a ring: that is, making a circular space amongst the spectators with a whip in his hand to force the refractory... A conjuror walked up to a table and executed several tricks with cups and balls: giving a boy beer to drink out of a funnel, making him blow through it to show that it was empty, and afterwards applying it to each of the boy's ears, from whence, through the funnel, the beer appeared to reflow and poured on the ground. Afterwards girls danced on the single and double slack wire, and a melancholy-looking clown ... said they were 'as clever as the barber and the blacksmith who shaved magpies at twopence a dozen'. The show concluded with a learned horse.

SHOW 15

Another, and a very good, menagerie — the admission 'only a penny!' It was GEORGE BALLARD'S Caravan, with '*The Lioness that attacked the Exeter mail — The great Lion — Royal Tiger — Large White Bear —*

48

Tiger Owls,' with monkeys and other animals... The chief attraction was the lioness.

Her attack on the Exeter mail was on a Sunday evening in the year 1816. The coach had arrived at Winterslow Hut, seven miles on the London side of Salisbury... At the moment when the coachman pulled up to deliver his bags, one of the leaders [of his team] was suddenly seized by some ferocious animal. This produced a great confusion and alarm. Two passengers who were inside the mail got out, ran into the house and locked themselves up in a room above-stairs. The horses kicked and plunged violently, and it was with difficulty that the coachman could prevent the coach from being overturned.

It was soon perceived by the coachman and guard, by the light of the lamps, that the animal that had seized the horse was a huge lioness. A large mastiff dog came up and attacked her fiercely, on which she quitted the horse and turned upon him. The dog fled, but was pursued and killed by the lioness within forty yards of the place. It appears that the beast had escaped from its caravan, which was standing on the roadside with others belonging to the proprietors of the menagerie, on their way to Salisbury Fair...

The horse, when first attacked, fought with great spirit, and if at liberty would probably have beaten down his antagonist with his fore feet, but in plunging he embarrassed himself in the harness. The lioness attacked him in the front, and springing at his throat, fastened the talons of her fore feet on each side of his neck close to the head, while the talons of her hind feet were forced into his chest... The expressions of agony in his tears and moans were most piteous and affecting... The coachman at first proposed to alight and stab the lioness with a knife, but was prevented...

Whether she had carried off with her as prey the dog she had killed, or from some other cause, she continued growling and howling in so loud a tone as to be heard for nearly half a mile. All had called out loudly to the guard to despatch her with his blunderbuss [carried as a defence against highwaymen], which he appeared disposed to do, but the owner cried out to him, 'For God's sake do not kill her! She cost me £500 and she will be quiet as a lamb if not irritated.' This arrested his hand... She was afterwards easily enticed by the keepers and placed in her usual confinement...

SHOW 16

Exhibition of Real Wonders

This announcement ... was inscribed over the show with the usual notice, '*Only a Penny!*' — 'The Wonders of the Deep!' — 'The

Prodigies of the Age!' and 'The Learned Pig!'... The printed bill is a curiosity:

To be Seen in a Commodious Pavilion in this Place

REAL WONDERS!
SEE AND BELIEVE.

Have you seen

THE BEAUTIFUL DOLPHIN
The Performing Pig & the Mermaid?

If not, pray do! as the exhibition contains more variety than any other in England. Those ladies and gentlemen who may be pleased to honour it with a visit will be truly gratified.

TOBY,
The Swinish Philosopher and Ladies' Fortune Teller.

That beautiful animal appears to be endowed with the natural sense of the human being. He is in colour the most beautiful of his race; in symmetry the most perfect; in temper the most docile; and far exceeds anything yet seen for his intelligent performances. He is beyond all conception: he has a perfect knowledge of the alphabet, understands arithmetic, and will spell and cast accounts, tell the points of the globe, the dicebox, the hour by any person's watch, &c.

The Real Head of
MAHOWRA,
THE CANNIBAL CHIEF.

At the same time, the public will have an opportunity of seeing what was exhibited so long in London under the title of

THE MERMAID:

The wonder of the deep! Not a facsimile or copy, but the same curiosity...

The great prodigies of this show were the 'performing pig' and the performing show-woman. She drew forth the learning of the *swinish philosopher* admirably. He told his letters and 'got into spelling' with his nose, and could do a sum of two figures... He routed out those of the company who were in love or addicted to indulgence; and peremptorily grunted that a round, fat, oily-faced personage at my elbow 'loved good eating, and a pipe, and a jug of good ale...'

The *Beautiful Dolphin* was a fish-skin stuffed. The *Mermaid* was the last manufactured imposture of that name, exhibited for half-a-crown in Piccadilly the year before. The *Real Head of Mahowra, the cannibal chief,* was a skull that might have been some English clodpole's, with a dried skin over it, and bewigged; but it looked sufficiently terrific when the lady show-woman put the candle in at the neck and the flame illuminated the yellow integument over the holes where eyes, nose and a tongue had been. There was enough for a penny.

The 'mermaid' showcloth

SHOW 17

Another 'only a penny!' with pictures 'large as life' on the showcloths outside ... and the following inscription:

ALL ALIVE!
No False Paintings!

THE WILD INDIAN,

THE

GIANT BOY

And the
DWARF FAMILY,

Never here before.

TO BE SEEN ALIVE!

Mr Thomas Day was the reputed father of the dwarf family, and exhibited himself as small enough for a great wonder; as he was. He was also proprietor of the show, and said he was thirty-five years of age and only thirty-five inches high. He fittingly descanted on the living personages in whom he had a vested interest. There was a boy six years old, only twenty-seven inches high. The *Wild Indian* was a civil-looking man of colour.

The *Giant Boy*, William Wilkinson Whitehead, was fourteen years of age on the 26th of March last, stood five feet two inches high, measured five feet round the body ... thirty-one inches round the thigh, and weighed twenty-two stone [308 lb, 139 kg]... He was born at Glasgow ... of fair complexion, an intelligent countenance, active in motion and of sensible speech. He was lightly dressed in plaid to

show his limbs, with a bonnet of the same. The artist with me
sketched his appearance exactly as we saw him...

SHOW 18

Holden's Glass Working and Blowing

Having seen exhibitions of the same kind, and the evening getting
late, I declined entering, though 'only a penny!'

SHOW 19

The paintings flared on the showcloths with this inscription:

They're all Alive Inside! Be assured They're All Alive!

The Yorkshire Giantess — Waterloo Giant — Indian Chief

Only a Penny!

An overgrown girl was the Yorkshire Giantess... The abdication of
such an Indian Chief as this, in favour of Bartholomew Fair, was
probably forced upon him by his tribe.

SHOW 20

Greatest of all Wonders! — Giantess and Two Dwarfs

Only a Penny!

The dwarfs inside were dwarfish, and the 'Somerset girl, taller than any man in England' (for so said the showcloth), arose from a chair ... to the height of six feet nine inches and three-quarters, with, 'Ladies and gentlemen, your most obedient.' She was goodlooking and affable, and obliged the ladies and gentlemen by taking off her tight-fitting slipper and handing it round. It was of such dimensions that the largest man present could have put his booted foot into it. She said her name was Elizabeth Stock and that she was only sixteen years old.

SHOW 21

CHAPPELL — PIKE

This was a very large show, without any showcloths or other announcement outside ... except a clown and several male and female performers who strutted the platform in their exhibiting dresses... The clown grimaced and, assisted by others, bawled 'Only a penny!' till the place filled... There was slack-rope dancing, tumbling and other representations as at Ball's theatre, but better executed.

SHOW 22

WOMBWELL

The front ... was entirely covered by painted showcloths representing the animals, with the proprietor's name in immense letters above, and the words *The Conquering Lion* very conspicuous. There were other showcloths along the whole length of the side, surmounted by this inscription stretching out in one line of large letters —

NERO AND WALLACE, THE SAME LIONS THAT FOUGHT AT WARWICK

One of the front showcloths represented one of the fights. A lion stood up with a dog in his mouth, crunched between his grinders. The blood ran from his jaws. His left leg stood upon another dog squelched by his weight. A third dog was in the act of flying at him ferociously, and one, wounded and bleeding, was fearfully retreating. There were seven other showcloths on this front, with the words NERO AND WALLACE between them...

Sixpence was the entrance money... No disorder without [in the fair] was equal to the disorder within Wombwell's. There was no passage at the end through which persons might make their way out.

Perhaps this was part of the proprietor's policy, for he might imagine that the universal disgust that prevailed in London while he was manifesting his brutal cupidity at Warwick [*see pages 30–33*] had not subsided, and that it was necessary his showplace here should appear to fill well on the first day of the fair...

Be that as it may, his show when I saw it was a shameful scene. There was no person in attendance to exhibit or point out the animals... A loutish fellow with a broomstick stood against one of the dens, from whom I could only obtain this information, that it was not his business to show the beasts, and that the showman would begin at a proper time. I patiently waited... At length I discovered ... that the showman, who was evidently under the influence of drink, had already made his way one-third along the show. With great difficulty I forced myself through the sweltering press somewhat nearer to him, and managed to get opposite to Nero's den, which he had by that time reached and clambered into, and into which he invited any of the spectators who chose to pay him sixpence each, as many of them did for the sake of saying that they had been in the den with the noble animal that Wombwell, his master, had exposed to be baited by bulldogs... The man was as greedy of gain as his master, and therefore, without the least regard to those who wished for general information concerning the different animals, he maintained his post as long as there was a prospect of getting the sixpences.

Pressure and heat were now so excessive that I was compelled to struggle my way, as many others did, towards the door...

Wombwell ... is undersized in mind as well as form, 'a weazen, sharpfaced man' with a skin reddened by more than natural spirits...

Here ends my account of the various shows... The following bill was slipped into my hand by a man stationed to give them away:

SERIOUS NOTICE,
IN PERFECT CONFIDENCE

The following extraordinary comic performances at

Sadler's Wells

can only be given during the present week. The proprietors, therefore, most respectfully inform that fascinating sex, so properly distinguished by the appropriate appellation of

THE FAIR!

and all those well-inclined gentlemen who are happy enough to protect them, that the amusements will consist of a romantic tale of mysterious horror and broad grin, never acted, called —

THE ENCHANTED
GIRDLES;
OR
WINKI THE WITCH
And the Ladies of Samarcand

———

A most whimsical burletta, which sends people home
perfectly exhausted from uninterrupted risibility, called

THE LAWYER, THE JEW
AND
THE YORKSHIREMAN

———

With, by request of 75 distinguished families, and a party of 5,
that never-to-be-sufficiently-praised pantomime, called

Magic in Two Colours,
OR,
FAIRY BLUE & FAIRY RED:
Or, Harlequin and the Marble Rock

———

It would be perfectly superfluous for any man in his senses to attempt
anything more than the mere announcement in recommendation of the
above unparalleled representations, so attractive in themselves as to
threaten a complete monopoly of the qualities of the magnet; and though
the proprietors were to talk nonsense for an hour, they could not assert a
more *important truth* than that they possess

The only Wells from which you may draw

WINE,

THREE SHILLINGS AND SIXPENCE
A full Quart

———

Those whose important avocations prevent their coming
at the commencement will be admitted for
HALF-PRICE, AT HALF-PAST EIGHT

N.B. A full Moon during the Week

———

[A full moon made people readier to be out late in ill-lit streets]

This bill is here inserted as a curious specimen of the method adopted to draw an audience to the superior entertainments of a pleasant little summer theatre, which to its credit discourages the nuisances that annoy every parent who takes his family to the boxes at the other theatres [*referring to the prostitutes cruising in the West End theatres*].

Hone follows his report with twenty-six pages of information about Bartholomew Fair and Smithfield over the centuries. Although he was impressed by some of the shows, his wish for moral improvement overrides that. He says the fair has become 'an annual scene of debauchery' (he does not venture to describe that) and 'must and will be put down'.

In 1826 he goes to have another look:

Crocodiles hatched by steam

SPITE OF Corporation resolutions, and references to the committee, and reports, and recommendations to abolish the fair, it is held again... It is going out like the lottery, by force of public opinion... There were this year only three shows at sixpence and one at twopence; all the rest were 'only a penny' [inferior shows for the poor].

The sixpenny shows were Clarke, with riders and tumblers; Richardson with his tragicomical company enacting *Paul Pry* [see pages 71–3], and wicked Wombwell with his fellow brutes. In the twopenny show were four lively little crocodiles about twelve inches long, hatched from the eggs at Peckham, by steam; two larger crocodiles; four cages of fierce rattlesnakes; and a dwarf lady.

In the penny shows were a glassblower, sitting at work in a glass wig with rows of curls all over, making pretty little teacups at threepence each and miniature tobacco pipes for a penny. He was assisted by a wretched-looking female, who was a sword-swallower at the last fair, and figured in this by placing her feet on hot iron and licking a poker, nearly red-hot, with her tongue. In 'Brown's Grand Company from Paris' there were juggling, tightrope dancing, a learned horse and playing on the saltbox with a rolling-pin, to a tune which is said to be peculiar to the pastime. The other penny shows were nearly as last year...

There was not one 'up-and-down' or roundabout... A person, apparently an agent of a religious society, was anxiously busy in the fair distributing a bill entitled 'Are you prepared to die?'

The fair took a while to die. In 1843 the authorities prohibited all showmen, thus making it a fair limited to merchandizing. The shows migrated to a field in Islington. Bartholomew Fair dwindled, and was formally proclaimed for the last time in 1855.

The great kaleidoscope rip-off

IN APRIL 1818 London was surprised by the sudden appearance of an optical instrument for creating and exhibiting beautiful forms, which derives its name from καλοσ *beautiful*, ειδοτ *a form*, and σκοπεω *to see*. The novelty was so enchanting that opticians could not manufacture kaleidoscopes fast enough to meet the universal desire for seeing the delightful and ever-varying combinations presented by each turn of the magical cylinder.

The kaleidoscope was invented by Dr David Brewster [1781–1868, Fellow of the Royal Society], to whom, had its exclusive formation been ensured, it must have produced a handsome fortune in the course of a single year. Unhappily, that gentleman was deprived of his just reward by fraudful anticipation. He says, '...In consequence of one of the patent instruments having been exhibited to one of the London opticians, the remarkable properties of the kaleidoscope became known before any number of them could be prepared for sale. The sensation excited in London by this premature exhibition of its effects ... can be conceived only by those who witnessed it... No fewer than two hundred thousand instruments have been sold in London and Paris during three months.'

Cuckoldom and cross-dressing

AT THE PLEASANT VILLAGE of Charlton on the north side of Black-heath, about eight miles from London, a fair is held annually on Saint Luke's Day [October 18]. It is called Horn Fair... An old newspaper states that it was formerly a custom for a procession to go from some of the inns in Bishopsgate, in which were a king, a queen, a miller, a counsellor, &c, and a great number of others with horns [symbols of cuckoldom] in their hats, to Charlton, where they went round the church [Saint Luke's] three times. This was accompanied by so many indecencies on Blackheath, such as the whipping of females with furze, &c, that it gave rise to the proverb of 'All is fair at Horn Fair'.

A curious biographical memoir, *Life of Mr William Fuller*, 1703, relates the custom of going to Horn Fair in women's clothes: 'I remember being there upon Horn-Fair day. I was dressed in my landlady's best gown and other women's attire... As we were coming back by water, all the clothes were spoiled by dirty water, &c, that was flung on us, for which I was obliged to present her with two guineas...'

The horn-bearing at this fair may be conjectured to have originated from the symbol accompanying the figure of Saint Luke: when he is represented by sculpture or painting he is usually in the act of writing, with an ox or cow by his side, whose horns are conspicuous... Though most of the painted glass in the windows of the church was destroyed during the troubles in the time of Charles I, yet many fragments remain of Saint Luke's ox with wings on his back, and goodly horns...

Horns still continue to be sold from the lowest to the best booth in the fair. They are chiefly those of sheep, goats and smaller animals, and are usually gilt and decorated... The fair is still a kind of carnival or masquerade. On Saint Luke's Day, 1825, though the weather was unfavourable to the customary humours, most of the visitors wore masks. Several were disguised in women's clothes, and some assumed whimsical characters... Horns were in the hat and bonnet of almost every person in the rout... [*This frolic lingered on until 1872.*]

Cornish hugs and Devonshire kicks

'Sam Sam's Son', a West Country contributor, reports on wrestling, and on a festival, the Saint Ives Knillian, that is still held — most recently in 1996.

THE MODE of wrestling in Cornwall is very different from that of Devonshire. The former is famous in the 'hug', the latter in kicking shins. No kicks are allowed in Cornwall, unless the players who are in the ring mutually agree to it.

A hat is thrown in as a challenge, which being accepted by another, the combatants strip and put on a coarse loose kind of jacket, of which they take hold and of nothing else. The play then commences. To constitute a fair fall, both shoulders must touch the ground at, or nearly, the same moment. To guard against foul play, to decide on the falls and manage the affairs of the day, four or six *sticklers* (as the umpires are called) are chosen...

The athletic exercise of wrestling thrives in the eastern part of Cornwall, particularly about Saint Austell and Saint Columb. At the latter place resides James Polkinhorne, the champion of Cornwall, and by many considered to be entitled to the championship of the four western counties. He keeps a respectable inn there, is a very good-looking, thickset man — still he does not look the man he is, 'he has that within that passes show'. A contest between him and Abraham Cann, the Devonshire champion, was expected in the course of this summer [1826]. Much chaffing passed between them for some time in the country papers, but it appears to be 'no go' — no fault of the Cornish hero... [*The match was fought: see below.*]

With a view of maintaining the superiority in amusements in which the Cornish delight, John Knill, Esq, of great eminence at Saint Ives, bequeathed the income of an estate to trustees, that the same might be distributed in a variety of prizes to those who should excel in racing, rowing and wrestling. These games [the Knillian] he directed should be held every fifth year forever around a mausoleum which he erected in 1782 on a high rock [Worvas Hill] near the town of Saint Ives.

The first celebration took place in July 1801, when according to the will of the founder a band of virgins, all dressed in white, with four matrons and a company of musicians, commenced the ceremony by walking in pairs to the summit of the hill, where they danced and chanted a hymn composed for the purpose round the mausoleum, in imitation of druids around the cromlechs of the departed brave.

> Quit the bustle of the bay.
> Hasten, virgins, come away,
> Hasten to the mountain's brow.
> Leave, oh! leave Saint Ives below.
> Haste to breathe a purer air,
> Virgins fair, and pure as fair.
> Quit Saint Ives and all her treasures,
> Fly her soft voluptuous pleasures.
> Fly her sons and all the wiles
> Lurking in their wanton smiles.
> Fly her splendid midnight halls,
> Fly the revels of her balls.

Early in the morning the roads from Helston, Truro and Penzance were lined with horses and vehicles of every description, while thousands of travellers on foot poured in... The wrestlers entered the ring; the troop of virgins, dressed in white, advanced with solemn step to notes of harmony; the spectators ranged themselves upon the hills... The sight was grand. Here the wrestlers exerted their sinewy strength; there the rowers in their various dresses of blue, white and red urged the gilded prows of their boats through the sparkling waves...

Although the Knillian survives, its sporting contests have faded away. And there is nothing now like the old west-country wrestling matches, with crowds of up to 10,000. Sam Sam's Son reports further on Cornwall v Devon:

I am really an admirer of Abraham Cann of Devon, whose behaviour in the ring no one can at all complain of. He *is* a fine fellow, but so is Polkinhorne, and beyond doubt the latter is much the better man... Cann, with his monstrous shoe and most horrible mode of kicking, has never yet been able to throw Polkinhorne... He [Cann] would find several awkward opponents if he would meet those from Westmorland, Carlisle and Cumberland, and play in their mode.

In the match, however, between Polkinhorne and Cann [in October

1826], the latter very properly received the stakes, on account of the former having quitted the ring on conceiving he had won the day by throwing two falls. The second throw, on reference to the umpires, was after some time deemed not a fair back fall... [*Devon men with heavy bets on Cann are said to have influenced this verdict.*]

I have seen in Cornwall more persons present at these games, when the prize has only been a gold-laced hat, a waistcoat or a pair of gloves, than ever attend the sports of Devon (where the prizes are very liberal, for they don't like to be kicked for a trifle) or even at the famed meetings of later days in London, at the Eagle in the City-road or the Golden Eagle in Mile End. How is this? Why, in the latter places six, eight or at farthest twelve standards [matches] are as much as a day's play will admit of; while in Cornwall I have seen forty made in one day... In Devon, what with the heavy shoes and thick padding, and time lost in equipment and kicking, half that number *cannot* be made in a day...

At a Cornish wrestling, a man's favourite play can be seen by the hitch or holdfast he takes... The off-hand play is that in which the men have each a gripe on his adversary's collar, or on the collar and opposite elbow or wrist; when by a sudden blow against the outside of the foot by the striker's inside (if strong enough), or by a corresponding twist of the collar, one lays the other flat on his back. This is called *playing with the toe*; but they never wear any shoes, and are generally barelegged from the knee downwards...

[Details follow on the *heave*, the *crook*, the *inlock*, the *clamp*, the *forward heave*, the *in-turn* and the *Cornish hug*.] The Devonshire men have no under-play, nor have they one heaver, and the do not understand or practise the hug. Visit a Devon ring, and you'll wait a tedious time after a man is thrown ere another appears. After undergoing the necessary preparation for a good kicking, &c, he enters and shakes his adversary by the hand, and kicks and lays hold when he can get a good opportunity. If he is conscious of superior strength he 'goes to work', and by strength of arms wrests him off his legs and lays him flat; or if too heavy for this, he carries him round by the hip.

But when the men find they are 'much of a muchness' it is really tiresome: caution is the word; the *shoe*, only, goes to work, and after dreadful hacking, cutting and kicking, one is at last thrown. The hardest shoe and the best kicker carries the day. Cann is a very hard kicker and a cautious wrestler.

The Irishman's legs [in a London match] bore ample testimony of the effects of Cann's shoe. He left him knee-deep in a stream of gore.

The Devon men never close with a Cornish adversary if they find he possesses any science... They therefore stand off, with only one hand in the collar, and kick. The Cornishman then attempts to get in, and the Devonman tries to confine one of his opponent's arms by holding him at the wrist and keeping him from coming in either over or under, and at every move of his leg kicking it... It will be plainly seen that a Cornishman cannot enter a Devon ring on anything like an equality. Wishing well to both counties...

What a glorious man our saint was

SEVERAL FAIRS, similar to those in the country parts of England as to tents and booths, are held in Ireland on Saint Patrick's day... It is a kind of rural fête with drinking and dancing, whereto is added fighting... The constant use of the shillelagh ... is a puzzling fact to Englishmen, who on their own holidays regard a shillelagh as a malicious weapon... Some years ago Patrick's day was welcomed in the smaller country towns or hamlets by every possible manifestation of gladness and delight. The inn, if there was one, was thrown open to all comers, who received an allowance of oaten bread and fish. This was a benev-

An Irishman all in his glory was there
With a sprig of shillelagh and shamrock so green.

Drawn by the Dublin-born artist William Henry Brooke, 1772–1860

olence from the host, and to it was added a 'Patrick's pot' or quantum of beer; but of late years whiskey is the beverage most esteemed…

In the city of Dublin, Patrick's day is still regarded as a festival from the highest to the lowest ranks of society… While the bells of churches and chapels are tuned to joyous notes, the piper and harper play up 'Patrick's Day in the Morning'. Old women with plenteous supplies of trefoil are heard in every direction crying 'Buy my shamrocks, green shamrocks!' and children have 'Patrick's crosses' pinned to their sleeves. These are small prints of various kinds. Some of them merely represent a cross, others are representations of Saint Patrick trampling the reptiles under foot… The following whimsical song is a particular favourite, and sung to 'his holiness' by all ranks in the height of convivial excitement:

> Saint Patrick was a gentleman, and he came from decent people.
> In Dublin town he built a church and on it put a steeple.
> His father was a Wollaghan, his mother an O'Grady,
> His aunt she was a Kinaghan and his wife a widow Brady.
>> Tooralloo tooralloo, what a glorious man our saint was,
>> Tooralloo tooralloo, O whack fal de lal de lal, &c.
>
> Och! Antrim hills are mighty high and so's the hill of Howth too,
> But we all do know a mountain that is higher than them both too.
> 'Twas on the top of that high mount Saint Patrick preached a sermon.
> He drove the frogs into the bogs and banished all the vermin.
>> *Tooralloo, &c —*
>
> No wonder that we Irish lads then are so blithe and frisky.
> Saint Patrick was the very man that taught us to drink whiskey.
> Och! to be sure, he had the knack and understood distilling
> For his mother kept a shebeen shop near the town of Enniskillen.
>> *Tooralloo, &c —*

Perhaps the first British publication, in 1826, of this original version of the song, created by two Cork men about 1815. It is still sung, with added stanzas and many minor changes (the saint soon had to lose his wife).

The blood must flow an inch

A reader tells of the hardy backswordmen of Wiltshire and their rivals.

THE NATIVES are a very strong and hardy set of men and are particularly fond of robust sports. Their chief and favourite amusement is backswording or singlestick, for which they are as greatly celebrated as the inhabitants of the adjoining counties, Somersetshire and Gloucestershire… They play with a large round stick, which must be three feet long, with a basket prefixed to one end as a guard for the hand. The combatants throw off their hats and upper garments, with the exception of the shirt, and have the left hand tied to the side... They brandish the stick over the head, guarding off the adversary's blows and striking him when the opportunity occurs. Great skill is often used in the defence. I have seen two men play for upwards of half an hour without once hitting each other. The blood must flow an inch from some part of the head before either party is declared victor.

Blackford the backsword player [see below] was a butcher residing at Swindon... His successor is a blacksmith at Liddington named Morris Pope, who is considered the best player of the day and generally carries off the prizes at the Hungerford Revel... To commence the fray, twenty very excellent players are selected from each county. The contest lasts a considerable time and is always severe, but the Wiltshire men are generally conquerors... But Hungerford Revel is not a scene of contention alone...

Here the writer describes rustic sports such as 'girls running for smocks', 'climbing the greasy pole', 'jumping in sacks for a cheese', and also:

Old women drinking hot tea for snuff. Whoever can drink it the quickest and hottest gets the prize.

Grinning through horse-collars. Several Hodges stand in a row, each holding a collar. Whoever can make the ugliest face through it gains the prize. This feat is also performed by old women, and certainly the latter are the most amusing.

Racing between old women for a pound of tea. This occasions much merriment, and it is sometimes astonishing to see with what agility the old dames run in order to obtain their favourite.

Hunting a pig with a soaped tail. ...The most laughable. Grunter with his tail well soaped is set off at the foot of a hill and is quickly pursued; but the person who can lay any claim to him must first catch him by the tail and fairly detain him with one hand. This is an almost impossible feat... Such is the obstinate nature of a pig that on being pulled one way he will strive all he can to go a contrary... I may mention a curious wager a few years ago between a pork-butcher and a waterman. The butcher betted the waterman that he would make a pig run over one of the bridges ... quicker than the waterman would row across the river... The waterman began to row with all his might and main, and the butcher catching hold of the tail of the pig endeavoured to pull him back, upon which the pig pulled forward and with great rapidity ran over the bridge, pulling the butcher after him...

Duck hunting. This sport generally concludes the whole. It is a very laughable, but certainly a very cruel amusement. They tie a poor unfortunate owl in an upright position to the back of a still more unfortunate duck and then turn them loose. The owl, presuming that his inconvenient captivity is the fault of the duck, very unceremoniously commences an attack on the head of the latter, who naturally takes to its own means of defence, the water. The duck dives with the owl on his back. As soon as he rises, the astonished owl opens wide his eyes, turns about his head in a very solemn manner, and suddenly recommences his attack on the oppressed duck, who dives as before. The poor animals generally destroy each other unless some humane person rescues them.

Like all other Wiltshire amusements, the Hungerford Revel always closes with good humour and conviviality, the ale flowing plentifully and the song echoing loud and gaily from the rustic revellers…

A correspondent at Purton, Wiltshire, recalls Blackford the backsword
player in his championship days, long years before:

He bore off the prizes then played for in London, Bath, Bristol and Gloucester… I recollect this frontispiece-despoiler broke fourteen heads one after another. In the fifteenth bout, however, he pretty nearly found his match in the person of Isaac Bushel, a blacksmith of this place, who could bite a nail asunder, eat a shoulder of mutton with appendages, or fight friend or foe for love or money. It was a saying, 'Bushel can take enough to kill a dozen men.' …When the Somerset youths played with the Wiltshire on a stage on Calne Green two years since, one of Blackford's descendants gave a feeling proof of head-breaking with other heads of this bloodletting art.

A wonder-working letter

A playful puzzle from a reader at Cheltenham.

I HAVE LONG MAINTAINED a distinguished station in our modern days, but I cannot trace my origin to ancient times, though the learned have attempted it. After the revolution of 1688 I was chief physician to the king; at least, in my absence he ever complained of sickness. Had I lived in ancient days, so friendly was I to crowned heads that Cleopatra would have got off with a sting; and her cold arm would have felt a reviving heat.

I am rather a friend to sprightliness than to industry; I have often converted a neutral pronoun into a man of talent; I have often amused myself with reducing the provident ant to indigence. I never meet a post-horse without giving him a blow; to some animals I am a friend, and many a puppy has yelped for aid when I have deserted him. I am a patron of architecture and can turn everything into bricks and mortar; and so honest withal that whenever I can find a pair of stockings, I ask for their owner. Not even Joseph Lancaster [educational reformer] has carried education so far as I have: I adopt always the system of interrogatories. I have already taught my hat to ask questions of fact, and my poultry questions of chronology.

With my trees I share the labours of my laundry; they scour my linen, and when I find a rent, 'tis I who make it entire. In short, such are my merits that whatever yours may be, you can never be more than half as good as I am.

Answer to the preceding

A *literary* character you view
Known to the moderns only — W.
I was physician to King William:
When absent, he would say, 'How — ill I am!'
In ancient days if I had liv'd, the asp
Which poison'd Egypt's queen had been a — Wasp;
And the death-coldness of th'imperial arm
With life reviving had again been — Warm.
A friend to sprightliness, that neuter It
By sudden pow'r I've changed into a — Wit.
The vainly-provident industrious ant
With cruel sport I oft reduce to — Want.
Whene'er I meet with an unlucky hack,
I give the creature a tremendous — Whack;
And many a time a puppy cries for help
If I desert capriciously the — Whelp.
A friend to architecture, I turn all
(As quick as Chelt'nham builders) into — Wall.
I'm honest, for whene'er I find some hose
I seek the owner, loud exclaiming — Whose?
Farther than Lancaster I educate,
My system's always to interrogate:
Already have I taught my very hat
Questions of fact to ask, and cry out — What?
Questions of time my poultry, for the hen
Cackles chronology, inquiring — When?
My laundry's labour I divide with ashes:
It is with them the laundress scours and — Washes;
And if an ugly rent I find, the hole
Instantly vanishes, becoming — Whole.
In short, my merits are so bright to view
How good soe'er you may be, just or true,
You can but halve my worth, for I am — *double you.*

Mrs Gilpin's horsemanship

Hone's friend Charles Lamb, under the pen-name 'A Sojourner at Enfield'
(he retired to this rural village in 1827), offers a jesting addition to William
Cowper's famous 'John Gilpin' poem:

> Then Mrs Gilpin sweetly said
>   Unto her children three,
> 'I'll clamber o'er this stile so high,
>   And you climb after me.'
>
> But having climbed unto the top
>   She could no further go,
> But sat, to every passer-by
>   A spectacle and show,
>
> Who said, 'Your spouse and you this day
>   Both show your horsemanship,
> And if you stay till he comes back
>   Your horse will need no whip.'

The sketch here engraved (probably from the poet's friend Romney)
was found with the above three stanzas in the handwriting of
Cowper, among the papers of the late Mrs Unwin. It is to be regretted

that no more was found of this little *episode*, as it evidently was intended to be, to 'The Diverting History of Johnny Gilpin'.

It is to be supposed that Mrs Gilpin, in the interval between dinner and tea, finding the time hang upon her hands during her husband's involuntary excursion, rambled out with the children into the fields at the back of The Bell (as what could be more natural?) and at one of those high awkward stiles for which Edmonton is so proverbially famed, the embarrassment represented, so mortifying to a substantial City madam, might have happened; a predicament which leaves her in a state which is the very antipodes to that of her too locomotive husband...

Now I talk of Edmonton stiles, I must speak a little about those of Enfield, its next neighbour, which are so ingeniously contrived — every rising bar to the top becoming more protuberant than the one under it — that it is impossible for any Christian climber to get over without bruising his (or her) shins as many times as there are bars. These inhospitable invitations to a flayed skin are planted so thickly, too, and are so troublesomely importunate at every little paddock here, that this, with more propriety than Thebes of old, might be entitled Hecatompolis: the Town of the Hundred Gates, or *stiles*.

The sketch is by Lamb's friend and fellow-punster, the comic writer Thomas Hood. The Bell at Edmonton was the country inn past which the unlucky Gilpin twice galloped instead of dining with his family.

A trio of merry epitaphs

At Penryn, Cornwall

Here lies William Smith: and what is somewhat rarish,
He was born, bred and hang'd in this here parish.

On a Miser

Here lies one who for med'cine would not give
A little gold, and so his life he lost.
I fancy now he'd wish again to live
Could he but guess how much his fun'ral cost.

At Staverton*

Here lies the body of Betty Bowden,
Who would live longer but she couden;
Sorrow and grief made her decay
Till her bad leg carried her away.

In Devon, Gloucestershire, Northamptonshire or Wiltshire?

A hundred thousand on the Serpentine

A HARD FROST is a season of holidays in London. The scenes exhibited are too agreeable and ludicrous for the pen to describe. They are for the pencil; and George Cruikshank's is the only one... He has hastily essayed the sketch in a short hour... Scarcely a tithe of either the time or space requisite has been afforded Mr Cruikshank for the subject. It conveys some notion however of part of the doings on the Serpentine in Hyde Park... The entire of this canal from the wall of Kensington Gardens to the extremity of the Knightsbridge end was, on Sunday the 15th of January 1826, literally a mob of skaters and gazers. At one period it was calculated that there were not less than a hundred thousand persons upon this single sheet of ice...

The Hyde Park river — which no river is;
The Serpentine — which is not serpentine,
When frozen, every skater claims as his
In right of common, there to intertwine
With countless crowds, and glide upon the ice...   *Hone*

The whims of Thomas Hood

After labouring on a mass of material about lotteries (see pages 277–82),
Hone gratefully turns in November 1826 to a review copy of *Whims and
Oddities*, written and illustrated by the whimsical Thomas Hood. He gives
it nearly nine pages, with some of Hood's own illustrations.

ALL THE WORLD knows, or ought to know, that among persons
called literary there are a few peculiarly *littery*, who master an article
through confusion of head and materials, and, having achieved the
setting of their thoughts and places to rights, celebrate the important
victory by the triumph of a short repose. At such a minute, after my
last toilsome adventure in the Lottery, sitting in my little room before
the fire and looking into it with the comfortable knowledge that the
large table behind me was 'free from all incumbrances', I yearned for a
recreative dip into something new, when Mr Hood's volume ... came
in the very nick. And as I amused myself, I resolved to be thenceforth,
and therefore, as agreeable as possible to my readers...

The first engraving that opened on me was of —

A DREAM

In this figure, 'a medley of human faces, wherein certain features
belong in common to different visages — the eyebrow of one, for
instance, forming the mouth of another', Mr Hood has successfully
'tried to typify a common characteristic of dreams, the entanglement
of divers ideas, to the waking mind distinct or incongruous, but by the
confusion of sleep inseparably ravelled up and knotted into Gordian
intricacies... In a dream, two separate notions will mutually involve
some convertible incident, that becomes, by turns, a symptom of both
in general, or of either in particular. Thus are begotten the most
extraordinary associations of thoughts and images — unnatural connections like those marriages of forbidden relationships where

mothers become cousins to their own sons or daughters, and quite as bewildering...'

Because it never happened that Mr Hood in his dreams fancied himself deprived of any sense, he was greatly puzzled by this question: '*How does a BLIND man dream?*'

'I mean,' says Mr H, 'a person with the opaque crystal from his birth. He is defective in that very faculty which, of all others, is most active in those night-passages, thence emphatically called visions. He has had no acquantance with external images, and has therefore none of those transparent pictures that, like the slides of a magic lantern, pass before the mind's eye and are projected by the inward spiritual light upon the utter blank. His imagination must be like an imperfect kaleidoscope... It is difficult to conceive such a man's dream.

'Is it a still benighted wandering, a pitchdark night progress, made known to him by the consciousness of the other senses? Is he still pulled through the universal blank by an invisible power, as it were, at the nether end of the string? — regaled sometimes with celestial voluntaries and unknown mysterious fragrances, answering to our more romantic flights; at other times with homely voices and more familiar odours, here of rank-smelling cheeses, there of pungent pickles or aromatic drugs, hinting his progress through a metropolitan street. Does he over again enjoy the grateful roundness of those substantial droppings from the invisible passenger [coins from passers-by], palpable deposits of an abstract benevolence — or, in his nightmares, suffer anew those painful concussions and corporeal buffetings from that (to him) obscure evil principle, the Parish Beadle?' [beating him for begging]...

Every town in England, and every village with inhabitants and wealth sufficient to consume a hogshead of 'brown moist' within a reasonable time, exhibits an empty sugar cask in the open street. It is every little grocer's pride, and every poor boy's delight...

If you desire an immediate living example to illustrate Thomas Malthus's principle that 'population always comes up to the means of subsistence', set out a sugar cask, and there will be a swarm of boys about it, from no one knows whither, in ten minutes. The first takes possession of the inside and is 'monarch of all he surveys'. Like the throne, it is an envied and an unquiet possession. From the emulous on all sides he receives vain addresses and remonstrances, and against their threatening hands is obliged to keep a sharp lookout; but his greatest enemy, for whom he keeps a sharp look *over*, is the grocer's man. A glimpse of that arch-foe 'frightens him from his impropriety' in a twinkling — unless, indeed, he fail to escape, when for certain his companions leave him 'alone in his glory'... The boy there [see illustration below], straddling like the Great Harry [Henry VIII], has had his wicked will of the barrel to satiety, and therefore vacates his place in favour of him of the hat, on whose nether end 'time hath written strange defeatures'. It is not so certain that the fine fat little fellow with his hands on the edge of the tub and the ends of his toes on the ground will ascend the side, as that he who stoops in front is enjoying the choicest pickings of the prize. The others are mere common feeders or gluttons who go for quantity; *he* is the epicure of the party —

> He seeks but little here below,
> But seeks that little *good* —

— and, of foretaste, he takes his place at the bunghole where the sugar crystallizes, and there revels in particles of the finest candies.

'I pity the poor child,' says Mr Hood, 'that is learned in alpha beta but ignorant of top and taw [marbles]' — and I pity every poor child who only knows that a sugar tub is sweet and is ignorant of the sweetest of its sweets...

> Ah! little think the gay, licentious proud —

who spend their money on bull's-eyes and hardbake, which are modern inventions, of the delicacies within a grocer's plain, upright and downright, good old, natural, brown-sugar tub —

O! there's nothing half so sweet in life

Wags and worthies

'Just popp'd in, you know!'

Mr Paul Pry in the Character of Mr Liston

That's another joke — isn't it?

Hone, a lover of the theatre, has some fun over the hit show of 1825, *Paul Pry*, starring the great comic actor John Liston. The character in the previous page is in fact Liston as Paul Pry — drawn by another theatre-lover, George Cruikshank. In a pastiche of Pry, using his catchphrases such as 'I hope I don't intrude', Hone advertises the fact that the first year of *The Every-Day Book* in book form, with index, is about to go on sale.

Letter from PAUL PRY
To the Editor of The Every-Day Book

SIR, I hope I don't intrude. I have called at Ludgate-hill [Hone's shop, No 45] many times to see you, and made many kind inquiries, but I am always informed you are 'not at home'; and what's worse, I never can learn when you'll be 'at home'... This looks very *odd*; I don't think it *correct*. Then again, on asking your people what *The Every-Day Book* is all about, they say it's about *every* thing; but that, you know, is no answer — is it? ... They say it's impossible to describe the contents of the book, but that all the particulars are in the index. That's just what I wanted; but behold! it is 'not out' — that is, it is not in, I mean not in the book... They say 'in a few days', but, bless you, I don't believe 'em, for though I let 'em know I've a world of things to communicate to you, when you've time to see me and let me ask you a few questions, they won't credit me, and why should I credit *them*?

I was not born yesterday, I assure you. I'm of a very ancient stock, and I've some notion you and I are kinsmen. Don't you think we are? I dare say there's a likeness, for I'm sure we are of the same disposition. If you aren't, how can you find out so much 'about *every* thing'? If I can make out that you are one of the *Pry* family it will be mutually agreeable — won't it? How people will stare — won't they?

I suppose you've heard how I've been used by Mr Liston — my private character exposed on the public stage, and the whole town roaring at the whole of the *Pry* family. But we are neither to be cried down nor laughed down, and so I'd have let the playgoers know, if the managers had allowed me to sing a song on new-year's night in imitation of Mr Liston when he's a-playing *me*. Will you believe it, they burst out a-laughing and would not let me go on the boards — they said the audience would suppose me to be the actor himself. What harm would that have done the theatre? Can you tell? They said it would hurt Mr Liston's feelings — never considering *my* feelings...!

They shall be matched, however, if you'll help me. I've copied out my song, and if you'll print it in *The Every-Day Book* it will drive 'em mad. I wish, of all things, that Mr Cruikshank could see me in the character of Liston. He could *hit* me, I know. Don't you think he could? — just as I am — 'quite correct' — like he did Guy Fawkes last 5th of November [page 158]. I never laughed so much in all my life as when I saw *that*. Bless you, I can mimic Liston all to nothing. Do get your friend George to your house some day — any day he likes — it's all one to me, for I call *every* day, and as I'm an 'every-day' man, you know, why, you might pop me at the head of the song in your *Every-Day Book*. That's a joke, you know. I can't help laughing — so droll...!

Here Hone prints 'Mr Paul Pry's song, intended to have been sung by him at the Theatre, in the Character of MR LISTON, on New Year's Eve.' It is about the old year 'going *off*'. The way he would have sung it 'is hinted at parenthetically'. Three stanzas of seven, to give an idea of Liston's patter:

(*Comfortably*)	'Twas better than the other —
(*Informingly*)	The one that went before —
(*Consolingly*)	But then there'll be *another* —
(*Delightedly*)	And that's *one* comfort more!
(*Alarmedly*)	I'm half afraid he's gone!
(*Kindlily*)	Must part with the old fellow!
(*Hastily*)	Excuse me — I must run — (*Exit*)
(*Returns*)	Forgot my umbrella.
(*Determinedly*)	I'll watch the *new* one, though,
(*Circumspectly*)	And see what he'll be at — (*Exit*)
(*Returns*)	Beg pardon — didn't bow — (*Bows and exit*)
(*Returns*)	Beg pardon — left my hat.

If you print this in *The Every-Day Book* it will send Liston into fits — it will kill him — won't it? But you know that's all right — if he takes me off I've a right to take him off — haven't I? I say, that's *another* joke — isn't it? Bless you, I could do as good as that forever. But I want to see you and ask how you go on. And I've lots of intelligence for you — *such* things as never were known in this world — all true, and on the very best authority... However, I'm in a great hurry and so you'll excuse me. Mind, though, I shall pop in every day...

Yours eternally,
PAUL PRY

Pryory Place, January 6, 1826

P.S. Don't forget the index — I want to learn all the particulars — *multum in parvo* — all quite correct.

P.S. I'm told you've *eleven* children — is it true? What day shall you have another? Today? *Twelfth* Day? That would be a *joke* — wouldn't it? I hope I don't intrude. I don't wish to seem curious.

Farewell to Cheap Tommy

From a contributor at Heanor, Derbyshire:

SIXTEEN OR SEVENTEEN years ago there appeared a singular character whose arrival excited a *sensation* and became an epoch in the village's history. Some boys who had been strolling to a distance brought an account that a little man, with a barrow as large as a house, was coming along the lane at 'a snail's gallop'.

Forth sallied a troop of gazers, who found a small, thickset, roundfaced man in an old red soldier's jacket and cocked hat, sitting on the handle of his barrow, which was built and roofed after the manner of a caravan... He sat very quietly as they came round him, and returned their greetings in a way short and dry, and which became markedly testy and impatient as they crowded more closely and began to ask questions. 'Not too fast, my masters, not too fast! My first answer can't overtake your twentieth question.'

At length he rose, and by the aid of a strong strap passed over his shoulders heaved up the handles of his barrow, and placing his head against it, like a tortoise under a stone, proceeded at a toilsome rate of some few hundred yards per hour. This specimen of patient endurance amazed the villagers. A brawny labourer would have thought it a severe toil to wheel it a mile, yet this singular being, outdoing the phlegmatic perseverance of an ass ... from county to county and from year to year urged on his ponderous vehicle...

It was soon found that he was not more singular in appearance than eccentric in mind. A villager, thinking to do him a kindness, offered to wheel his barrow, but what was the surprise of the gazers to see him present the man payment when he had moved it a considerable way, and on its being refused, to behold him quietly raise the barrow, turn it round and wheel it back to the identical spot whence the villager set out.

On reaching the hamlet he took up his quarters in a stable and opened his one-wheeled caravan, displaying a good assortment of cutlery ware. It was there I first saw him, and was struck with his grave and uncomplying air, more like that of a beadle stationed to keep off intruders than of a solicitous vendor of wares. He was standing with a pair of pliers, twisting wire into scissor-chains, keeping at the same time a shrewd eye upon the goods.

The prices were so wonderfully low that it was whispered the articles could not be good, or they were stolen; yet I did not perceive that either idea was sufficient to dissuade people from buying, or from attempting to get them still lower. Then it was that his character and temper showed themselves. He laid aside the goods attempted to be chaffered for, saying, 'You shall not have them at all. I tell no lies about them, nor shall you.' In fact his goods were *goods*. So much so that many of them are in use in the village to this day. He desired only such a profit as would supply the necessities of one who never slept in a bed, never approached a fire for the sake of its warmth, nor ever indulged in any luxury.

His greatest trial appeared to be to bear with the sordid spirit of the world. When this did not cross him he became smiling, communicative and, strange as it may seem, exceedingly intelligent. I well recollect my boyish astonishment when he quoted to me the maxims of Plato and Seneca, and when I heard him pouring out abundance of anecdote from the best sources...

He had a tame hedgehog which partook his fare, slept in a better nest than himself and was evidently a source of affectionate enjoyment. He was fond of children; but he had a stern spirit of independence which made him refuse gifts and favours unless permitted to make some return. My mother frequently sent him warm messes in the wintry weather, and he brought her a scissor-chain and a candlestick of brass wire.

He was a writer of anagrams, acrostics and so forth, and one epitaph written for one of his bystanders was —

> Too bad for heaven, too good for hell,
> So where he's gone I cannot tell.

He always slept with his barrow chained to his leg; and on Sundays kept himself totally shut up, except during service time, standing the day through reading his bible...

His stable became a sort of school, where he taught ... more useful knowledge than has emanated from many a philosopher, modern or antique. The goodwill he excited evidently pleased the old man. He came again, and again, till at length years rolled away without his reappearance and he was considered as dead. But not so. For ten or eleven years he was still going on his pilgrimage, a wanderer and an outcast, probably doing voluntary penance for some sin or unhappiness of youth; for he carefully kept aloof of his native country, Scotland, and though he spoke of one sister with tearful eyes, he had not seen her for many, many years.

In 1820 he had found his way to Midsomer Norton, near Bristol, where he was hooted into the town by a troop of boys, a poor, worndown object of the most apparent misery. This I accidentally learnt a short time ago from a little book, the memorial of his last days, written by the worthy clergyman of that place...

What tales would a history of those years have displayed! What scenes of solitary travel, exhaustion, suffering, insults and occasional sympathy and kindness...! *His barrow was gone!* Poverty had wrung from him, or weakness had compelled him to abandon, that old companion of his travels. I have often thought what must have been his feelings at that parting. Poor old man, it was his house, his friend, his dog, his everything. What energies had he not expended in propelling it from place to place. It could not have been left without a melancholy pang... But I cannot dwell upon the subject...

A final adieu to our old friend under every name of Thomas Hogg, Tam Hogg, or Cheap Tommy.

> If I forget thee, worthy old Tam Hogg,
>   May I forget that knives were ever cheap.
>   If I forget thy barrow huge and steep,
> Slow as a snail, and croaking like a frog —
> Peripatetic, stoic, 'cynic dog',
>   If from my memory perish thee or thine
>   May I be doomed to gnaw asunder twine
> Or shave with razor that has chipped a log!
>
> For in thy uncouth tabernacle dwelt
>   Honest philosophy; and oh! far more.
> Religion thy unstooping heart could melt,
>   Nor scorned the muse to sojourn at thy door.
> What pain, toil, poverty didst thou endure,
> Reckless of earth, so heaven might find thee pure!

Thompson the memory-corner man

John Thompson, a London auctioneer (1756–1836), was famed in his retirement for displaying a remarkable talent that won him the name Memory-Corner Thompson. A few of his feats when aged over sixty:

HE DREW from actual memory, in twenty-two hours at two sittings, in the presence of two well-known gentlemen, a correct plan of the parish of St James, Westminster, with parts of the parishes of St Marylebone, St Anne and St Martin; which plan contained every square, street, lane, court, alley, market, church, chapel and all public buildings, with all stable and other yards, also every public-house in the parish, and the corners of all streets with all minutiae, as pumps, posts, trees, houses that project and inject, bow-windows, Carlton House, St James's Palace, and the interior of the markets, without scale or reference to any plan, book or paper whatever.

He did the same with respect to the parish of St Andrew, Holborn, in the presence of four gentlemen, from eight to twelve one evening in a tavern; and he also undertook to draw the plan of St Giles-in-the-Fields, St Paul's Covent Garden, St Mary-le-Strand, St Clement's and three-fourths of St Marylebone or St George's.

He can tell the corner of any great and leading thoroughfare-street from Hyde Park-corner, or Oxford-street, to St Paul's; or from the New-road [now Euston-road] to Westminster Abbey; and the trade or profession carried on at such corner house. He can tell every public shop of business in Piccadilly, which consists of two hundred and forty-one houses, allowing him only twenty-four mistakes. He accomplished this in the presence of four gentlemen, after five o'clock, and proved it before seven in the same evening.

A house being named in any public street, he will name the trade of the shop either on the left or right hand of the same, and whether the door of such house so named is in the centre or on the right or left.

He can take an inventory, from memory only, of a gentleman's house from the attic to the ground floor, and afterwards write it out. He did this at Lord Nelson's at Merton, and likewise at the Duke of Kent's in the presence of two noblemen. He is known by the appellation of 'Memory-Corner Thompson'.

The plan of his house, called Frognal Priory, Hampstead, he designed, and built it externally and internally without any working drawing, but carried it up by the eye only.

Yet though his memory is so accurate in the retention of objects submitted to the eye, he has little power of recollecting what he hears. The dialogue of a comedy heard once or even twice would, after an interval of a few days, be entirely new to him.

Frognal Priory, a vast mansion of gothic and various other styles, and filled in his day with real and fake antiques, stood until the late 19th century.

Hut Alderson, bellman of Durham

The Bishop of Butterby: A Sketch by one of his Prebendaries

I remember reading in that excellent little periodical *The Cigar* of the red nose of the friar of Dillow, which served the holy man in the stead of a lantern when he crossed the fens at night to visit the fair lady of the sheriff of Gloucestershire. Whether the nose of the well-known eccentric now under consideration ever lighted his path when returning from Shincliffe feast or Houghton-le-Spring hopping … this deponent knoweth not. But certainly if ever nose could serve for such a purpose it is that of Hut Alderson, which is the reddest in the city of Durham — save and excepting, nevertheless, the nose of fat Hannah, the Elvet orange-woman. Yes, Hut, thou portly living tun! Thou

78

animated lump of obesity! Thou hast verily a most jolly nose! ...Many a time, I ween, thou hast mulled thine ale with it when sitting with thy pot-companions at Morralie's!

Hutchinson Alderson, the subject of the present biographical notice, is the well-known bellman of the city of Durham... I am informed by him, at one of his 'visitations', that he is a native of the place, where very early in life he was 'bound prentice to a shoemaker', and where, after the expiration of his servitude, he began business.

During the period of the threatened invasion of this nation by the French [in 1803] he enlisted in the Durham militia... Some have informed me he was a mere private, others that he was a corporal; and a wanton wag has given out that he was kept by the regiment to be used as a beacon in cases of extraordinary emergency. Certain it is that he was in the militia, and that during that time the accident occurred

And who gave thee that jolly red nose?
Brandy, cinnamon ale and cloves,
That gave me the jolly red nose.   *Old song*

which destroyed his hopes of military promotion and rendered him unable to pursue his ordinary calling — I allude to the loss of his right hand [when his gun exploded]... For some time after this calamity, Alderson's chief employment consisted in taking care of gentlemen's horses, and cleaning knives... He has also, at different periods, been one of the constables of the parish of St Mary le Bow.

About the year 1822 the office of bellman to the city of Durham became vacant by resignation, upon which Hut immediately offered himself... It is in that capacity our artist has represented him... But Hut Alderson is the wearer of other dignities.

About three miles from Durham is a beautiful little hamlet called Butterby, and in ancient deeds *Beautrove* and *Beautrovensis*, from the elegance of its situation... The seclusion of its walks, the deep shade of its lonely glens and the many associations connected with it, independently of its valuable mineral waters, conspire to render it a favourite place of resort...

In olden time Butterby had a church dedicated to Saint Leonard, of which not a visible vestige is remaining... Yet to hear many of the inhabitants of Durham talk, a stranger would naturally believe that the hamlet is still in possession of this sacred edifice; for 'Butterby church' is there spoken of, not as a plate adorning the antiquarian page, nor even as a ruin to attract the gaze of the moralizing tourist, but as a real, substantial *bona fide* structure. The fact is that in the slang of Durham ... a Butterby churchgoer is one who does not frequent any church, and when such a one is asked, 'What church have you attended today?' the customary answer is, 'I have been attending service at Butterby.'

About the year 1823 there appeared in one of the London journals an account of a marriage said to have been solemnized at Butterby church between two parties who never existed but in the fertile brain of the writer of the paragraph, 'By the Rev Hutchinson Alderson, rector'. From that time Hut Alderson began to be designated a clergy- man, and was speedily dubbed A.M. Merit *will* rise, and therefore the A.M. became D.D., and Alderson himself enjoyed the waggery ... and gave out that Butterby was a bishop's see, that the late parochial church was a cathedral, and in fine that the late humble rector was a lordly bishop — THE RIGHT REVEREND HUTCHINSON ALDERSON LORD BISHOP OF BUTTERBY, or HUT BUT.

Having thus dubbed himself, he next proceeded to the proper formation of his cathedral; named about ten individuals as prebends (among whom were the writer of this sketch and his good friend his assistant artist), chose a dean and archdeacon and selected a few more humble individuals to fill the different places of sexton, organist, vergers, bellringers, &c... A cathedral is nothing without a tutelary saint, and accordingly Butterby church has been dedicated to Saint Giles. Several articles have been written and privately circulated, descriptive of the splendid architecture of this imaginary edifice ... and its saint has been exalted in song...

SAINT GILES: His Holie Legend

[*To the tune of 'The Night Before Larry was Stretched'*]

O did ye ne'er hear of Saint Giles,
  The saint of fam'd Butterby steeple?
There ne'er was his like seen for miles.
  Pardie, he astonied the people!
His face was as red as the sun,
  His eyes were a couple of sloes, sir.
His belly was big as a tun
  And he had a huge bottle nose, sir.
    O what a strange fellow was he!

Of woman he never was born,
  And wagers have been laid upon it.
They found him at Finchale one morn
  Wrapp'd up in a heavenly bonnet.
The prior was taking his rounds
  As he was wont after his *brick* fast.
He heard most celestial sounds
  And saw something in a tree stick fast
    Like a bundle of dirty old clothes.

Quite frighten'd, he fell on his knees
  And said thirteen aves and ten credos,
When the thing in the tree gave a sneeze,
  And out popp'd a hand, and then three toes.
Now when he got out of his faint
  He approach'd, with demeanour most humble,
And what should he see but the saint,
  Not a copper the worse from his tumble,
    But lying all sound wind and limb.

Says the prior, 'From whence did you come,
  Or how got you into my garden?'
But the baby said nothing but mum
  And for the priest cared not a *farden.*
At length the saint open'd his gob
  And said, 'I'm from heaven, d'ye see, sir.
Now don't stand there scratching your nob
  But help me down out of the tree, sir,
    Or I'll set your convent ablaze!'...

In sanctity he pass'd his years,
    Once or twice exorcis'd a demoniac;
And to quieten his doubts and his fears
    Applied to a flask of old cognac.
To heaven he show'd the road fair,
    And if he saw sinner look glum or sad
He'd tell him to drive away care,
    And say, 'Take a swig of good rum, my lad,
      And it will soon give your soul ease.'

*Six more stanzas tell of his miracles and his passing. Then the contributor gives
'a specimen of the ridiculous interruptions Hut meets with when crying':*

THREE RINGS — *Ding dong! ding dong! ding dong!*

Hut To be sold by auction —
1 Boy Speak up, speak up, Hut!
Hut Hod your jaw. — At the Queen's Heed in —
2 Boy The town of Butterby.
Hut I'll smash your heed wi' the bell! — the Queen's Heed in the Bailya — a large collection of —
2 Boy Pews, pulpits and organs.
Hut I'll rap your canister! — of valuable buiks, the property of —
1 Boy The Bishop of Butterby.
Hut Be quiet, you scamp! — of a gentleman from Lunnon. The buiks may be viewed any time between the hours of one and three, by applying to —
2 Boy Tommy Sly —
Hut — Mr Thwaites on the premises. The sale to commence at seven o'clock in the evening *prizizely*.
All Huih! hooeh! hooeh!
Hut I'll smash some o' your heeds wi' the bell! I knaw thee, Jack! Mind an' I doan't tell thee mither noo, thou daft fule!

Prescribing according to the patient

FEW INHERITED better qualities or were more eccentric than the late Dr John Lettsom [1744–1815; a Quaker]. While he associated with literary men, communicated with literary works, and wrote and published his medical experience, he gave gratuitous aid to the needy and apportioned his leisure to useful and practical purposes...

    The doctor was once called in to attend a sick lady and her maid-servant. On entering the passage he was asked by the nurse into the lady's chamber. 'Very well,' said he mildly, 'but is there not a servant ill also?' 'Yes, sir,' was the reply. 'Then let me prescribe for her first,' he rejoined, 'as her services will be first wanted...' By the second visit the servant was convalescent. 'I generally find this the case,' observed the doctor goodhumouredly to his friend. 'Servants want physic *only*, but their mistresses require more skill than physic. This is owing to the difference between scrubbing the stairs and scrubbing the teeth...' [The mistress has too little exercise or useful activity.]

Whenever a friend borrowed a book from the doctor's library, he rarely lent it but with this stipulation, that the supposed value of the book should be deposited, with the name of the borrower and the title of the volume with date, in the vacant place till the book was restored. 'Though attended with some pains, I find this a good plan,' said the doctor. 'Many of my sets would otherwise be imperfect. I feel pleasure in lending my books (many I give away), but I like to see my library, like my practice, as regularly conducted as possible...'

The doctor, having been called to a poor lone woman, pitied her desolate situation so much that he shed tears. Her person and room were squalid; her language and deportment indicated that she had seen better days. He took a slip of paper out of his pocket and wrote with his pencil the following very rare prescription to the overseers of the parish in which she resided:

> A shilling *per diem* for Mrs Maxton: Money,
> not Physic, will cure her.   *Lettsom*

A chimley clean as a new pin

CERTAIN REWARDS allowed by act of parliament to firemen, turn-cocks and others who first appear with their engines and implements at premises sworn to be on fire were claimed at the public office, Marlborough-street ... and resisted on the ground that the chimney, which belonged to a brewery, and was more than eighty feet high, was not and could not be on fire.

A witness to that end gave a lively specimen of familiar statement and illustration. He began by telling the magistrate that he was a sweep-chimney by profession — a piece of information very unnecessary, for he was as black and sooty a sweep as ever mounted a chimney-top — and then went on in this fashion:

'This here man (pointing to the patrol), your wortship, has told a false affidavit. I knows that 'ere chimley from a hinfant, and she knows my foot as well as my own mother. The way I goes up her is this. I goes in all round the boiler, then I twists in the chimley like the smoke, and then up I goes with the wind, for, your wortship, there's a wind in her that would blow you out like a feather if you didn't know her as well as I do, and that makes me always go to the top myself, because there isn't a brick in her that doesn't know my foot.

'So that you see, your wortship, no soot or blacks is ever in her. The wind won't let 'em stop. And besides, they knows that I go up her regular. So that she always keeps herself as clean as a new pin. I'll be bound the sides of her is as clean this minute as I am (not saying much for the chimley). Therefore, your wortship, that 'ere man as saw two yards of fire coming out of her did not see no such thing, I say; and he has told your wortship, and these here gentlemen present, a false affidavit, I say.

'I was brought up in the chimley, your wortship, and I can't a-bear to hear such things said — lies of her. And that's all as I knows at present, please your wortship.'

The Times, 5th January, 1826

Woolley the miser ploughs a furrow

THE PEN of a country gentleman communicates an account of a remarkable character created by 'love of the *gun*'.

About sixty years ago at Loscoe, a small village in Derbyshire, lived James Woolley, notorious for three things, the very good clocks he made, his eccentric system of farming, and the very great care he took of his money. He was, like Elwes and Dancer [famous misers], an old bachelor... It was a favourite maxim with him, and ever upon his lips, that 'fine wives and fine gardens are mighty expensive things'. He consequently kept at a very respectful distance from both. He had, indeed, an unconquerable dread of anything 'fine' or that approached in any way that awful and ghostlike term 'expensive'.

It would seem that Woolley's avaricious bias was not, as is generally the case, his first ruling passion... 'When young,' says John Blackner in his *History of Nottingham* (1815), 'he was partial to shooting, but being detected at his sport upon the estate of the depraved William Andrew Horne, Esq, of Butterly (who was executed on the 11th of December 1759 at Nottingham for the murder of a child), and compelled by him to pay the penalty, he made a vow never to cease from labour ... till he had obtained sufficient property to justify him in following his favourite sport without dreading the frowns of his haughty neighbour.

'He accordingly fell to work and continued at it till he was weary, when he rested, and "to it again" — a plan which he pursued without any regard to night or day. He denied himself the use of an ordinary bed, and of every other comfort as well as necessary, except of the meanest kind. But when he had acquired property to qualify him to carry a gun, he had lost all relish for the sport; and he continued to labour at clockmaking, except when he found an opportunity to traffic in land, till he had amassed a considerable fortune, which he bequeathed to one of his relations. I believe he died about 1770' [actually 1786: he figures worthily in histories of clockmakers].

It must have been a singular spectacle to anyone except Woolley's neighbours, who were the daily observers of his habits, to have seen a man worth upwards of £20,000 up at five in the morning brushing away with his bare feet the dew as he fetched up his cows from the pasture, his shoes and stockings carefully held under his arm to prevent them from being injured by the wet; though by the by, a glance at them would have satisfied anyone they had but little to fear from the dew or anything else.

A penny loaf boiled in a small piece of linen made him an excellent pudding. This with a halfpenny worth of small beer from the village alehouse was his more than ordinary dinner, and rarely sported unless on holidays or when he had a friend or tenant to share the luxury.

Once in his life Woolley was convicted of liberality. He had at great labour and expense of time made what he considered a clock of considerable value, and as it was probably too large for common purposes he presented it to the corporation of Nottingham, for the Exchange [it does not survive]. In return he was made a freeman of the town. They could not have conferred on him a greater favour. The honour mattered not — but election dinners were things which powerfully appealed through his stomach to his heart. The first he attended was productive of a ludicrous incident. His shabby and vagrant appearance nearly excluded him from the scene of good eating, and even when the burgesses sat down to table no one seemed disposed to accommodate the miserly old gentleman with a seat. The chairs were quickly filled. Having no time to lose, he crept under the table and thrusting up his head forced himself violently into one, but not before he had received some heavy blows on the bare skull.

The most prominent incident in his history was a ploughing scheme of his own invention. He had long lamented that he kept horses at a great expense for the purposes of husbandry. To have kept a saddle-horse would have been extravagant. And at last fancying he could do without them, they were sold, and the money carefully laid by. This was a triumph — a noble saving! The winter passed away, and his hay and corn-stacks stood undiminished. Ploughing time however arrived, and his new plan must be carried into effect.

The plough was drawn from its inglorious resting-place and a score of men were summoned from the village to supply the place of horses.

At the breakfast-table he was not without fears of a famine: he could starve himself, but a score of brawny villagers, hungry, and antici-pating a hard day's work, would eat, and drink too, and must be satisfied. They soon proceeded to the field, where a long-continued drought had made the ground almost impenetrable. The day became excessively hot, and the men tugged and puffed to little purpose. They again ate heartily and drank more good ale than the old man had patience to think of. And difficult as it was to force the share through the unyielding sward, it was still more difficult to refrain from laughing out at the grotesque figure their group presented. They made many wry faces, and more wry furrows, and spoiled with their feet what they had not ploughed amiss.

But this was not all. Had a balloon been sent up from the field it could scarcely have drawn together more intruders. He tried, but in vain, to keep them off. They thronged upon him from all quarters. His gates were all set open or thrown off the hooks, and the fences broken down in every direction. Woolley perceived his error. The men, the rope traces and the plough were sent home in a hurry, and with some blustering and many oaths the trespassers were got rid of. The fences were mended and the gates replaced, and having to his heart's content gratified his whim, he returned to the oldfashioned custom of plough-ing with horses until in his brain's fertility he could discover some-thing better and less 'expensive'.

shooting and property: To have the right to shoot game, commoners had to own property of an annual rental value of at least £100, a large sum then. Flouters of the law risked three months in jail.

Huck'n, the dumb creatures' friend

A correspondent recalls an unconventional Wiltshire veterinary surgeon.

DR GIBBS, commonly called 'Huck'n', was an extraordinary individ-ual who followed the profession of an itinerary veterinary surgeon in the west of England. His ways were different from his neighbours', and his appearance was so singular that a stranger might have taken him for a tramping tinker. Like George Morland [the artist], he had an unfortunate predilection for 'signs' [that is, inn or alehouse signs], under whose influence he was generally to be found. He would 'keep it up to the last' with his last shilling...

To love for his profession he added a love for old pastimes, customs and revelries. He was a man in the fullest extent of the word... Zeal-ous in his friendships, he exercised the virtues of humanity by aiding and even feeding those who were in severe distress. He spent much, for his means were considerable — they were derived from his great practice. His knowledge of his art was profound. A horse's life was as safe in his hands as the writer's would be in Sir Astley Cooper's [noted surgeon, 1768–1841].

In his person Huck'n was muscular and he stood above the middle size. His habits gave him an unwieldy motion. His complexion was sandy, his aspect muddled; large eyebrows penthoused his small glassy blue eyes; a wig of many curls, perking over his bald forehead, was closed by a bush of his own hair of another colour behind; his whiskers were carroty, and he usually had an unshorn beard.

It was when he entered a stable or cowpen, in his leather apron half-crossed, with his drug-pouch at his side, that he appeared in a skilful light. His thick holly walking-stick with a thong run through the top was tried in the service, as its worn appearance testified and many an animal's mouth could witness. He rarely pulled the drenching horn or fleam [instrument for bleeding cattle] from his pocket, but he rolled his tongue over his beloved 'pigtail' [chewing tobacco], juicily deposited in the nook of a precarious tooth, and said, 'Huck'n!' Hence his *nom de guerre* — and hence the proverb that outlives him, 'He that can *chew* like Huck'n may *cure* like Huck'n.' The meaning of this emphatic monosyllable remains a secret. Some of the superstitious conjectured that he used it ... as a charm to scare the witches from riding the cattle. This liberty is verily believed by many to exist to this day. Hence a horseshoe is nailed to the sill of the stable-door, that the midnight hags of 'air and broom' may not cross the iron barrier.

It is thirty years since Huck'n flourished. If he had a home it was at Hullavington, near Malmesbury [Wiltshire], where as a pharmacist, farrier and phlebotomist of high character and respectability, to his patients (who are known to evince more patience than most of the human species) he was very attentive. He would cheerfully forgo his cheerful glass, his boon companions, his amusing anecdotes, necessary food and nocturnal rest to administer to the comfort of a poor dumb creature, and remain day and night till life departed or ease returned. Were he alive he would tell us that in our intercourse with the brute creation we should exercise humane feelings and bestir ourselves to assuage the acute pain betokened by agonizing looks and groans in suffering animals.

Huck'n was an improvident man. Under more classical auspices he might have stood first in his profession, but he preferred being 'unadorned — adorned the most'. He lived to assist the helpless, and died in peace. Let persons of higher pretensions do more.

Tom Airay and his thespian dalesmen

From Grassington, West Yorkshire (which is still a 'favourite mountain village'), a contributor tells of an unsung actor-manager.

AT THIS SEASON [December] everything appears dull and lifeless in the neighbourhood of my favourite mountain village. In my younger days it was otherwise. Christmas was then a festival, enlivened by a round of innocent amusements... We had a theatre...

Gentle reader! Should you ever visit Skipton-in-Craven, go on the market-day and stand opposite to the vicarage-house in the high-street. There you will see a cart with this inscription, 'Thomas Airay, Grassington and Skipton Carrier'. Keep your eye on that cart, and about the hour of three in the afternoon you will behold approach the owner, a little, fat old man with reddish whiskers and a jolly face that John Liston or John Reeve [comic actors] would not be ashamed to possess. In that countenance a mere tyro in physiognomy may discover a roguish slyness, a latent archness, a hidden mine of fun and good humour. Then when Airay walks, mark his stately gait and tell me if it does not proclaim that he has worn the sock and buskin and trod the thespian floor. He was the manager of the Grassington theatre...

I fancy some rigid moralist bestowing a cold glance on poor Tom and saying to himself, 'Ah, old man, this comes of acting. Had you in your youth followed some industrious pursuit, not joined an idle strolling company, instead of now being a country carrier you might have been blessed with a comfortable independence!' Think not so harshly of Airay. Though not the manager of a patent theatre nor of one 'by royal authority', he never was a stroller nor an associate with vagabonds, nor did he ever, during his theatrical career, quake under the terrors of magisterial harshness or fear the Vagrant Act.

> No idle, worthless wandering man was he
>   But in the dales of honest parents bred.
> Trained to a life of honest industry,
>   He with the lark in summer left his bed;
> Through the sweet calm by morning twilight shed,
>   Walking to labour by that cheerful song...

Tom Airay's sole theatre was at Grassington, and that was only 'open for the season' — for a few weeks in the depth of winter, when the inclemency of the weather, which in these mountain parts is very severe, rendered the agricultural occupations of himself and companions impossible to be pursued. They chose rather to earn a scanty pittance by acting than to trouble their neighbours for eleemosynary support. The *corps dramatique* of Tom Airay consisted chiefly of young men (they had no actresses) who moved in the same line of life as the manager and whose characters were equally respectable ... for setting aside our hero's occasionally getting tipsy at some of the neighbouring feasts, nothing can be said against him ... and if report speak truth, [he] has realized about a thousand pounds.

Few of Tom Airay's company are living... There was honest Peter W——, whose face peeped from behind the green curtain like a full moon. He was accounted a bit of a wag: ever foremost in mischief, he more than once almost blew up the stage by gunpowder, half suffocated the audience by asafoetida, and was wont to put hot cinders in the boots of his associates. He has 'left the mimic scene to die indeed', and sleeps peacefully under the beautiful lime-trees of Kirkby Malhamdale churchyard...

Then there was Isaac G——, the fiddler and comic singer: *he* exists no longer. There was Waddilove, and Frankland of Hetton, and Bill Cliff the Skipton poet and bailiff — all dead! There were also the Hetheringtons, and Jack Solomon the besom-maker, and Tommy Summersgill the barber and clockmaker, and Jack L—— the politician of Threshfield, who regarded John Wilkes [the 18th-century polemical politician] as his tutelary saint, and settled in the Illinois, from whence he occasionally sends a letter to his old friends, informing them what a paltry country England is, what a paradise the new world is, and how superior the American rivers are... Besides these, there were fifteen or sixteen others from Arncliffe, Litton, Conistone, Kilnsey and the other romantic villages that enliven our heath-clad hills.

The Grassington theatre, or rather playhouse, for it never received a loftier appellation ... was an old limestone 'lathe', the Craven word for barn, with huge folding doors, one containing a smaller one through which the audience was admitted to the pit and gallery, for there were no boxes. Yet on particular occasions, such as when the Duke of Devonshire or Earl of Thanet goodnaturedly deigned to patronize the performances, a 'box' was fitted up by railing off a part of the pit, and covering it, by way of distinction, with brown paper painted to represent drapery. The prices were pit sixpence and gallery threepence...

The stage was lighted by five or six halfpenny candles... The scenery was respectable; and though sometimes by sad mishap the sun or moon would take fire and expose the tallow candle behind it, was very well managed... The dresses, as far as material went, were good, though not always in character. An outlaw of the forest of Arden sometimes appeared in the guise of a Craven wagoner, and the holy friar 'whose vesper bell is the bowl, ding-dong' would wear a bob wig, cocked hat and the surplice of a modern church dignitary.

These slight discrepancies passed unregarded by the audience...
There were no prying editors to criticize and report.

The audience was always numerous (no empty benches *there*)... I
have known the village lawyer, the parson of the parish and the
doctor comfortably seated together, laughing heartily at Tom Airay
strutting as Lady Randolph [in John Home's drama *Douglas*], his huge
Yorkshire clogs peeping from beneath a gown too short to conceal his
corduroy breeches, and murdering his words... All the actors had a
bad pronunciation. Cicero was called *kikkero* (which, by the by, is
probably the correct one); Africa was called *Afryka*, fatigued was
fattygewed and pageantry was always called *paggyantry*. Well do I
remember Airay exclaiming, 'What *pump*, what *paggyantry* is there
here!' and on another occasion saying, '*Ye damons o' deeth, come sattle
my swurd!*'

The company would have spoken better had they not, on meeting
with a 'dictionary word', applied for information to an old schoolmaster, who constantly misled them and taught them to pronounce in
the most barbarous mode he could devise; yet such was the awe
wherewith they were accustomed to regard this dogmatical personage, and the profound respect they paid to his abilities, that they
received his deceiving tricks with thankfulness...

The plays usually performed at Grassington were of the regular
drama, the productions of Shakespeare, Dryden, Otway and George
Lillo. *George Barnwell* [Lillo's popular drama, dating from 1731] has
many a time caused the Craven maids to forget 'Turpin' and 'Nevison'
and bloody squires, and weep at the shocking catastrophe of the
grocer's apprentice. Melodramas were unknown to them, and happy
had it been for the dramatic talent of this country if they had remained
unknown elsewhere, for since these innovations, mastiff dogs, monkeys and polichinellos have followed in rapid succession, and what
monstrum horrendum will next be introduced is difficult to conceive...

Grassington being too poor to support a printer, the playbills were
written, and by way of making the performances better known, the
parish bellman was daily employed to cry the play in a couplet
composed by the manager. I only remember one —

> 'Guy in His Youth' our play we call.
> At six to the haymow hie ye all!

...Their performances were always of a moral character. If any
indelicate sentiment or expression occurred in their plays, it was
omitted; nothing was uttered that could raise a blush on the female
cheek. Nor were the audiences less moral than the manager: not an
instance can be recorded of riot or indecency...

The lubrication of lawyers

IT IS AFFIRMED of Sir William Blackstone [1723–80] that so often as he sat down to the composition of his *Commentaries on the Laws of England*, he always ordered a bottle of wine wherewith to moisten the dryness of his studies. And in proof that other professional men some-times solace their cares by otherwise disporting themselves, there is a kind of catch, the words of which, having reference to their art or mystery, do so marvellously inspire them that they chant it with more glee than gravity to a right merry tune:

> A woman having settlement
>   Married a man with none.
> The question was, he being dead,
>   If that she *had* was gone?
>
> Quoth Sir John Pratt, 'Her settlement
>   *Suspended* did remain,
> Living the husband — but, him dead,
>   It doth revive again.'
>
> CHORUS OF PUISNE JUDGES
> *Living the husband — but, him dead,*
>   *It doth revive again.*

A chief justice in the stocks

Sir John Pratt (1657–1725), a judge of some note, was the father of a more notable one, Charles Pratt, 1st Earl Camden (1714–94), our next character.

AS CHIEF JUSTICE of the Common Pleas he was distinguished for having discharged the celebrated John Wilkes from the Tower. By that decision, general warrants were pronounced illegal… He was equally distinguished for opposing the opinion of prerogative lawyers in matters of libel.

It is pleasantly related of him that while chief justice, being upon a visit to Lord Dacre [*his brother-in-law*] at Aveley in Essex, he walked out with a gentleman, a very absent man, to a hill at no very great distance from the house, upon the top of which stood the stocks of the village. The chief justice sat down upon them, and … having a mind to know what the punishment was, he asked his companion to open them and put him in. This being done, his friend took a book from his pocket, sauntered on and completely forgot the judge…

In the meantime, the chief justice, being tired of the stocks, tried in vain to release himself. Seeing a countryman pass by, he endeavoured to move him to let him out... 'No no, old gentleman,' said the countryman, 'you was not set there for nothing,' and left him, until he was released by a servant of the house dispatched in quest of him.

Some time after, he presided at a trial in which a charge was brought against a magistrate for false imprisonment and for setting in the stocks. The counsel for the magistrate ... made light of the whole charge, and more especially setting in the stocks, which he said everybody knew was no punishment at all.

The chief justice rose, and leaning over the bench said in a half-whisper, 'Brother, have you ever been in the stocks?'

'Really my lord, never.'

'Then I have,' said the judge, 'and I assure you, brother, it is no such trifle as you represent.'

Run to hear Blind Willie singin'

A Newcastle contributor opens by quoting from 'Blind Willie Singing' by Robert Gilchrist, one of many Tyneside songmakers of that time:

> Lang may wor Tyneside lads sae true,
> In heart byeth blithe an' mellow,
> Bestow the praise that's fairly due
> To this bluff, honest fellow —
> And when he's hamper'd i' the dust,
> Still i' wor memory springin'
> The times we've run till like to brust
> To hear Blind Willie singin'.

WILLIAM PURVIS, or as he is generally styled, Blind Willie, is a well-known character and native of Newcastle... He was born blind, and is the son of Margaret Purvis, who died in All Saints' workhouse, February 7, 1819, in her hundredth year...

He has long been celebrated for his minstrelsy throughout the northern counties, but more particularly so in Northumberland. In Newcastle, Willie is respected by all. From the rudest to the gentlest heart, all love him — children seize his hand as he passes — and he is ever an equally welcome guest at the houses of the rich and the hovels of the pitmen. The hoppings of the latter are cheered by the soul-inspiring sound of his viol. Nay, he is, I may truly say, a very particle of a pitman's existence, who, after a hard day's labour, considers it a pleasure of the most exquisite nature to repair to some neighbouring pot-house, there to enjoy Willie's music and listen to the rude ballads he is in the habit of composing and singing to the accompaniment of his own music.

Poor Willie! May he live long and live happy. When he dies [it was in 1832, aged 80] many a tear will fall from eyes that seldom weep... Willie will die, but not his fame will die. In many of those humorous provincial songs with which Newcastle abounds more than any other town I am acquainted with — the very airs as well as the words of which possess a kind of local nationality — Blind Willie is the theme... Several of them have been sung for years, and I venture to prophesy will be sung by future generations...

One of Willie's greatest peculiarities is thus alluded to by Mr John Sykes [in his book *Local Records*, Newcastle, 1824]: 'He has travelled the streets of Newcastle time out of mind without a covering upon his head. Several attempts have been made, by presenting him with a hat, to induce him to wear one, but after having *suffered* it for a day or two, it is thrown aside...'

One song credited to Blind Willie is 'Buy Broom Buzzems' (*If you want a buzzem for to sweep your hoose / Come to me, ma hinnies...*). Are others known?

'From a large quarto engraving published at Newcastle'

William the Walking Post

In the *Sporting Magazine* Hone learns of a postman, William Brockbank, 'whose daily pedestrian achievements occasioned public notice' in the first decade of the 19th century:

HE WAS the Walking Post from Manchester to Glossop in Derbyshire, a distance of sixteen miles, which he performed every day, Sundays excepted; returned the same evening; and personally delivered the letters, newspapers, &c in that populous and commercial country to all near the road, which made his daily task not less than thirty-five miles or upwards. What is more extraordinary, he

> This daily course of duty *walk'd*

in less than twelve hours a day, and never varied a quarter of an hour from his usual time of arriving at Glossop.

Brockbank was a native of Millom in Cumberland, and had daily walked the distance between Whitehaven and Ulverston, frequently under the necessity of wading the river at Muncaster... Including the different calls he had to make at a short distance from the road, his daily task was not less than forty-seven miles.

Joe the samphire gatherer

> The crows and choughs that wing the midway air
> Show scarce so gross as beetles. Halfway down
> Hangs one that gathers samphire: dreadful trade!   *King Lear*

THE CLIFFS in the range eastward of Dover to the Foreland are the most precipitous, but not so high as Shakespeare's... It was in this range of Dover cliffs that Joe Parsons, who for more than forty years had exclusively gathered samphire, broke his neck in 1823. Habit had rendered the highest and most difficult parts of these awful precipices as familiar to this man as the level below. Where the overhanging rock impeded his course, a rope, fastened to a peg driven into a cliff above, served him to swing himself from one projection to another. In one of these dangerous attempts this fastening gave way and he fell to rise no more.

Joe had heard of Shakespeare, and felt the importance of a hero. It was his boast that he was a king too powerful for his neighbours, who dared not venture to disturb him in his domain; that nature alone was his lord, to whom he paid no quittance. All were free to forage on his grounds, but none ventured.

Joe was twice wedded. His first rib frequently attended and looked to the security of his ropes, and would sometimes terrify him with threats to cast him loose. A promise of future kindness always ended the parley, and a thrashing on the next quarrel placed Joe again in peril. Death suddenly took Judith from this vale of tears: Parsons awoke in the night and found her brought up in an everlasting road-stead. Like a true philosopher and a quiet neighbour, Joe took his second nap, and when day called out the busy world to begin its matin labour, Joe called in the nearest gossip to see that all was done that decency required for so good a wife.

His last helpmate survives her hapless partner. No one has yet taken possession of his estate. The inquisitive and firm-nerved stranger casts his eyes below in vain: he that gathered samphire is himself gathered. The anchored bark, the skiff, the choughs and crows, the fearful precipice, and the stringy root growing in unchecked abundance, bring the bard and Joe Parsons to remembrance, but no one now attempts the dreadful trade.

A passion for fatal nooses

IN A LECTURE at the Leeds Philosophical Hall, Mr Michael Sadler [1780–1835, MP, a founder of the Leeds Literary and Philosophical Society] mentioned as a strange instance of perverted taste the case of a respectable gentleman in the county of Derby who has a strong penchant for halters in which malefactors have been executed, and who, having made friends with the Jack Ketches [hangmen] of all the neighbouring counties, has collected a large number of nooses which have done their duty, and which now hang as lines of beauty, with the names of their former tenants attached to each, round a museum in his house. He is known as 'a cut-and-come-again customer' to the finisher of the law in London.

   lines of beauty: a play on William Hogarth's sinuous 'Line of Beauty'

Keeping the rival clocks reet

The Durham contributor of 'Hut' the bellman (pages 77–81) tells of another of the city's oddities.

WILLEY WALKER, a well-known Durham character, who has discovered a new solar system different from all others, is a beadsman of the cathedral... In Durham there are two clocks which, if I may so express myself, are both *official* ones; viz, the cathedral clock and the jail or county clock. The admirers of each are about equal, some of the inhabitants regulating their movements by one and some by the other. Three or four years ago it happened, during the middle of the winter, that the two clocks varied considerably: there was *only* three-quarters of an hour's difference between them. The citizens cared very little about the *slight* discrepancy, but it was not at all relished by the guard of the London and Edinburgh mail, who spoke on the subject to the late John Bolton [1761–1821, a good clockmaker], the regulator of the county clock. John immediately posted off to the cathedral, where he met Willey Walker, and the following dialogue is said to have passed between them:

Bolton   Willey, why doan't ye keep t' abba clock reet? There's a bit difference between it and mine.

Willey   Why doan't ye keep yours so? It never gans reet.

Bolton   Mine's set by the sun, Willey! (Bolton was an astronomer.)

Willey   By the sun! Whew! whew! whew! Why, are ye turned fule? Nebody would think ye owt else! And ye pretend to be an astronomer, and set clocks by t' sun in this *windy* weather! Ther's nae depending on it. The winds, man, blaw sa, they whisk the sun about like a whirligig...!

Bolton was a very eccentric character and a great natural genius. From a very obscure origin he rose to considerable provincial celebrity. Such was his contempt of London artists that he described himself on his sign as being 'from Chester-le-Street, not London'. He was an indefatigable collector of curiosities, and had a valuable museum which most strangers visited. His advertisements were curious compositions, often in doggerel verse...

Bolton built some excellent organs and turret clocks. For one of the latter which he made for North Shields, he used to say he was not paid; and the following notice in his shop, in large characters, informed his customers of the fact: *'North Shields clock never paid for!'*

The half-guinea husband

On the 7th of October, 1736, a man and his wife at Rushall in Norfolk ... 'having some words', the man went out and hanged himself. The coroner's inquest found it self-murder and ordered him to be buried in the crossways; but his wife sent for a surgeon and sold the body for half a guinea. The surgeon feeling about the body, the wife said, 'He is fit for your purpose. He is as fat as butter.' The deceased was thereupon put into a sack, with his legs hanging out, and being thrown upon a cart, conveyed to the surgeon's.

Gentleman's Magazine

The noted John Cooke of Exeter

An Exeter correspondent gently mocks a local hero.

CORPORATIONS in old times kept fools, and there are still traces of the custom. The antiquary admires the carving of a fool, 'a motley fool', at the porchway of the King John tavern at Exeter, and contemplates it as probably the faithful representation of an obsolete servant of that ancient city; while the traveller endeavours to obtain a sight of the 'noted Captain Cooke, all alive! alive!' — the most public and not the least important officer of its lively corporation.

A tract ... denominated 'A Pamphlet called Old England for Ever!' is the production of Captain Cooke himself; and a lithographed print represents that noted personage 'drawn from *nature'*, in his full costume as 'Captain of the Sheriff's troop at 74 assizes for the county of Devon'... The captain calls his literary production 'a pamphlet of patriotic home achievements during the late direful war from 1793 to 1815'; and accordingly it is a series, to adopt his own words, of 'twenty-two years multifarious but abridged memoirs, novelties, anecdotes, genealogy and bulletins, by the author's natural instinct'.

The first most important information resulting from the captain's natural instinct is that 'the Duke of Wellington, Marshal Blucher, the allied officers and armies defeated the atheist, the enemy of the Sabbath and of peace to the world, on Sunday, 18th of June, 1815, at half after eight o'clock in the evening... I built a cottage that year, and have a tablet over my door, *Waterloo Cottage, in memory of Europe's victory ...*'

'I was born,' says the captain, 'at the Rose and Crown public-house on the old bridge in the borough town of Ashburton, 1765; where a good woollen-manufactory has been carried on; and it has produced a great character or so, for learning', and 'has been as famous for a beverage called *Ashburton Pop* as London is for porter. I recollect its sharp feeding [sic] good taste, far richer than the best small beer, more of the champagne taste, and what was termed a good sharp bottle. When you untied and hand-drew the cork, it gave a report louder than a popgun, to which I attribute its name. Its contents would fly up to the ceiling. If you did not mind to keep the mouth of the stone bottle into the white quart cup, it filled it with froth but not over a pint of clear liquor.

'Three old cronies would sit an afternoon six hours, smoke and drink a dozen bottles, their reckoning but eightpence each and a penny for tobacco. The pop was but twopence a bottle. It is a great loss to the town, because its recipe died with its brewer about 1785...'

From the never-enough-sufficiently-to-be-lamented and for-ever-departed Pop, the captain returns to himself... [*He is apprenticed at 15 to 'the head saddler in Exeter'; succeeds to his business; is saddler to Lord Heathfield and 'other colonels of dragoons, connoisseurs of saddlery'.*]

> Tho' I did not know the use of grammar,
> I was well supported by my hammer.
> I sticked to my King, leather and tools,
> And, for order, wrote a set of shop rules.
> Working with the hands only is but part,
> The head's the essential to make the work smart...

'Now,' says the captain, 'for my *sixty home achievements* during the late war for my king and country.' Alas! ...The captain's sixty achievements ... are past the arithmetician's art to enumerate...

Foremost stands 'the labour I took in pleasing and accommodating my customers'; and almost next, 'the many hours I have knocked my head, as it were, against Samuel Johnson to find words for handbills and advertisements all at my own expense, to avoid inflammatory pamphlets [counter radical ones]. I gloried in the name of John Bull, and shall to my life's end. I went into the pothouses at Exeter, and treated with mugs round, and gave loyal toasts and sentiments...

'From the attention I paid to the nobility, gentry, dragoon and militia officers, &c, when they tarried at Exeter or its neighbourhood, it was a pleasure and an honour mixed with fatigue. Besides my own business, I procured for them gratis [arranged deals for] manors, estates, houses, lodgings, carriages, horses, servants, fish, fowl, hunting, shooting and trout fishing. I may say John Cooke, saddler of Exeter, is known from England to the Indies...

'I had two direction-posts at my door during the war that no one had in the kingdom beside; one to the various places and distances, from Exeter to London 170 miles, &c, &c; the other a large sheet of paper written as a daily monitor gratis, a bulletin of news, to cheer people in the worst of times, to guide them in the constitutional [anti-reform] road. *I even made myself a direction-post*, and wore a conspicuous breastplate painted with this motto, "Fear God, honour the king, and revere his ministers"...

'I used to rise, before we had firemen, at the dead of night or morning with my apprentices, at any alarm of fire, desiring all women, children and lookers-on, if they did not help they were of harm, being in the way. I put in my bulletins, You are to take the left of all you meet in riding, and the right in walking. I was the means of the watering cart to lay the dust of the streets in summer...

'I saw Buonaparte at Torbay [as a prisoner in the Bellerophon], exact like his picture; a huge stiff broad back, strong neck, big calf to

98

his legs, he looked about fifty [he was 46], and about five feet eight; resembling a country master-builder, a sturdy one, full of thought, as about a building...

'I end this pamphlet. Four words: thought is the quickest; time the wisest; the laws of necessity the strongest; truth the most durable. This from a Devonshire Jog-trot, who has done enough to be termed a public character in his way; a John Bull tradesman.'

JOHN COOKE, *Waterloo Cottage*

Captain John Cooke 'drawn from nature'

A calendar
of customs

Next came fresh Aprill full of lustyhed
And wanton as a kid whose horne new-buds.
Upon a bull he rode, the same which led
Europa floting through th'Argolick fluds.
His hornes were gilden all with golden studs
And garnishèd with garlonds goodly dight
Of all the fairest flowres and freshest buds
Which th'earth brings forth; and wet he seem'd in sight
With waves through which he waded for his love's delight.

Spenser, *The Faerie Queene*, VII, vii

The customs that Hone recorded could make a generous book in themselves. Some survive; others he caught in their last days. Many were a creative way for the poor to beg cash or food as well as an occasion for carousing. No doubt the censure of moralistic people was one cause of their decline.

This selection moves through the year, but leaves Christmas and new-year jollities for a chapter of their own.

Drawing lots for love

FRANCIS DOUCE, whose attainments include more erudition concerning the origin and progress of English customs than any other antiquarian possesses ... observes in his *Illustrations of Shakespeare* [1807] concerning Saint Valentine's day:

'It was the practice in ancient Rome during a great part of the month of February to celebrate the Lupercalia, which were feasts in honour of Pan and Juno, whence the latter deity was named Februata, Februlis and Februlla... Amidst a variety of ceremonies, the names of young women were put into a box, from which they were drawn by the men as chance directed. The pastors of the early Christian church, who by every possible means endeavoured to eradicate the vestiges of pagan superstitions, and chiefly by some commutations of their forms ... appear to have chosen Saint Valentine's day for celebrating the new feast... It should seem, however, that it was utterly impossible to extirpate altogether any ceremony to which the common people had been much accustomed...'

Henri Misson, a learned traveller who died in England about 1721 [1719], describes the amusing practices of his time: 'On the eve of the 14th of February, Saint Valentine's day, the young folks of England and Scotland, by a very ancient custom, celebrate a little festival. An equal number of maids and bachelors get together, each writes their true or some feigned name upon separate billets which they roll up and draw by lots, the maids taking the men's billets and the men the maids', so that each of the young men lights upon a girl that he calls his valentine, and each of the girls upon a young man which she calls hers... But the man sticks faster to the valentine that is fallen to him than to the valentine to whom he is fallen... The valentines give balls and treats to their mistresses, wear their billets several days upon their bosoms or sleeves, and this little sport often ends in love...'

In some places at this time, and more particularly in London, the lad's valentine is the first lass he sees in the morning who is not an inmate of the house; the lass's valentine is the first youth she sees...

A correspondent communicates to *The Every-Day Book* a singular custom which prevailed many years since in the west of England. Three single young men went out together before daylight on Saint Valentine's day with a clapnet to catch an old owl and two sparrows in a neighbouring barn. If they were successful, and could bring the birds to the inn without injury before the females of the house had risen, they were rewarded by the hostess with three pots of purl [spiced ale] in honour of Saint Valentine, and enjoyed the privilege of demanding at any other house in the neighbourhood a similar boon.

This was done ... as an emblem that the owl, being the bird of wisdom, could influence the feathered race to enter the net of love as mates on that day, whereon both single lads and maidens should be reminded that happiness could alone be secured by an early union...

Two hearts made one: 'What be this?'

THE TENDER PASSION in the two-mile-an-hour Jehu [carter] of an eight-horse wagon puzzles him mightily. He 'sighs and drives, sighs and drives, and drives and sighs again', till the approach of this festival enables him to buy a valentine with a 'halter' and a 'couple o' hearts' transfixed by an arrow in the form of a weathercock, inscribed

> I'll be yours, if you'll be mine.
> I am your pleasing valentine.

This he gets his name written under by the shopkeeper, and will be quite sure that it is his name before he walks after his wagon, which he has left to go on, because neither that nor his passion can brook delay. After he is out of the town, he looks behind him lest anybody should see, and for a mile or two on the road ponders on the 'two hearts made one' as a most singular device, and with admired devotion. He then puts it in the trusty pocket under his smock which holds the wagon-bill, and flogs his horses to quicken their pace towards the inn where she who is his heart's delight has been lately promoted to the rank of under-kitchenmaid, *vice* her who resigned on being called 'to the happy estate of matrimony' by a neighbouring carter.

He gives her the mysterious paper in the yard. She receives it with a 'What be this?' and with a smack on the lips, and a smack from the whip on the gown. The gods have made him poetical, and from his recollection of a play he saw at the statute-fair he tells her that 'love, like a worm in the bud, has played upon his Lammas cheek' ever since last Lammastide, and she knows it has, and she's his valentine.

Valentines by the twopenny post

Where *can* the postman be? I say.
He ought to *fly* — on such a day!
Of *all* days in the year, you know,
It's monstrous rude to be so *slow*.
The fellow's so *exceeding* stupid —
Hark! *There* he is! Oh, the dear Cupid!   *Hone*

The twopenny postman of 1825 is transformed by the artist Samuel
Williams into a mock Cupid, equipped with arrows and bow as well
as his postman's horn and pouch, mounted on a shabby ass

TWO HUNDRED THOUSAND letters beyond the usual daily average
annually pass through the twopenny post-office in London on Saint
Valentine's day. 'Two hundred thousand twopences,' said an old
gentleman as he read this in a March newspaper, 'are four hundred
thousand pence' — and he was going to cast up the amount —

'Why, papa,' said his daughter, 'that's just the number of young
folks there must be in love with each other. That's the way to reckon.'

Fighting-cocks for Shrovetide

THE CRUELTY of cockfighting was a chief ingredient of the pleasure which intoxicated the people on Shrove Tuesday... The earliest mention of cockfighting in England is by Fitz-Stephens, who died in 1191. He mentions this as one of the amusements of the Londoners, together with the game of football. The whole passage is worth transcribing:

'Yearly at Shrovetide, the boys of every school bring fighting-cocks to their masters, and all the forenoon is spent at school to see these cocks fight together. After dinner all the youth of the city goeth to play at the ball in the fields. The scholars of every study have their balls; the practisers also of all the trades have every one their ball in their hands. The ancienter sort, the fathers and the wealthy citizens, come on horseback to see these youngsters contending at their sport, with whom in a manner they participate by motion, stirring their own natural heat in the view of the active youth, with whose mirth and liberty they seem to communicate.'

Cockfighting was prohibited in England under Edward III and Henry VIII, and even later; yet Henry himself indulged his cruel nature by instituting cockfights, and even James I took great delight in them. And within our own time games have been fought, and attendance solicited by public advertisement, at the Royal Cockpit, Whitehall, which Henry VIII built.

In 1835 new laws against cockfighting were enacted; yet matches are still held in secret.

Threshing the fat hen

THIS SINGULAR CUSTOM is almost obsolete, yet it certainly is practised even now [1825] in at least one obscure part of the kingdom. A reasonable conjecture is that the fowl was a delicacy to the labourer, and therefore given to him on this festive day for sport and food.

> At Shrovetide, to shroving; go thresh the fat hen.
> If blindfold can kill her, then give it thy men.
> Maids: fritters and pancakes enough see you make.
> Let slut have one pancake for company sake.

So directs Thomas Tusser in his *Five Hundreth Good Pointes of Husbandrie*, 1620. On this, his annotator, *Tusser Redivivus*, 1710, annexes an account of the custom: 'The hen is hung at a fellow's back, who has also some horse-bells about him. The rest of the fellows are blinded and have boughs in their hands with which they chase this fellow and his hen about some large court or small enclosure. The fellow with his hen and bells shifting as well as he can, they follow the sound and sometimes hit him and his hen. Other times, if he can get behind one of them they thresh one another well-favouredly.

'But the jest is, the maids are to blind the fellows, which they do with their aprons, and the cunning baggages will endear their sweethearts with a peeping-hole, whilst the others look out as sharp to hinder it. After this the hen is boiled with bacon, and store of pancakes and fritters are made.

'She that is noted for lying a-bed long, or any other miscarriage, hath the first pancake presented to her, which most commonly falls to the dog's share at last, for no one will own it their due.

'Thus were youth encouraged, shamed, and feasted at very little cost, and always their feasts were accompanied with exercise. The loss of which laudable custom is one of the benefits we have got by smoking tobacco.' Old Tusser himself denotes ... that this was a sport in Essex and Suffolk.

John Brand (*see next page*) was informed by a Mr Jones that when he was a boy in Wales, the hen that did not lay eggs before Shrove Tuesday was considered useless, and to be on that day threshed by a man with a flail. If he killed her he got her for his pains.

All the fun of hen-threshing

Schoolboys throwing at cocks

THIS BRUTAL PRACTICE on Shrove Tuesday is still [1825] conspicuous in several parts of the kingdom. John Brand affirms that it was retained in many schools in Scotland within the last century, and he conjectures, 'Perhaps it is still in use.' A little inquiry on his part would have discovered it in English schools.

He proceeds to observe that the Scotch schoolmasters 'were said to have presided at the battle and claimed the runaway cocks, called fugees, as their perquisites'. To show the ancient legitimacy of the usage he instances a petition of 1355 from the scholars of the school of Ramera to their schoolmaster for a cock he owed them upon Shrove Tuesday, to throw sticks at...

No decently circumstanced person, however rugged his disposition from neglect in his childhood, will in our times permit one of his sons to take part in the sport... Country gentlemen threw at the cock formerly: there is not a country gentleman now who would not discourage the shocking usage.

The Rev John Brand (1744–1806), was for 22 years secretary of the Society of Antiquaries. See Bibliography for his and other works cited by Hone.

Tinsel, flauntery and cross-dressing

ON SHROVE TUESDAY, according to an old author, 'Men ate and drank and abandoned themselves to every kind of sportive foolery, as if resolved to have their fill of pleasure before they were to die.'

The preparing of bacon, meat, and the making of black-puddings, for good cheer after the coming Lent, preceded the day itself, whereon, besides domestic feasting and revelry, with dice and card-playing, there was immensity of mumming.

The records of Norwich testify that in 1440 one John Gladman, who is there called 'a man who was ever trewe and feythfull to God and to the kyng' and constantly disportive, made a public disport with his neighbours, crowned as king of Christmas, on horseback, having his horse bedizened with tinsel and flauntery, and preceded by the twelve months of the year, each month habited as the season required. After him came Lent, clothed in white and herring-skins, on a horse with trappings of oyster-shells 'in token that sadness should follow, and an holy tyme'... They rode through the city accompanied by others in whimsical dresses, 'makyng mirth, disportes and playes'. Among much curious observation on these Shrovetide mummings in *The Popish Kingdome* [1570] it is affirmed that of all the merrymakers —

The chiefest man is he and one that most deserveth praise
Among the rest, that can find out the fondest kind of plays.
On him they look, and gaze upon, and laugh with lusty cheer,
Whom boys do follow, crying 'fool' and suchlike other gear.
He in the meantime thinks himself a wondrous worthy man, &c.

...Some of the rout carried staves, or fought in armour. Others, disguised as devils, chased all the people they came up with... Men wore women's clothes, and women dressed as men entered their neighbours' or friends' houses. Some were apparelled as monks; others arrayed themselves as kings, attended by their guards and royal accompaniments. Some disguised as old fools pretended to sit on nests and hatch young fools. Others wearing skins and dresses became counterfeit bears and wolves, roaring lions and raging bulls; or walked on high stilts, with wings at their backs, as cranes...

Apprentices grow less licentious

SHROVE TUESDAY was until late years the great holiday of the apprentices... Their licentious disturbances stand recorded in the annals of many a fray. Mixing in every neighbouring brawl to bring it if possible to open riot, they at length assumed to determine on public affairs, and went in bodies with their petitions and remonstrances to the bar of the house of commons... But this is not the place to notice their manners further. The successors to their name are of another generation. They have been better educated, live in better times, and having better masters will make better men. The apprentices whose situation is to be viewed with anxiety are the outdoor apprentices [not living in] of poor persons, who can scarcely find homes, or who being orphans leave the factories or workrooms of their masters at night to go where they can, and do what they please, without paternal care or being the creatures of anyone's solicitude, and are yet expected to be or become good members of society.

Shroving for pankiak

William Barnes (1801–86), schoolmaster and scholar, and later to win fame as a Dorset poet, sent this article in 1831. (See also page 240.)

IN SOME of the villages of Dorsetshire and Wiltshire the boys at Shrovetide still keep a custom called lent-crocking, which originated in the carnival of Roman Catholic times, and consists in going round in the evening to pelt the doors of the inhabitants with pieces of broken crockery. In Dorsetshire ... the leader goes up and knocks at the door, leaving his followers behind him armed with a good stock of potsherds — the collected relics of the washing-pans: jugs, dishes and plates that have been the victims of concussion in the unlucky hands of careless housewives...

When the door is opened, the hero, who is perhaps a farmer's boy with a pair of black eyes sparkling under the tattered brim of his brown milking-hat covered with cow's hair and dirt like the inside of a blackbird's nest, hangs down his head and, with a corner of his mouth turned up into an irrepressible smile, pronounces in the dialect of his county the following lines, composed for the occasion, perhaps, by some mendicant friar whose name might have been suppressed with the monasteries by Henry VIII.

> I be come a-shrovin
> Vor a little pankiak,
> A bit o' bread o' your biakin
> Or a little truckly cheese
> O' your own miakin.
> If you'll gi' me a little I'll ax no moore.
> If you don't gi' me nothin I'll rottle your door.

Sometimes he gets a piece of bread and cheese; and at some houses he is told to be gone, when he calls up his followers to send their missiles in a rattling broadside against the door...

The broken pots and dishes originally signified that, as Lent was begun, those cooking vessels were of no use and were supposed to be broken; and the cessation of flesh-eating is understood in the begging of pancakes and bread and cheese.

'Ah! you April fool!'

IT IS customary on this day for boys to practise jocular deceptions...

Thirty years ago, when buckles were worn on shoes, a boy would meet a person in the street with 'Sir, if you please, your shoe's unbuckled,' and the moment the accosted individual looked towards his feet the informant would cry, 'Ah! you April fool!'

Twenty years ago, when buckles were wholly disused, the urchin-cry was 'Sir, your shoe's untied,' and if the shoe-wearer lowered his eyes he was hailed as his buckled predecessor had been, with the said 'Ah! you April fool!'

Now, when neither buckles nor strings are worn, because in the year 1825 no decent man has a *shoe* to his foot ['Hessian' topboots are the fashion], the waggery of the day is 'Sir, there's something *out* of your pocket.' 'Where?' 'There!' 'What?' 'Your *hand*, sir. — Ah! you

'There's something out of your pocket... Something on your face...'

April fool!' Or else some lady is humbly bowed to and gravely addressed with 'Ma'am, I beg your pardon, but you've *something on your face*!' 'Indeed, my man! What is it?' 'Your nose, ma'am. — Ah! you April fool!'

> Then indoor, young ones club their wicked wits
> And almost frighten servants into fits —
> 'Oh, John! James! John! — oh, quick! oh! Molly, oh!
> Oh, the trapdoor! oh, Molly! down below!'
> 'What, what's the matter!' scream, with wild surprise,
> John, James and Molly, while the young ones' cries
> Redouble till they come; then all the boys
> Shout, 'Ah! you April fools!' with clamorous noise,
> And little girls, enticed downstairs to see,
> Stand peeping, clap their hands, and cry 'tee-hee!'
> Each jibing boy escapes a different way,
> And meet again, some trick 'as good as that' to play.　　*Hone*

Pay for your shoes, if you please

DURHAM, 1826:   On Easter Sunday it is a common custom here for a number of boys to assemble in the afternoon, and as soon as the clock strikes four, scour the streets in parties and accost every female they may happen to meet with 'Pay for your shoes, if you please,' at the same time stooping to take them off; which if they do, and do not immediately get a penny or twopence, they will actually carry off by main force. I have known the boys have at least a dozen odd shoes.

But generally something is given, which in the evening they either spend in public-houses, or divide.

On Easter Monday the women claim the same privilege towards the male sex. They begin much earlier in the day and attack every man and boy they can lay hold of to make them *pay for their shoes*. If the men happen to wear boots and will not pay anything, the girls generally endeavour to seize their hats and run off. If a man catches the girl with the hat it is usually thrown or handed about to the great amusement of the spectators, till the person is baffled out of a sixpence to redeem the right of wearing it again. But this, like all other old customs, is now chiefly practised by a few children.

Hone adds: A contributor to the *Gentleman's Magazine* in August 1790 says that at Ripon in Yorkshire 'on Easter Sunday, as soon as the service of the church is over the boys run about the streets and lay hold of every woman or girl they can and take their buckles from their shoes. This farce is continued till the next day at noon, when the females begin and return the compliment upon the men, which does not end till Tuesday evening. Nay, I was told that, some years ago, no traveller could pass through the town without being stopped and having his spurs taken away unless redeemed by a little money...'

Whooping after a stag

Citizens of London long claimed a right to hunt stags in Epping Forest under a grant of *free warren* made by King Henry III in 1226. By Hone's time the right was asserted in a boisterous Easter Monday event, of great benefit to innkeepers. The frolic died out in the 1860s (unlawful developers had sharply encroached on the once-vast forest). Hone prints an account of the hunt of 1826 by 'Simon Youngbuck' in *The Morning Herald*.

THE HUNTSMEN of the east were all abroad by nine o'clock, trotting fair and softly down the road on great nine-hand sky scrapers, nimble daisy-cutting nags, flowing-tailed chargers and ponies no bigger than the learned one at Astley's [circus]. Some were in job-coaches [hired] at two guineas a day; some in three-bodied nondescripts, some in gigs, some in cabs, some in drags, some in short stages and some in long stages; while some on no stages at all footed the road, smothered by dust driven by a black, bleak northeaster full in the teeth.

Every gentleman was arrayed after his own particular taste, in blue, brown or black — in dress-coats, long coats, short coats, frock-coats, greatcoats and no-coats; in drab-slacks and slippers; in gray-tights and black-spurred Wellingtons; in nankeen bomb-balloons, in city-white cotton-cord unmentionables [breeches] with jockey toppers, and in Russian-drill down-belows as a memento of the late czar. The ladies all wore a *goose-skin* under-dress, in compliment to the northeaster.

At that far-famed spot, the brow above Fairmead Bottom, by twelve o'clock there were not less than three thousand merry lieges then and there assembled. It was a beautiful set-out. Fair dames 'in purple and in pall' reposed in vehicles of all sorts, sizes and conditions whilst seven or eight hundred mounted members of the hunt wound in and out 'in restless ecstasy', chatting and laughing with the fair, sometimes rising in their stirrups to look out for the long-coming cart of the stag... The pollard oaks which skirt the bottom on either side were filled with men and boys.

But where the deuce is the stag all this while? One o'clock, and no stag. *Two* o'clock, and no stag! ...The secret is this. There are buttocks of boiled beef and fat hams, and beer and brandy in abundance, at The Roebuck public-house low down in the forest; and ditto at The Bald-faced Stag on the top of the hill; and ditto at The Coach and Horses at Woodford Wells; and ditto at The Eagle at Snaresbrook; and if the stag had been brought out before the beef, beer, bacon and brandy were eaten and drunk, where would have been the use of providing so many good things?

So they carted the stag from public-house to public-house, and showed him at threepence a head to those ladies and gentlemen who never saw such a thing before, and the showing and carting induced a consumption of eatables and drinkables, an achievement which was helped by a band of music in every house playing hungry tunes to help the appetite. And then when the eatables and drinkables were gone, and paid for, they turned out the stag.

Precisely at half-past two o'clock the stag-cart was seen coming over the hill by The Baldfaced Stag, and hundreds of horsemen and gigmen rushed gallantly forward to meet and escort it to the top of Fairmead Bottom amidst such whooping and hallooing as ... would have done Carl Maria von Weber's heart good to hear. And then when the cart stopped and was turned tail about, the horsemen drew up in long lines, forming an avenue wide enough for the stag to run down.

For a moment all was deep, silent, breathless anxiety, and the doors of the cart were thrown open, and out popped a strapping four-year-old red buck, fat as a porker, with a chaplet of flowers round his neck, a girth of divers-coloured ribbons and a long blue and pink streamer depending from the summit of his branching horns. He was received, on his alighting, with a shout that seemed to shake the heaven's concave, and took it very graciously, looking round him with great dignity as he stalked slowly and delicately forward down the avenue prepared for him, and occasionally shrinking from side to side as some super-valorous cockney made a cut at him with his whip.

Presently he caught a glimpse of the hounds and the huntsmen waiting for him at the bottom, and in an instant off he bounded, sideways, through the rank, knocking down and trampling all who crowded the path he chose to take; and dashing at once into the cover, he was out of sight before a man could say Jack Robinson!

Then might be seen gentlemen running about without their horses, and horses galloping about without their gentlemen, and hats out of number brushed off their owners' heads by the rude branches of the trees; and everybody asking which way the stag was gone, and nobody knowing anything about him; and ladies beseeching gentlemen not to be too venturesome; and gentlemen gasping for breath at the thoughts of what they were determined to venture; and myriads of people on foot running hither and thither in search of little eminences to look from. And yet nothing at all to be seen...

Meanwhile the stag, followed by the keepers and about six couple of hounds, took away through the covers towards Woodford. Finding himself too near the haunts of his enemy, man, he there turned back, sweeping down the bottom for a mile or two and away up the enclosures towards Chingford; where he was caught nobody knows how, for everybody returned to town, except those who stopped to regale afresh and recount the glorious perils of the day...

A lift from the damsels

In John Brand's *Popular Antiquities*, 1813 edition, Hone finds a City
gentleman's account of an experience in Shropshire:

I WAS sitting alone last Easter Tuesday at breakfast at The Talbot in Shrewsbury when I was surprised by the entrance of all the female servants of the house, handing in an armchair, lined with white and decorated with ribbons and favours of different colours. I asked them what they wanted. Their answer was, they came to *heave* me. It was the custom of the place on that morning, and they hoped I would take

a seat in their chair. It was impossible not to comply with a request very modestly made, and to a set of nymphs in their best apparel and several of them under twenty. I wished to see all the ceremony, and seated myself accordingly.

The group then lifted me from the ground, turned the chair about, and I had the felicity of a salute [kiss] from each. I told them I supposed there was a fee due upon the occasion, and was answered in the affirmative; and having satisfied the damsels in this respect, they withdrew to heave others... On Easter Monday, between nine and twelve, the men heave the women in the same manner...

In Lancashire, Staffordshire, Warwickshire and some other parts of England there prevails [1825] this custom of *heaving* or *lifting* at Eastertide. This is performed mostly in the open street, though sometimes it is insisted on and submitted to within the house. People form into parties of eight or a dozen or even more for the purpose...

A Warwickshire correspondent: Easter Monday and Easter Tuesday were known by the name of *heaving-day*, because on the former day it was customary for the men to heave and kiss the women, and on the latter for the women to retaliate upon the men. The women's heaving-day was the most amusing. Many a time have I passed along the streets inhabited by the lower orders of people and seen parties of jolly matrons assembled round tables on which stood a foaming tankard of ale. There they sat in all the pride of absolute sovereignty, and woe to the luckless man that dared to invade their prerogatives! As sure as he was seen he was pursued — as sure as he was pursued he was taken — and as sure as he was taken he was heaved and kissed, and compelled to pay sixpence for 'leave and licence' to depart.

Hone adds a stern comment: Conducted as *lifting* appears to have been by the blooming lasses of Shrewsbury, and acquitted as all who are actors in the usage anywhere must be of even the slightest knowledge that this practice is an absurd performance of the resurrection, still it must strike the reflective mind as at least an absurd custom... It has been handed down to us from the bewildering ceremonies of the Romish church, and may easily be discountenanced into disuse by opportune and mild dissuasion... [*and much more in this vein*].

John Clare's village maidens

The poet John Clare sends an account of customs still practised in his
village of Helpston, Northamptonshire, on Saint Mark's Eve, April 25.

ON ST MARK'S EVE it is still a custom with us for young maidens to make the *dumb cake*, a mystical ceremony which has lost its origin, and in some counties may have ceased altogether.

The number of the party never exceeds three. They meet in silence to make the cake, and as soon as the clock strikes twelve they each break a portion off to eat, and when done they walk up to bed backwards without speaking a word, for if one speaks the spell is broken. Those that are to be married see the likeness of their sweethearts hurrying after them as if wishing to catch them before they get into bed; but the maids, being apprised of this beforehand (by the cautions of old women who have tried it), take care to unpin their clothes before they start, and are ready to slip into bed before they are caught by the pursuing shadow.

If nothing is seen, the desired token may be a knocking at the doors or a rustling in the house as soon as they have retired. To be convinced that it comes from nothing else but the desired cause, they are always particular in turning out the cats and dogs before the ceremony begins. Those that are to die unmarried neither see nor hear anything, but they have terrible dreams, which are sure to be of new-made graves, winding-sheets and churchyards, and of rings that will fit no finger or which if they do, crumble into dust as soon as put on...

On this same night too, the more stouthearted watch the church porch. They go in the evening and lay in the church porch a branch of a tree, or a flower large enough to be readily found in the dark, and then return home to wait the approach of midnight. They are to proceed to the porch again before the clock strikes twelve, and to remain in it till it has struck. As many as choose accompany the maid who took the flower or branch, and is to fetch it again, as far as the church gate and there wait until their adventuring companion returns — who, if she is to be married within the year, is to see a marriage procession pass by her with a bride in her own likeness hanging on the arm of her future husband. As many bridesmen and maidens as appear to follow them, so many months is the maid to wait before her marriage. If she is to die unmarried, then the expected procession is to be a funeral, consisting of a coffin covered with a white sheet, borne on the shoulders of shadows that seem without heads.

This custom, with all its contingent 'hopes and fears', is still practised, though with what success I am unable to determine. The imagination may be wrought to any height in such matters, and doubtless some persuade themselves that they see what the story describes.

And odd character at Helpston whose name is Ben Barr, and whom the villagers call, and believe as, 'the prophet', watches the church porch every year and pretends to know the fate of everyone in the village round, and who shall be married or die in the year; but as a few pence generally purchase a good omen, he seldom prophesies the deaths of his believers.

Hone comments: This Ben Barr of Helpston must be a useful fellow to timid believers in such affairs. He seems to have created for himself a place of trust and profit. If he is only a wag he may enjoy his emoluments with his humour, and do no harm; but should he assume to foretell mischief to his believers he is, legally speaking, a 'sturdy rogue'. The seeing of supernatural sights by a paid proxy is a novelty in the annals of superstition...

Junketings on May Day

A NATIVE of Penzance in Cornwall relates to the editor of *The Every-Day Book* that it is an annual custom there on May-eve for a number of young men and women to assemble at a public-house and sit up till the clock strikes twelve, when they go round the town with violins, drums and other instruments, and by sound of music call upon others who had previously settled to join them. As soon as the party is formed, they proceed to different farmhouses within four or five miles of the neighbourhood, where they are expected as regularly as May morning comes; and they there partake of a beverage called junket made of raw milk and rennet, or running as it is there called, sweetened with sugar, and a little cream added. After this they take tea and 'heavy country cake', composed of flour, cream, sugar and currants; next, rum and milk; and then a dance.

After thus regaling, they gather the may. While some are breaking down the boughs others sit and make the 'May music'. This is done by cutting a circle through the bark at a certain distance from the bottom of the may branches, then, by gently and regularly tapping the bark all round, from the cut circle to the end, the bark becomes loosened and slips away whole from the wood; and a hole being cut in the pipe, it is easily formed to emit a sound … and becomes a whistle.

The gathering and the May music being finished, they then 'bring home the may' by five or six o'clock in the morning, with the band playing and their whistles blowing. After dancing throughout the town they go to their respective employments…

On the first Sunday after May Day it is a custom with families at Penzance to visit Rose Hill, Poltier and other adjacent villages by way of recreation. These pleasure-parties usually consist of two or three families together. They carry flour and other materials with them to make the 'heavy cake' … at the pleasant farm-dairies which are always open for their reception. Nor do they forget to take tea, sugar, rum and other comfortable things for their refreshment, which, by paying a trifle for baking and for the niceties awaiting their consumption, contents the farmers for the house-room and pleasure they afford their welcome visitants.

Here the young ones find delicious junkets with sour milk or curd cut in diamonds, which is eaten with sugar and cream. Newmade cake, refreshing tea and exhilarating punch satisfy the stomach, cheer the spirits and assist the walk home in the evening.

Frolicking mayers in Hertfordshire

A contributor at Hitchin, Hertfordshire, tells of curious doings on May 1:

SOON AFTER three o'clock in the morning a large party of the townpeople and neighbouring labourers parade the town, singing the Mayers' Song. They carry in their hands large branches of may, and they affix a branch either upon or at the side of the doors of nearly every respectable house in the town. Where there are knockers they place these branches within the handles.

That which was put into our knocker was so large that the servant could not open the door till the gardener came and took it out. The larger the branch is that is placed at the door, the more honourable to the house, or rather to the servants of the house. If in the course of the year a servant has given offence to any of the mayers, then instead of a branch of may a branch of elder with a bunch of nettles is affixed to her door. This is considered a great disgrace and the unfortunate subject of it is exposed to the jeers of her rivals. On May morning, therefore, the girls look with some anxiety for their may-branch, and rise very early to ascertain their good or ill fortune…

Throughout the day, parties of these mayers are seen dancing and frolicking in various parts of the town. The group that I saw today … was composed as follows. First came two men with their faces blacked, one of them with a birch broom in his hand and a large artificial hump on his back, the other dressed as a woman all in rags and tatters, with a large straw bonnet on and carrying a ladle. These are called 'Mad Moll and her husband'.

Next came two men: one most fantastically dressed with ribbons

Mad Moll and her humpbacked 'husband' lead the dance, the gaudy 'Lord' brandishes his sword, the musicians can be seen on left

and a great variety of gaudy coloured silk handkerchiefs tied round his arms from the shoulders to the wrists and down his thighs and legs to his ankles. He carried a drawn sword in his hand. Leaning upon his arm was a youth dressed as a fine lady, in white muslin, and profusely bedecked from top to toe with gay ribbons. These, I understood, were called the 'Lord and Lady' of the company. After these followed six or seven couples more, attired much in the same style as the lord and lady, only the men were without swords.

When this group received a satisfactory contribution at any house, the music struck up from a violin, clarinet and fife, accompanied by the long drum, and they began the merry dance, and very well they danced, I assure you. The men-*women* looked and footed it so much like *real* women that I stood in great doubt as to which sex they belonged to, till Mrs J—— assured me that women were not permitted to mingle in these sports.

While the dancers were merrily footing it, the principal amusement to the populace was caused by the grimaces and clownish tricks of Mad Moll and her husband. When the circle of spectators became so contracted as to interrupt the dancers, then Mad Moll's husband went to work with his broom, and swept the road-dust all round the circle into the faces of the crowd, and when any pretended affronts were offered (and many were offered) to his wife, he pursued the offenders, broom in hand. If he could not overtake them, whether they were males or females, he flung his broom at them. These flights and pursuits caused an abundance of merriment...

The Mayers' Song is a composition, or rather a medley, of great antiquity, and I was therefore very desirous to procure a copy of it... [and] at length succeeded in obtaining it from one of the mayers. The following is a literal transcript of it:

> Remember us poor mayers all,
>   And thus we do begin
> To lead our lives in righteousness,
>   Or else we die in sin.
>
> We have been rambling all this night
>   And almost all this day,
> And now returnèd back again
>   We have brought you a branch of may.
>
> A branch of may we have brought you
>   And at your door it stands.
>   It is but a sprout
>   But it's well budded out
> By the work of our Lord's hands.

The hedges and trees they are so green,
    As green as any leek.
Our heavenly father He watered them
    With his heavenly dew so sweet.

The heavenly gates are open wide,
    Our paths are beaten plain,
And if a man be not too far gone
    He may return again.

The life of man is but a span,
    It flourishes like a flower.
We are here today and gone tomorrow,
    And we are dead in an hour.

The moon shines bright and the stars give a light
    A little before it is day,
So God bless you all, both great and small,
    And send you a joyful May.

Town and country maypoles

THE MAYPOLE nearest to the metropolis that stood the longest within the recollection of the editor was near Kennington Green [Lambeth], at the back of the houses at the south corner of the Workhouse-lane leading from the Vauxhall-road to Elizabeth-place ... nearly opposite to the Black Prince public-house. It remained till about the year 1795, and was much frequented by milkmaids.

A delightfully pretty print of a merrymaking round about the maypole supplies an engraving on the next page illustrative of the prevailing tendency of this work, and the simplicity of rural manners. It is not so sportive as the dancings about the maypole near London formerly; there is nothing of the boisterous rudeness which must be well remembered by many old Londoners on May Day...

The late Dr Samuel Parr [1747–1825], the fascinating converser, the skilful controverter, the first Greek scholar and one of the greatest and most influential men of the age, was a patron of May Day sports. Opposite his parsonage-house at Hatton, near Warwick ... stood the parish maypole, which on the annual festival was dressed with garlands, surrounded by a numerous band of villagers. The doctor was 'first of the throng' and danced with his parishioners the gayest of the gay. He kept the large crown of the maypole in a closet of his house, from whence it was produced every May Day, with fresh flowers and streamers... He always spoke of this festivity as one wherein he joined with peculiar delight to himself, and advantage to his neighbours. He was deemed eccentric, and so he was; for he was never proud to the humble nor humble to the proud. His eloquence and wit elevated humility, and crushed insolence; he was a champion to the oppressed, a foe to the oppressor, a friend to the friendless and a brother to him who was ready to perish...

Hone knew the scholarly and kindly Parr (that rarety among Church of England parsons of his day, a strong Whig), and as a tribute to him he named his youngest son Samuel Parr Hone.

It is a pleasant sight to see
A little village company
Drawn out upon the first of May
To have their annual holiday —
The pole hung round with garlands gay,
The young ones footing it away;
The aged cheering their old souls
With recollections and their bowls ;
Or, on the mirth and dancing failing,
Their oft-times-told old tales re-taleing.   *Hone*

Gathering the May-dew

A less charming scene is reported by an Edinburgh man in 1826:

ALLOW ME, without preface, to acquaint you with a custom of *gathering the May-dew* here on the first of May.

About four o'clock in the morning there is an unusual stir, a great opening of area gates and ringing of bells, and a 'gathering' of folk of all clans, arrayed in all the colours of the rainbow; and a hurrying of gay throngs of both sexes through the King's Park to Arthur's Seat. In the course of half an hour the entire hill is a moving mass of all sorts and sizes. At the summit may be seen a company of bakers and other craftsmen, dressed in kilts, dancing round a maypole. On the more level part 'next door' is usually an itinerant vendor of whisky or mountain (not May) dew, your approach to whom is always indicated by a number of bodies carelessly lying across your path, not dead, but

'From a slight sketch accompanying the communication,
Mr George Cruikshank's pencil depicts the action'

drunk... The strong light thrown upon the various groups by the rising sun gives a singularly picturesque effect... The ever-varying and unceasing sounds of the bagpipes and tabors and fifes, *et hoc genus omne*, almost stun the ear.

About six o'clock the appearance of the gentry, toiling and *pechin* [panting] up the ascent, becomes the signal for serving men and women to march to the right-about, for they well know that they must have the house clean and everything in order earlier than usual on May-morning... By nine or ten, were it not for the drunkards who are staggering towards the 'gude town', no one would know that anything particular had taken place...

Norfolk's Floralian hornblowers

Town and country people held all sorts of floral parades on May Day, collecting money. A classically-minded reader reports from Norfolk:

IN NO PLACE where the custom of celebrating May Day still continues does it present so close a resemblance to its Roman origin as at [King's] Lynn.

The Lynn garland is made of two hoops of the same size, fixed transversely and attached to a pole or staff... Bunches of flowers, interspersed with evergreens, are tied round the hoops, from the interior of which festoons of blown birds' eggs are usually suspended, and long strips of various-coloured ribbons are also pendant from the top. A doll, full-dressed ... is seated in the centre, thus exhibiting a humble but not inappropriate representation of Flora surrounded by the fragrant emblems of her consecrated offerings...

The garlands are carried forth in all directions about the town, each with an attendant group of musicians (hornblowers*), collecting eleemosynary tributes... The horns, used only on this occasion, are those of bulls and cows, and the sound produced by them when blown in concert ... is not unlike the lowing of a herd of the living animals.

Forgetful of their youthful days, numberless anathemas are ejaculated by the elder inhabitants at the tremendous hurricane of monotonous sounds throughout the day. Though deafening in their tones, there appears something so classically antique in the use of these horns that the imagination cannot forbear picturing the hornblowers as the votaries of Io and Serapis (the Egyptian Isis and Osiris) ... sounding their *Io Pæans* to the honour of Flora.

*Hone's note:*By sound of trumpet all the courtesans in Rome were called to the Floralian sports, where they danced, it is said (though greatly to be doubted) in a state of nudity about the streets, with the trumpets blown before them.

Village girls come garlanding

A Northampton reader describes similar garlands, and sends a picture:

THE GIRLS from the neighbouring villages of Kingsthorpe, &c, on the morning of May Day come into the town with May garlands which they exhibit from house to house (to show, as the inhabitants say, what flowers are in season), and usually receive a trifle from each house. The garland is composed of two hoops crossing each other vertically, and covered with flowers and streamers of various coloured ribands. These are affixed to a staff about five feet long by which it is carried, and in each of the apertures between the hoops is placed a smartly dressed doll. The accompanying sketch will convey some idea of the garland...

The dancing milkmaids vanish

In London thirty years ago
      When pretty milkmaids went about,
It was a goodly sight to see
      Their May Day pageant all drawn out:

Themselves in comely colours dressed,
      Their shining garland in the middle,
A pipe and tabor on before
      Or else the foot-inspiring fiddle.

They stopped at houses where it was
      Their custom to cry 'Milk below!'
And while the music played, with smiles
      Joined hands, and pointed toe to toe…

Such scenes and sounds once blessed my eyes
      And charmed my ears — but all have vanished!
On May Day now no garlands go
      For milkmaids, and their dance, are banished…   *Hone*

THE MILKMAIDS' 'GARLAND' was a pyramidical frame, covered with damask, glittering on each side with polished silver plate and adorned with knots of gay-coloured ribbons and posies of fresh flowers, surmounted by a silver urn or tankard. The garland, being placed on a wooden horse, was carried by two men … sometimes preceded by a pipe and tabor but more frequently by a fiddle. The gayest milkmaids followed the music, others followed the garland, and they stopped at their customers' doors and danced.

The plate in some of these garlands was very costly. It was usually borrowed of the pawnbrokers for the occasion, upon security. One person in that trade was particularly resorted to… He furnished out the entire garland, and let it at so much per hour, under bond from responsible householders for its safe return… One set of milkmaids would hire the garland from ten o'clock till one and another set … from one o'clock till six; and so on, during the first three days of May. It was customary with milk-people of less profitable walks to make a display of another kind…

A London reader remembers: A beautiful country girl … more gaily attired than on any other day, with floral ornaments in her neat little hat and on her bosom, led her cow by a rope depending from its horns, garlanded with flowers and knots of ribbons. The horns, neck and head of the cow were decorated in like manner. A fine net, like those upon ladies' palfreys, tastefully stuck with flowers, covered Bess's back, and even her tail was ornamented with products of the

124

spring and silken knots. The proprietess of the cow, a neat, brisk little matronly body, followed on one side in holiday array, with a sprig in her country bonnet, a blooming posy in her kerchief, and ribbons on her stomacher. This scene was in Westminster, near the old abbey.

Ah! *those* were the days.

And now there are even battery cows

In the milkmaids' dance pictured here, the 'garland' is smaller than the one described in the previous page, but it is still a costly display of silverware with posies. Housewives throw coins from their windows.

A lesser garland, on a damask bed
Was carried on a skilful porter's head.
It stopped at every customer's street-door
And all the milkmaids ranged themselves before.
The fiddler's quickening elbow quicker flew,
And then he stamped, and then the galliard grew.

Then cows the meadows ranged and fed on grass,
And milk was sometimes watered. Now, alas!
In huge first-floors each cow, a prisoned guest,
Eats rancid oilcake in unnat'ral rest;
Bids from her udder unconcocted flow
A stream a few short hours will turn to — foh!
Milk manufactories usurp the place
Of wholesome dairies...   *Hone*

Perhaps the first reference in verse to dairy industrialization. As early as 1794, a survey reported nearly 4,000 cows in the range of farms from Paddington to Islington. By the 1820s some dairies had 500 cows or more, 'prisoned' and fed with oilcake. ('First-floor' here means ground-level.)

Song, dance, strawberries and cream

A reader remembers a May Day scene at Chepstow in the Wye Valley:

MY ATTENTION was arrested by one of the prettiest processions I remember to have enjoyed ... milkmaids dancing and serenading round an old man, whose few grey hairs were crowned by a wreath of wild flowers. He held a blossomy hawthorn in his right hand, and a staff with cowslips and bluebells in his left. A cow's horn hung across his shoulders, which he blew on arriving at a house. The youths and lasses were more than thirty in number. Their arms, heads and necks were surrounded by clusters of lilies of the valley and wild roses.

Then came an apple-cheeked dame with a lowcrowned broad-brim hat ... her petticoat short; blue worsted stockings; a highheeled pair of shoes with silver buckles... In one hand she held a brass kettle, newly scoured. It was full of cream. In the other, a basket of wood strawberries. To whoever came up to her with a saucer or basin she gave a portion of her cream and fruit, with the trimmest curtsey I ever saw made by a dainty milkwoman betwixt earth and sky. She was Aunt Nelly, and her 'bough-bearer', called Uncle Ambrose, was known for singing a song, ''Twas on one moonshiny night'... Six goats, harnessed in flowers, carried utensils in milking and butter-making; and the farmer of the party rode on a bull, also tastily dressed...

The language of May Day boughs

It was formerly a custom in Cheshire for young men to place *birchen boughs* on May Day over the doors of their mistresses, and mark the residence of a scold by an *alder bough*. There is an old rhyme which mentions peculiar boughs for various tempers, an *owlder* (alder) for a scolder, a *nut* for a slut, &c.

The famed Helston Furry in 1826

ON THE 8th OF MAY at Helston in Cornwall is held what is called 'the Furry'. The word is supposed by Richard Polwhele [*The History of Cornwall*, 1803] to have been derived from the old Cornish word *fer*, a fair or jubilee...

Report by a man who was present in 1826 (the festival continues much the same, though without such practices as the river-jump punishment):

This festival commences at an early hour. The morning is enlivened by the sound of drum and fife; and music, harmony and dance are the sports of 'high and low' from morn to night. Some of the oldest townsmen chant some *ancient ditties* — not very comprehensible, 'nor is the melody thereof enchanting'...

Every consideration but mirth, music and feasting is set at naught. Should any persons be found at work they are instantly seized, set astride on a pole and jolted away on men's shoulders, amidst thousands of huzzas, &c, and at last sentenced to leap *over* the river (which by the by is none of the narrowest). The result which therefore frequently happens is — they jump *into it*. The payment of a certain fine towards the expenses of the day saves them from this cooling.

At nine in the morning the mob gathers round the various seminaries [schools] and countless voices demand a holiday for all in them, which is acceded to. A collection from the housekeepers [householders] is then commenced towards the general fund. While this is going on, the young folks of both sexes go to the gardens of the neighbourhood and return at twelve with their heads dressed out with gay flowers, oak branches, &c. On entering the town they are joined by a band of music. They dance through the streets to the Flora Tune. In their progress they go through every house and garden they please without distinction. All doors are opened, and in fact it is thought much of by the householders to be thus favoured.

The older branch of the population dance in the same manner. It is to be noticed they have select parties and at different hours; no two sets dance together, or at the same time. Then follows the gentry, which is really a very pleasing sight on a fine day from the noted respectability of this rich borough... The appearance of the ladies is enchanting. Added to their personal charms, in ballroom attire, each tastefully adorned with beautiful spring flowers in herself appears to the gazer's eye a Flora...

The next set is the soldiers and their lasses; then come the tradesmen and their wives; journeymen and their sweethearts; and 'though last not least', the male and female servants in splendid livery. Best

bibs and tuckers are in request, and many pretty brunettes are to be found in their Sunday finery, with healthy smiling looks, which on such a day as this are sure to make sad havoc with the hearts of the young men.

In the evening a grand ball is always held at the assembly rooms [now the Angel Hotel], to which this year were added the performance of *The Honey Moon* [by John Tobin, 1805] at the theatre by Dawson's company of comedians, Powell's celebrated troop of horse at the Circus, and Mr Ingleby's sleight of hand at the rooms...

Workshops go on parade

IN THE PLEASANT little city of Lichfield (celebrated for the neatness of its streets and the beauty of its splendid cathedral) ... it is the custom on that day [Whit Monday] for a procession, accompanied with musicians, flags, &c, to be formed, composed of part of the corporation, with its inferior officers, &c, who are joined by several of the best mechanics of the place, each of whom carries a representation in miniature of his separate workshop and mode of trade, the figures being so formed as to be put in motion by machinery... These representations are about two feet square and are fixed at the top of a pole about two yards high, decorated with flowers, &c. The procession walks from the guildhall to a high hill ... called Greenhill (but which is now nearly surrounded by houses), where a temporary booth has been erected, with a small space of ground enclosed at the front with boards. This booth is also decorated with flowers, and hence the fair has derived the appellation of the Greenhill Bower...

[*The mechanics' displays are set up and judged for prizes*.] The machines remain and are put in motion and exhibited by their owners until the evening. The booth itself is filled with refreshments; and men being stationed at the gates to prevent the entrance of disorderlies, every well-dressed person is admitted at once...

Sheffield feasts for Charles II

IN MANY of the larger towns the traces of the ancient wake are nearly worn out, and this is pretty much the case with ... our great national emporium for cutlery, files, edge-tools and the better kinds of plated goods. Only in a few ancient and primitive families do roast beef, plum-pudding and an extra allowance of Yorkshire stingo, gracing on Trinity Sunday a large table begirt with some dozen of happy and happy-faced town and country cousins, show that the venerable head of the family and his antique dame have not forgotten Sheffield Feast Day... [*But sundry local feasts are kept up.*] Besides those of the Wicker and Little Sheffield, which are suburban, Broad-lane and Scotland-street in the town itself have their respective feasts too.

At Little Sheffield and in Broad-lane the zest of the annual festivity is often heightened by assraces; footraces, masculine, for a hat; footraces, feminine, for a chemise; grinning-matches; and, though less frequently, the humours and rattle of a mountebank and his merry andrew. Occasionally too changes in imitation of those on the church-bells are rung, by striking with a hammer or a short piece of steel on six, eight or ten long bars, each suspended by twine from the roof of a workshop, and the entire set chosen so as to resemble pretty nearly a ring of bells, both in diversity and in sequence of tone. (When the period for which an apprentice is bound, seven years, expires, his 'loosing' is held by himself and shopmates. Then are these steel bells made to jangle all day. At night the loosing is farther celebrated by a supper and booze...)

Scotland Feast, however, in point of interest, bears away the bell from all the other district revels of Sheffield. It is so called from Scotland-street, already mentioned: a long, hilly and very populous one situated in the northern part of the town. On the eve of the feast, which is yearly held on the 29th of May, the anniversary of the restoration of our second Charles, parties of the inhabitants repair into the neighbouring country; whence, chiefly however from Walkley Bank, celebrated as Sheffield schoolboys too well know for birch trees [*birch rods for flogging them*], they bring home at dead of night or morning's earliest dawn from sixteen to twenty well-sized trees, besides a profusion of branches.

The trees they instantly plant in two rows, one on each side of the street, just without the kerbstone of the flagged pavement. With the branches they decorate the doors and windows of houses, the sign-boards of drinking-shops, and so on. By five or six in the morning Scotland-street, which is not very wide, has the appearance of a grove. And soon, from ropes stretched across it, three, four or five superb garlands delight the eyes and dance over the heads of the feast-folk. These garlands are composed of hoops wreathed round with foliage and flowers, fluttering with variously coloured ribands, rustling with assidue [arsedine – gilt tinsel] and gay with silver tankards, pints, watches, &c.

Before the door of the principal alehouse the largest tree is always planted. The sign of this house is, if memory do not deceive me, the Royal Oak... Certain it is that duly ensconced among the branches of the said tree may always be seen the effigy, in small, of King Charles the Second. To commemorate indeed the happy concealment and remarkable escape of the merry monarch at Boscobel [hidden in an oak] should seem to be the object of creating a sylvan scene at Scotland Feast... It needs scarcely to be added that dancing, drinking and other merrymaking are, as a Scotsman would say, *rife*...

Morris dancers come to town

A London reader admires some performers from the country:

IN JUNE 1826 I observed a company of these 'bold peasantry, the country's pride', in Rosoman-street, Clerkenwell. They consisted of eight young men, six of whom were dancers. The seventh played the pipe and tabor, and the eighth, the head of them, collected the pence in his hat and put the precious metal into the slit of a tin painted box, under lock and key, suspended before him. The tune the little rural-noted pipe played to the gentle pulsations of the tabor is called

> Moll in the wad and I fell out,
> And what d'ye think it was about?

This may be remembered as one of the once popular street songs of the late Charles Dibdin's composition [songwriter, 1745–1814]. The dancers wore particoloured ribands round their hats, arms and knees, to which a row of small latten bells were appended, somewhat like those which are given to amuse infants in teeth-cutting, that tinkled with the motion of the wearers.

These rustic adventurers 'upon the many-headed town' came from a village in Hertfordshire. Truly natural and simple in appearance, their features, complexion, dress and attitude perfectly corresponded. Here was no disguise, no blandishment, no superhuman effort. Their shape was not compressed by fashion, nor did their hearts flutter in an artificial prison [a jibe at fashionable waspwaisted gentlemen]...

The 'set-to', as they termed it, expressed a vis-à-vis address; they then turned, returned, clapped their hands before and behind, and made a jerk with the knee and foot alternately,

> Till toe and heel no longer moved.

Though the streets were dirty and the rain fell reluctantly, yet they heeded not ... but 'danced and smiled, and danced and smiled again.' ...At intervals the little pretty pipe drew the fancy, as it were, piping to a flock in the valley by the shade of sweet trees... O! methought, what difference is here by comparison with the agile-limbed aërials of St James's and these untutored clowns! Yet something delightful

130

comes home to the breast and speaks to the memory of a rural-born creature, and recalls a thousand dear recollections...

Lubin Brown, the piper, was an arch dark-featured person. His ear was alive to Doric melody, and he merrily played and tickled the time to his note. When he stopped to take breath, his provincial dialect scattered his wit among the gapers, and his companions were well pleased with their sprightly leader... I observed his eye ever alert to the movement and weariness of his six choice youths. He was a chivalrous fellow. He had won the prize for 'grinning through a horse-collar' at the revel, thrown his antagonist in the wrestling ring and 'jumped twenty yards in a sack' to the mortification of his rivals who lay vanquished on the green.

The box-keeper ... informed me that 'he and his companions in

Early morris dancers (fool with coxcomb, ass's ears and bells, and piper with tabor), as published in *The Year Book*. They and nine others can be seen in a stained-glass window of about 1500, originally at Betley Court, Staffordshire, now in the Victoria and Albert Museum, shown in the same room as the Great Bed of Ware.

sport' had charmed the village lasses round the maypole, and they intended sojourning in town a week or two, after which the box would be opened and an equitable division take place, previous to the commencement of mowing and hay-harvest. He said it was the third year of their pilgrimage; that they had never disputed on the road, and were welcomed home by their sweethearts and friends, to whom they never omit the carrying a seasonable gift...

Be merry all harvest-time long

IT IS the advice of the most popular of our old writers on husbandry [Thomas Tusser, *Five Hundreth Good Pointes of Husbandrie*] that —

> In harvest time, harvest folke, servants and all,
> Should make all together good cheer in the hall,
> And fill out the black bole of bleith to their song,
> And let them be merry all harvest-time long.
> Once ended thy harvest, let none be beguilde.
> Please such as did please thee, man, woman and child.
> Thus doing, with alway such help as they can,
> Thou winnest the praise of the labouring man.
>
> [*black bole*, leathern pot for ale; *bleith*, mirth, pleasure

Tusser Redivivus [1710] says... 'A good supper must be provided, and everyone that did anything towards the *inning* must now have some reward, as ribbons, laces, rows of pins to boys and girls, if never so small, for their encouragement, and, to be sure, plum-pudding. The men must now have some better than best drink...'

Ceres and the kern baby

'I HAVE SEEN,' says William Hutchinson in his *A View of Northum-berland* [1778], 'in some places an image apparelled in great finery, crowned with flowers, a sheaf of corn placed under her arm and a sickle in her hand, carried out of the village in the morning of the conclusive reaping day, with music and much clamour of the reapers, into the field, where it stands fixed on a pole all day; and when the reaping is done, is brought home in like manner. This they call the harvest queen, and it represents the Roman Ceres.'

John Brand says, 'An old woman, who in a case of this nature is respectable authority, at a village in Northumberland, informed me that not half a century ago they used everywhere to dress up something similar to the figure above described at the end of the harvest, which was called a harvest doll or *kern baby* [corn dolly]...

We have reaped, we have mowed

When a good harvest meant the difference between a tolerable life and misery, every county had its emotion-laden rituals. Readers sent Hone many examples. One recalls scenes in Gloucestershire and Suffolk:

YOU HAVE touched upon a subject in one of your sheets which in my youth used to animate my soul and bring every energy of my mind and of my body into activity. I mean, harvest. Yes, sir, in my younger days I was introduced into the society of innocence and industry, but I know not how it was, Dame Fortune kicked me out, and I was obliged to dwell in smoke and dirt, in noise and bustle, in wickedness and strife, compared with what I left...

[*In Gloucestershire*] Look yonder, and see the whole of the troop of men, women and children congregated together. They are about to bring home the last load. You have seen election chairings, Mr Editor; these are mere jokes to it. This load should come from the farthest field... A large bough is placed in the centre, the women and children are placed on the load, boys on the horses, they themselves trimmed with cowslips and boughs of leaves, and with shouts of 'harvest home' the horses are urged forward and the procession comes full gallop to the front of the farmhouse... Now he who has the loudest and the clearest voice mounts upon a neighbouring shed, and with a voice that would do credit to your city crier shouts aloud —

> We have ploughed, we have sowed,
> We have reaped, we have mowed,
> We have brought home every load.
> Hip, hip, hip, *harvest home!*

— and thus, sir, the whole assembly shout 'huzza'. The strong ale is then put round, and the cake which Miss made with her own hands. The load is then driven round to the stackyard or barn, and the horses put into the stable. John puts on a clean white frock and William a clean coloured handkerchief. The boys grease their shoes to look smart, and all meet in the house to partake of the harvest supper... Here, Mr Editor, is pomp without pride, liberality without ostentation, cheerfulness without vice, merriment without guilt...

They say that old persons are old fools, and although I am almost blind, yet I cannot resist telling you of what I have also seen in my boyish days in Suffolk... At the commencement of harvest one is chosen to be 'my lord'. He goes first in reaping and mowing, and leads in every occupation.

Now, sir, if you were to pass within a field or two of this band of husbandmen, 'my lord' would leave the company, and approaching

AUGUST

The fields are all alive with sultry noise
Of labour's sounds and insects' busy joys.
The reapers o'er their glittering sickles stoop,
Startling full oft the partridge coveys up.
Some o'er the rustling scythe go bending on,
And shockers follow where their toils have gone.

John Clare, *The Shepherd's Calendar*

you with respect, ask of you a *largesse*. Supposing he succeeded, which I know he would, he would hail his companions and they would thus acknowledge the gift: my lord would place his troop in a circle — suppose fifteen men and that they were reaping, each one would have a hook in his hand, or if hoeing of turnips he would bring his hoe. My lord then goes to a distance, mounts the stump of a tree or a gatepost, and repeats a couplet (forgive the treachery of my memory, for I forget the words)... At the conclusion, each with his reaphook pointing with his right hand to the centre of the circle, and with intent as if watching and expecting, they utter all together a groan as long as four of your breves... Then, as if impelled together, their eyes are lifted to the heavens above them, their hooks point in the same direction, and at the same time they change the doleful groan to a tremendous shout, which is repeated three distinct times...

> In Norfolk, the circle of men, with linked hands held high, would cry *Halloo! Lar-r-r-r-r-r-g-e-esse!* three times, and one blew a trumpet. The largesse was spent at the alehouse. 'A tea table is set out for the women; the men finding more virtue in the decoction of Sir John Barleycorn.'

A goddess in the Cotswolds

As a Wiltshire lady travelled past Hawkesbury, Gloucestershire, she was deeply moved by a harvest-home. She sends a passage from her journal:

AS WE APPROACHED the isolated hamlet we were aware of a may-pole, that unsophisticated trophy of innocence, gaiety and plenty; and as we drew near, saw that it was decorated with flowers and ribands fluttering in the evening breeze. Under it stood a wagon with its full complement of men, women, children, flowers and corn; and a handsome team of horses tranquilly enjoying their share of the finery and revelry of the scene, for scarlet bows and sunflowers had been lavished on their winkers with no niggard hand.

On the first horse sat a damsel, no doubt intending to represent Ceres. She had on, of course, a white dress and straw bonnet — for could Ceres or any other goddess appear in a rural English festival in any other costume? A broad yellow sash encompassed a waist that evinced a glorious and enormous contempt for classical proportion and modern folly [tight corsetry]... I ascertained ... that she was good-natured, that she enjoyed the scene as a downright English joke — and that she had the most beautiful set of teeth I ever beheld. (What a stigma on all tooth-doctors, tooth-powders and tooth-brushes!)

There was something very affecting in this simple festival, and I felt my heart heave, and the fields looked indistinct for some minutes...

Hone commissions this engraving to illustrate the
Cotswold scene, and adds some verse of his own

The last in-gathering of the crop
Is loaded, and they climb the top
And there huzza with all their force
While Ceres mounts the foremost horse.

'Gee-up!' the rustic goddess cries,
And shouts more loud and long arise.
The swagging cart, with motion slow
Reels careless on; and off they go!

Crying the neck and 'we yen!'

A Devon correspondent sends this in July 1826:

AFTER THE WHEAT is all cut, on most farms in the north of Devon the harvest people have a custom of 'crying the neck' [or 'knack'; a corn dolly]... An old man or someone else well acquainted with the ceremonies used ... when the labourers are reaping the last field of wheat, goes round to the shocks and sheaves and picks out a little bundle of all the best ears he can find. This bundle he ties up very neat and trim, and plaits and arranges the straws very tastefully. This is called 'the neck'...

After the field is cut out, and the pitcher once more circulated, the reapers, binders and the women stand round in a circle. The person with the neck stands in the centre, grasping it with both his hands. He first stoops and holds it near the ground, and all the men forming the ring take off their hats, stooping and holding them with both hands towards the ground. They then all begin at once in a very prolonged and harmonious tone to cry 'the neck!', at the same time slowly raising themselves upright and elevating their arms and hats above their heads; the person with the neck also raising it on high. This is done three times.

They then change their cry to 'we yen!' — 'way yen!' — which they sound in the same prolonged and slow manner as before, with singular harmony and effect, three times. This last cry is accompanied by the same movements of the body and arms as in crying the neck... Well, after having thus repeated 'the neck' three times and 'we yen' or 'way yen' as often, they all burst out into a kind of loud and joyous laugh, flinging up their hats and caps into the air, capering about and perhaps kissing the girls.

One of them then gets the neck and runs as hard as he can down to the farmhouse, where the dairymaid or one of the young female domestics stands at the door prepared with a pail of water. If he who holds the neck can manage to get into the house ... unseen or openly, by any other way than the door at which the girl stands with the pail of water, then he may lawfully kiss her; but if otherwise, he is regularly soused with the contents of the bucket.

On a fine still autumn evening the 'crying of the neck' has a wonderful effect at a distance, far finer than that of the Turkish muezzin which Lord Byron eulogizes so much and which he says is preferable to all the bells in christendom. I have once or twice heard upwards of twenty men cry it, and sometimes joined by an equal number of female voices. About three years back, on some high

The harvest-men ring summer out
With thankful song and joyous shout,
And when September comes, they hail
The autumn with the flapping flail.   *Hone*

grounds where our people were harvesting, I heard six or seven necks cried in one night, although I know that some of them were four miles off... But I think that the practice is beginning to decline of late, and many farmers and their men do not care about keeping up this old custom. I shall always patronize it myself, because I take it in the light of a thanksgiving. By the by, I was about to conclude without endeavouring to explain the meaning of the words 'we yen'. I had long taken them for Saxon ... but I think that I am wrong. I asked an old fellow about it the other day, and he is the only man who ever gave me a satisfactory explanation. He says that the object of crying the neck is to give the surrounding country notice of the *end* of harvest, and that they mean by 'we yen' *we have ended...*

The neck is generally hung up in the farmhouse, where it remains sometimes three or four years.

Rushbearing grows luxurious

A report from Rochdale, Lancashire:

A FEW YEARS AGO I was told by an old man, now deceased, that he remembered the rushes to have been borne on the shoulders of the country people in bundles, some very plain, others ornamented with ribands, garlands, &c, to the churchyard at Rochdale; that they were there dried, previous to being put into the church, and that these rushbearers received a small compensation from the churchwardens. This was before churches were floored with wood. The rushes were strewed for the purpose of rendering the congregation more comfortable and saving their feet from being chilled by the stone pavements, and in some instances the clay floors.

In many churches rushes are used in the same manner in the present day... The old homely method of rushbearing on the shoulders has given place to the more luxurious and gorgeous display of the rush-cart and banner. The load of rushes is decorated with carnations and other flowers, and a person rides upon the top. The carts are sometimes drawn by horses gaily caparisoned, but more frequently by young men to the number of twenty or thirty couple, profusely adorned with ribands, tinsel, &c. They are generally preceded by men with horse-bells about them, grotesquely jumping from side to side and jingling the bells. After these is a band of music and sometimes a set of morris dancers ... followed by young women bearing garlands.

Then comes the banner made of silk of various colours, joined by narrow riband fretted, the whole profusely covered on both sides with roses, stars, &c, of tinsel... The banners are generally from four to five yards wide and six to eight yards long, having on either side in the centre a painting of Britannia, the king's arms or some other device. The whole procession is flanked by men with long cart-whips, which they keep continually cracking to make a clear path...

Great rivalry exists between the young men of the neighbouring villages which shall produce the best-formed cart and banner, and it not unfrequently happens that when two of them meet in the street a scuffle takes place, and many bloody noses are the result... A collection is made ... from the gentry and other inhabitants, which enables them to sacrifice very freely at the shrine of John Barleycorn...

Places near Rochdale holding these rival displays, the writer says, are Ashworth, Littlebro', Minbrow, Shaw, Oldham, Royton, Middleton, Heywood and Whitworth.

French and English jibes and kisses

IT IS NOT my intention to trouble you [*a contributor writes*, 1831] with a contrast between the rival nations as respects sobriety, courtesy, honesty, wanton mischief and good manners, for I fear it will little suit our national vanity and conceit... My object is ... to show how much may be learned from that fine people [the French] by men of antiquarian taste and knowledge...

It is evident to me that our ancient national manners and customs may be still seen in France in many curious instances. The greatest insult or sign of contempt which a Frenchman can show to anyone is by a most significant action which I cannot adequately express in words: he puts his thumb to his mouth, seizing the nail of it with his teeth as if about to bite it, and he then draws out the arm towards his adversary with a curious and very significant grin.

This was anciently the practice in England. The thumb ... represented a fig, and the action expressed 'I don't care a fig for you,' an expression which is still retained. It was called giving a man 'the fico'. In Yorkshire we have amongst our lowest orders a still more contemptuous and ludicrous word as a substitute for 'fig', and one which will make every Yorkshireman who reads this laugh heartily. But to prove that this action was anciently in England as it is now in France: in Shakespeare's play of *Romeo and Juliet*, 'I will bite my thumb at them, which is a disgrace to them if they bear it.' — 'Dags and pistols! To bite his thumb at me!'

...To bite the ear, on the other hand, was anciently an expression of endearment, and it is still so far retained by the French that to pull a man gently by the ear is the most sure token of good will. This, as appears from Mr Barry O'Meara's first volume of *Napoleon in Exile* [1822] ... was the practice of that extraordinary man when in high good humour. Indeed, I have known persons of great respectability pull one by the ear, gently, in England. But formerly it was common, as appears from the plays both of Shakespeare and Jonson.

Another specimen of our ancient manners is seen in the French embrace. The gentlemen ... lay hands on the shoulders and touch the sides of each other's cheek; but on being introduced to a lady they say to her father, brother or friend, *Permettez-moi*, and salute [kiss] each of her cheeks...

And was not this the custom in England in Elizabeth's reign? Let us read one of the epistles of the learned Erasmus, which being translated is in part as follows:

'If you knew the advantages of Britain, truly you would hasten thither with wings to your feet... For, just to touch on one thing out of many here, there are lasses with heavenly faces; kind, obliging, and you would far prefer them to all your Muses. There is, besides, a practice never to be sufficiently commended. If you go to any place you are received with a kiss by all — if you depart on a journey you are dismissed with a kiss — you return, kisses are exchanged — they come to visit you, a kiss the first thing — they leave you, you kiss them all round. Do they meet you anywhere — kisses in abundance...

'How soft they are, how fragrant! On my honour you would wish not to reside here for ten years only, but for life.'

Swearing on the horns at Highgate

'HAVE YOU been sworn at Highgate?' is a question frequently asked in every part of the kingdom... The village of Highgate takes its name from the gate across the public road into London, opposite the chapel, which is sometimes erroneously called the church, for it is in fact only a chapel-of-ease to Hornsey church. This road runs through land belonging to the bishopric of London... This gate, from being on the great northern eminence towards London, was called the *high*-gate...

It seems probable that the first dwelling erected here was the gate-house. The occupier of the inn of that name holds it under a lease from the bishop, under which lease he also farms [collects] the bishop's toll. In the year 1769 the old gatehouse, which extended over the road, was taken down and the present common turnpike-gate put up...

'Swearing on the horns' ... is a jocular usage of the place, from beyond the memory of man, especially encouraged by certain of the villagers to the private advantage of public landlords. On the drawing up of coaches at the inn-doors, particular invitations were given to the company to alight, and after as many as could be collected were got into a room for purposes of refreshment, the subject of being 'sworn at Highgate' was introduced...

[*The horns, fixed on a stout staff, are held in front of the person to be sworn. All present take off their hats, and the landlord recites the oath in a loud voice.*] What is called the oath … has been taken down in writing from the lips of different persons who administer it… The following may be depended on… [*Here it is, with slight cuts* :]

Upstanding and uncovered! Silence!

You must acknowledge me to be your adopted father, I must acknowledge you to be my adopted son (or daughter). If you do not call me father you forfeit a bottle of wine. If I do not call you son I forfeit the same.

And now, my good son, if you are travelling through this village of Highgate and you have no money in your pocket, go call for a bottle of wine at any house you think proper to go into, and book it to your father's score. If you have any friends with you, you may treat them as well.

But if you have money of your own, you must pay for it yourself. For you must not say you have no money when you have, neither must you convey the money out of your own pocket into your friends' pockets, for I shall search you as well as them, and if it is found that you or they have money, you forfeit a bottle of wine for trying to cozen and cheat your poor old ancient father.

You must not eat brown bread while you can get white, except you like the brown the best. You must not drink small beer while you can get strong, except you like the small the best. You must not kiss the maid while you can kiss the mistress, except you like the maid the best, but sooner than lose a good chance you may kiss them both…

A word or two of advice. Keep from all houses of ill repute and every place of public resort for bad company. Beware of false friends, for they will … inveigle you into houses where you may lose your money and get no redress. Keep from thieves of every denomination. And now, my good son, I wish you a safe journey through Highgate and this life…

So now, my son, God bless you! Kiss the horns, or a pretty girl if you see one here, which you like best, and so be free of Highgate!

If a female be in the room she is usually saluted [kissed]; if not, the horns *must* be kissed… The swearer-in commands 'silence!' and then addressing himself to his newmade son, he says,

I have now to acquaint you with your privilege as a freeman of this place. If at any time you are going through Highgate and want to rest yourself, and you see a pig lying in a ditch, you have liberty to kick her out and take her place; but if you see three lying together you must only kick out the middle one and lie between the other two. God save the king!

…Now in the year 1826 there are nineteen licensed houses in this village, and at each of these houses the horns are kept and the oath administered… [*The list*: Gatehouse (stag's horns), Mitre (stag's), Green Dragon (stag's), Red Lion & Sun (bullock's), Bell (stag's), Coach & Horses (ram's), Castle (ram's), Red Lion (ram's), Wrestler's (stag's), Bull (stag's), Lord Nelson (stag's), Duke of Wellington (stag's), Crown (stag's), Duke's Head (stag's), Cooper's Arms (ram's), Rose & Crown (stag's), Angel (stag's), Flask (ram's), Fox and Crown (ram's).]

The Fox and Crown ... commonly called the Fox and the Fox Under the Hill, is nearly at the top of the road from Kentish Town to Highgate, and ... is certainly the most remarkable house for swearing on the horns. Guiver, the present landlord (January 1826), came to the house about Michaelmas 1824 ... and very soon finding that much of the custom of his house depended on the 'custom of Highgate' ... he procured habiliments and an assistant ... and exercises his faculties so as to dignify the custom. Robed in a domino, with a wig and mask, and a book wherein is written the oath ... he reads it through a pair of spectacles. The staff with the horns is held by an old villager who acts as clerk and at every full stop calls aloud, 'Amen!'

...An old inhabitant who formerly kept a licensed house says, 'In my time nobody came to Highgate in anything of a carriage without being called upon to be sworn in. There was so much doing in this way at one period that I was obliged to hire a man as a swearer-in. I

Hone took his artist-friend Cruikshank with him to the Fox and Crown to record the scene. The landlord Guiver, masked, reads the oath. In his report, Hone adds cryptically that Cruikshank 'has waggishly misrepresented one of the figures' — meaning that the man being sworn is a comically fat version of himself.

have sworn in from a hundred to a hundred and twenty in a day. Bodies of tailors used to come up here from town, bringing five or six new shopmates with them to be sworn...' As prerequisite for admission to sundry convivial societies, now no more, the freedom of Highgate was indispensable...

Concerning the origin of this custom ... a probable account is to this effect — that Highgate being the place nearest to London where cattle rested on their way from the north for sale in Smithfield, certain graziers were accustomed to put up at The Gatehouse for the night, but as they could not wholly exclude strangers ... they brought an ox to the door, and those who did not choose to kiss its horns after going through the ceremony described were not deemed fit members of their society.

A reader sends in a song from a pantomime, *Harlequin Teague,* performed at the Haymarket Theatre in August 1742. Its references to small beer, brown bread, kissing, &c, show that the droll content of the oath goes back a long way. Three stanzas of five:

> Spend not with cheaters nor cozeners your life
>> Nor waste it on profligate beauty,
> And when you are married, be kind to your wife
>> And true to all petticoat duty.
> Dutiful, beautiful, kind to your wife
>> And true from the cap to the shoe-tie.
>>> *Dutiful, &c —*
>
> To drink to a man when a woman is near
>> You never should hold to be right, sir,
> Nor unless 'tis your taste, to drink small for strong beer
>> Or eat brown bread when you can get white, sir.
> Manniken, canniken, good meat and drink
>> Are pleasant at morn, noon and night, sir.
>>> *Manniken, &c —*
>
> To kiss with the maid when the mistress is kind
>> A gentleman ought to be loth, sir,
> But if the maid's fairest, your oath does not bind,
>> Or you may, if you like it, kiss both, sir.
> Kiss away, both you may, sweetly smack night and day
>> If you like it — you're bound by your oath, sir.
>>> *Kiss away, &c —*

Many of the Highgate pubs survive (though rebuilt), and so does the custom in a small way. Once a year the mayor of either Camden or Haringey borough performs the ceremony at either The Gatehouse or The Wrestler's, using the ram's horns from The Cooper's Arms.

Faire May deckt all with dainties

Then came faire May, the fayrest mayd on ground,
Deckt all with dainties of her season's pryde,
And throwing flowres out of her lap around.
Upon two brethren's shoulders she did ride,
The twinnes of Leda, which on eyther side
Supported her like to their soveraine Queene.
Lord! how all creatures laught when her they spide,
And leapt and daunct as they had ravisht beene!
And Cupid self about her fluttred all in greene.

Spenser, *The Faerie Queene*, VII, vii

London scenes,
London life

SEARS SC

First view of the New River
from London

THIS IS SEEN immediately on coming in view of Sadler's Wells, a place of dramatic entertainment. After manifold windings and tunnellings from its source, the New River passes beneath the arch in the engraving and forms a basin within a large walled enclosure, from whence diverging main pipes convey the water to all parts of London. At the back of the boy angling on the wall is a public-house with tea-gardens and a skittle-ground ... the Sir Hugh Myddelton's Head [*rebuilt 1831; demolished 1891*]. A portrait of Sir Hugh hangs in front of the house. To this stream, as the water nearest London favourable to sport, anglers of inferior note repair:

> Here boys their penny lines and bloodworms throw,
> And scare, and catch, the 'silly fish' below.
> Backstickles bite, and biting up they come,
> And now a minnow, now a miller's thumb.
> Here too experienced youths of better taste
> And higher aim resort, who bait with paste
> Or push beneath a gentle's shining skin
> The barbèd hook and bury it within.
> The more he writhes the better: if he die
> Not one will touch him of the finny fry.
> If in strong agony the sufferer live
> Then doth the 'gentle angler' joy receive.
> Down bobs the float, the angler wins the prize,
> And now the gentle, now the gudgeon dies.   *Hone*

The old theatre, after various alterations, was replaced in 1931 by one that survived until 1996 — to be succeeded by another... Sir Hugh Myddelton was (to quote Hone) 'a man renowned in English annals for having abundantly supplied London with water by conducting the New River from Ware in Hertfordshire'. He almost bankrupted himself in creating this aqueduct, nearly forty miles long, in 1609–13. It still contributes to London's supply. Within London most of it is covered over, but a pleasant tree-lined stretch, New River Walk, can be seen in Islington.

Up the sweetly flowing river

THIS GENTLE RIVER meanders through countless spots of surprising beauty and variety within ten miles of town. When I was a boy I thought Sadler's Wells arch, opposite the Sir Hugh Myddelton (a house immortalized by Hogarth), the prime part of the river; for there, by the aid of a penny line and a ha'porth of gentles and bloodworms 'mixed', bought of old Turpin who kept the little fishing-tackle shop, the last house by the river's side at the end next St John's-street, I essayed to gudgeon gudgeons.

But the prime gudgeon-fishing then was at 'the Coffin', through which the stream flows after burying itself at The Thatched House under Islington road [now Essex-road], within half a stone's-throw of a cottage endeared to me, in later years, by its being the abode of 'as much virtue as can live' [*Charles Lamb's house during 1823–27, in Duncan-terrace: preserved and plaqued*].

Past The Thatched House [*a pub of this name survives*] towards

Canonbury there was The Horseshoe, now no more, and the enchanting rear, since despoiled, of the gardens to the retreats of Canonbury-
place. And all along the river to the pleasant village of Hornsey there
were delightful retirements on its banks, so 'far from the busy haunts
of men' that only a few solitary wanderers seemed to know them.

'At the pleasant village of Hornsey' ... a scene that vanished long ago

Since then I have gone 'over the hills and far away' to see it sweetly
flowing at Enfield Chase [*where his friend Charles Lamb retired*], near
many a 'cottage of content', as I have conceived the lowly dwellings to
be which there skirt it, with their little gardens, not too trim, whence
the inmates cross the neat iron bridges of the New River Company...
Pursuing the river thence to Theobalds [Hertfordshire], it presents to
the 'contemplative man's recreation' temptations that old Izaak
Walton himself might have coveted to fall in his way...

immortalized by Hogarth: in his painting and print 'Evening', 1737

148

The Compleat Angler, eighteen-pence

Fishing and Walton lead Hone to say that among his collected pieces of early printing is an almanac of 1654 that contains 'what was perhaps the earliest advertisement of Walton's Compleat Angler'.

IT IS on the back of the dedication leaf to *Hemeroscopeion*, 'Anni Ærae Christianæ 1654'. The almanac was published of course in the preceding year, which was the year wherein Walton's work was printed.

> There is published a Booke of Eighteen-pence price, called
> *The Compleat Angler, Or, The Contemplative Man's Recreation*:
> being a Discourse of Fish and Fishing. Not unworthy the perusall.
> Sold by *Richard Marriott* in S. *Dunstan's* Church-yard *Fleetstreet*.

This advertisement I deem a bibliomaniacal curiosity. Only think of the first edition of Walton as a 'booke of eighteen-pence price'! [*One sold at auction in 1993 for $32,500.*] And imagine the good old man on the day of publication walking from his house 'on the north side of Fleet-street, two doors west of the end of Chancery-lane', to his publisher and neighbour just by, 'Richard Marriott in S. Dunstan's Churchyard', for the purpose of inquiring 'how the book went off'.

There is, or lately was, a large fish in effigy at a fishing-tackle maker's in Fleet-street, near Bell-yard, which whenever I saw it, after I first read Walton's work many years ago, reminded me of him and his pleasant book and its delightful ditties, and brought him before me, sitting on 'a primrose bank' turning his 'present thoughts into verse'.

Tucking up the highwaymen

On Jerry Abershaw, hanged 1795, and the decline of robbery on the road.

ABERSHAW was the last of the great highwaymen who, when people carried money [gold] about them, robbed every night, and sometimes in the open day, on Bagshot, Wimbledon, Finchley and other commons and high roads in the neighbourhood of London. Some of these highwaymen of the 'old school' lived in the wretched purlieus of Saffron-hill [*later the haunt of Fagin in Oliver Twist*], and would mount in the afternoon at the end of Field-lane, at Holborn Bridge, as openly as travellers setting out from an inn.

On the order-in-council in 1797 which prohibited the Bank from paying in specie, gold went out and banknotes came in; and as these were easily concealed, and when stolen were difficult to pass [their numbers being noted], the business of 'the highway' fell off and highwaymen gradually became extinct.

Jerry Abershaw was the most noted because he was the most desperate and most feared of these marauders. He was a reckless desperado who, pistol in hand, would literally have 'your money or your life', and perhaps both. He was as famous in his day as Sixteen-String Jack [Jack Rann, hanged 1774] or the Flying Highwayman. He shot several persons ... and the concourse of people at his execution was innumerable. It was in the height of summer; and the following Sunday being fine, London seemed a deserted city, for hundreds of thousands went to see Abershaw hanging in chains [on Wimbledon Common]. His fame will outlast his gibbet, which I suppose has been down years ago...

John Townsend the Bow-street officer's interesting examination before the police committee of the House of Commons in June 1816 contains some curious particulars respecting Abershaw, the pirates, 'the dangers of the *road*' and hanging matters toward the close of the last century.

Q   The activity of the officers of Bow-street has infinitely increased of late years?

A   No doubt about it; and there is one thing which appears to me most extraordinary, when I remember in very likely a week there should be from ten to fifteen highway robberies. We have not had a man committed for a highway robbery lately; I speak of persons on horseback. Formerly there were two, three or four highwaymen, some on Hounslow Heath, some on Wimbledon Common, some on Finchley Common, some on the Romford Road. I have actually come to Bow-street in the morning, and while I have been leaning over the desk had three or four people come in and say, 'I was robbed by two highwaymen in such a place,' 'I was robbed by a single highwayman in such a place.'

People travel now safely, by means of the horse-patrol that Sir Richard Ford [chief Bow-street magistrate from 1800] planned... There are no footpad robberies or road robberies now but merely jostling you in the streets. They used to be ready to pop [shoot] at a man as soon as he let down his glass [carriage window].

Q   You remember the case of Abershaw?

A   Yes. I had him tucked up where he was. It was through me...

Q   Do you think any advantages arise from a man being put on a gibbet after his execution?

A   Yes, I was always of that opinion; and I recommended Sir William Scott to hang the two men that are hanging [on gibbets] down the river. I will state my reason. We will take for granted that those men were hanged as this morning for the murder of those revenue officers:

150

they are by law dissected; the sentence is that afterwards the body is
to go to the surgeons for dissection. There is an end of it — it dies.

But look at this: there are a couple of men now hanging near the
Thames, where all the sailors must come up, and one says to the other,
'Pray, what are those two poor fellows there for?' — 'Why,' says another, 'I will go and ask.' They ask. 'Why, those two men are hung and
gibbeted for murdering His Majesty's revenue officers.' And so the
thing is kept alive. If it was not for this, people would die and nobody
would know anything of it.

In Abershaw's case I said to the sheriff, 'The only difficulty in
hanging this fellow upon this place is its being so near Lord Spencer's
house.' But we went down, and pointed out a particular place. He was
hung at the particular pitch of the hill where he used to do the work. If
there was a person ever went to see that man hanging, I am sure there
was a hundred thousand.

I received information that they meant to cut him down. I said to
Sir Richard Ford, 'I will counteract this... I will go and sit up all night,
and have eight or ten officers at a distance, for I shall nail these
fellows,' for I talked cant [slang] language to him. However ... nobody
ever came... They would have come down and sawed the gibbet and
taken it all away...

Q Do you think, from your long observation, that the morals and
manners of the lower people in the metropolis are better or worse than
formerly?

A I am decidedly of opinion that with respect to the present time and
the early part of my time, such as 1781, 2, 3, 4, 5, 6 and 7, where there
is one person convicted now ... there were five then. We never had an
execution wherein we did not grace that unfortunate gibbet at the Old
Bailey with ten, twelve, thirteen, sixteen and twenty; and forty I once
saw, at twice [two sets of twenty]...

*Townsend recalls a conversation he had with a man acquitted on a capital
charge — a man he had arrested:*

Says he, 'Townsend, you heard what the chief baron said to me. A fine
flowery speech, was it not?'

'Yes.'

'But he did not answer the question I put to him.'

Now how could he? After all that the chief baron said to him after
he was acquitted — giving him advice — this word was everything.
Says he, 'My lord, I have paid great attention to what you have been
stating to me... I return my sincere thanks to the jury for their good-
ness. But your lordship says you lament very much that a man of my
abilities should not turn my abilities to a better use. Now, my lord, I

have only this reply to make: I am ready to go into any service … if your lordship will but find me a master.'

Why, what was the reply to that? 'Jailer, take the prisoner away.'

Why, who would employ him? It is really farcical… Where is there anybody to take these wretches? They have said to me, 'Sir, we do not thieve from disposition, but we thieve because we cannot get employ- ment: our character is damned and nobody will have us.'

And so it is…

Jerry Abershaw's fame did indeed long outlast his gibbet. At the time Hone was publishing this in 1831, if he had bought a little book called *The Fal-Lal Songster* he would have found a slang ditty, 'Jerry Abershaw's Will', which opens, 'Vhen the noted Jerry Abershaw vas cast for death/And vas sentenced to exhibit in chains O!' Two stanzas of sixteen —

> At last he vas ordered for to quit his dingy cage,
>> Which made his pals and blowens look so shy O, *flash girls*
> And be ready to go off in the eight o'clock stage
>> Down to Vimbleton, the Surrey air to try O!

> He said his mother told him he vould die in his shoes
>> 'Cause he boned his father's tatler from his fob O, *stole his watch*
> But to prove she told a lie, while his scrag was in the noose
>> As a legacy he kicked them to the mob O.

All the humours of Garratt

During each general election in the 18th century, irreverent voteless people held an uproarious mock election in the hamlet of Garratt, beyond Wandsworth village (the name survives in Garratt-lane). The candidates dressed in finery, called themselves 'Sir' or 'Lord', had great parades and made speeches satirizing the corruption of their betters.

In 1826 there was talk of reviving the event. Hone went to seek firsthand information and was told the man to see was 'old Jack Jones the sawyer', Master of the Horse for four Garratt elections, most recently in 1796. 'You'll find him by the waterside,' Hone was told. 'Anybody'll tell you of him. If you don't find him at home, he is most likely at The Plume of Feathers.'

He was. The interview began unpromisingly:

HE TALKED of the 'famous doings' and 'such sights as were never seen before, nor never would be seen again'; and he dimmed the hope of particular information by 'quips and quirks and wanton wiles'; and practised the 'art of ingeniously tormenting', by declarations of un- bounded knowledge, and that 'he *could* a tale unfold' but would not, because, as he said, 'Why should I make other people as wise as I am?' Yet there was a string which 'discoursed most excellent music' — it was of himself and of the fame of his exploits…

John Jones's topic was not a dry one, nor was John Jones dry, but in the commencement he had preferred 'a little porter to anything else in the world', except, and afterwards accepted, 'a drop of something by itself', and by degrees he became communicative...

Hone prints a mass of material from many sources. A few extracts must serve.
First, information about the custom's origin that a Wandsworth resident gave to
an antiquary, Andrew Ducarel, at the time of an election in 1754:

I have been informed that about 60 or 70 years ago some watermen belonging to this town went to The Leather Bottle, a public house at Garratt, to spend a merry day, which being the time of a general election for members of parliament, in the midst of their frolic they took it into their heads to choose one of their company a representative of that place...

This local usage from that small beginning has had a gradual increase... [The 1754 election] has been performed with uncommon pomp and magnificence, in the plebeian mode of pageantry... I have herewith sent you handbills of the candidates... Their pseudo-titles, as you will observe, are Lord Twankum, Squire Blow-me-down and Squire Gubbins. Lord Twankum's right name is John Gardiner, and he is gravedigger to this parish; Blow-me-down is Willis, a waterman; and Squire Gubbins, whose name is Simmonds, keeps a public-house, the sign of The Gubbins Head, in Blackman-street, Southwark.

On to 1781, when the candidates are Sir Jeffery Dunstan, Sir William Blase,
Admiral Sir Christopher Dashwood, Sir John Harper, Sir William Swallowtail
and Sir John Gnawpost, and more than 50,000 people flock to Wandsworth to
enjoy the fun:

Sir William Swallowtail was one William Cock, a whimsical basket-maker of Brentford, who deeming it proper to have an equipage every way suitable to the honour he aspired to, built his own carriage, with his own hands, to his own taste. It was made of wicker, and drawn by four high hollow-backed horses whereon were seated dwarfish boys, whimsically dressed for postilions. In allusion to the American war, two footmen rode before the carriage tarred and feathered. The coachman wore a wicker hat... Sir John Harper was by trade a weaver... He made his grand entry ... in a phaeton and six bays, with postilions in scarlet and silver, surrounded by thousands of supporters.

Old John Jones recalls for Hone a song that was printed for sale in the streets about
this election of 1781 . A few stanzas:

> At Garratt, lackaday, what fun!
> To see the sight, what thousands run!
> Sir William Blase and all his crew —
> Sure it was a droll sight to view.

Sir William Swallowtail came next
In basket-coach, so neatly dressed,
With handbells playing all the way.
For Swallowtail, my boys, huzzay!

Sir Christopher Dashwood so gay,
With drums and fifes did sweetly play.
He in a boat was drawn along
Amongst a mighty gazing throng.

On Sir John Harper next we gaze
All in his carriage, and six bays,
With star upon his breast, so fine
He did each candidate outshine.

The handbell player was Thomas Cracknell, who at that time was a publican at Brentford and kept The Wilkes's Head [*polling in John Wilkes's famous elections was at Brentford*]. He had been a cow-boy in the service of Lady Holderness; and after he took that public-house he so raised its custom that it was a place of the first resort in Brentford 'for man and horse'. With an eye to business as well as a disposition to waggery, he played the handbells ... as much for the good of The Wilkes's Head as in honour of his neighbour Cock the basketmaker... Cracknell afterwards became a rectifier or distiller at Brentford.

Beside Blase in his carriage rode 'my Lady Blase', got up as a 'broad caricature of the fashion of the times'. A Wandsworth woman tells how she helped to rig her out:

'I remember her very well, and so I ought, for I had a good hand in the dressing of her. I helped to put together many a good pound of wool to make her hair up. I suppose it was more than three feet high at least. And as for her stays, I also helped to make them, down in Anderson's barn. They were neither more nor less than a washing tub without the bottom, well covered, and bedizened outside to look like a stomacher... As she sat in his boat, she was one of the drollest creatures, for size and dress, that ever was seen. I was quite a girl at the time, and we made her as comical and as fine as possible.'

Hone continues: Sir Solomon Hiram, another Garratt candidate, was a shrewd, clever carpenter of Battersea named Thomas Solomon... The motto on his carriages was 'Gin gratis! Porter for nothing!' Our living chronicler, John Jones, says that on the day of election Sir Solomon Hiram was 'dressed like an old king in a scarlet coat with gold lace, large sleeves with very large hanging cuffs, a wig such as George the Second wore, with large falling curls and the tail in a silk bag. He held a roll of parchment in his hand, and looked for all the world like a king.'

Nor must 'old John Jones' himself be forgotten, for he rode as Master of the Horse at four elections in a marvellous proper dress. He was mounted on the largest dray horse that could be got, in the full regimentals of the Surrey yeomanry, grey, blue and red. He had a cap on his head twenty-three inches high, and bore in his hand a sword seven feet long and four inches wide, like the sword of the Ancient and Honourable Lumber Troop. His boots were up to his hips, and he wore wooden spurs thirteen inches long, with steel rowels three inches in diameter. The mane of his horse was plaited with ears of corn, denoting a plentiful harvest and the coming cheapness of bread; and he had two pages to lead his horse.

The Garratt Cavalry or troop of horse guards of which John Jones was the commander were forty boys of all ages and sizes, for whom flannel uniforms were purposely made of the exact pattern of the Surrey yeomanry.

Besides the hustings at Garratt, scaffoldings and booths were erected in Wandsworth at every open space. These were filled with spectators to the topmost rows, and boys climbed to the tops of the poles. Flags and colours were hung across the road... For accommodation to view the humours of the day extraordinary prices were paid.

For eleven years, up to 1796, the 'MP and mayor' of Garratt was a merry, dwarf-ish cripple, Sir Jeffery Dunstan — such a noted character that the printshops vied in issuing prints of him (more than a dozen versions survive) .

This distinguished individual was a child of chance — a foundling. He was picked up in the year 1759 at a churchwarden's door in Saint Dunstan's-in-the-East, and ... was reared in the workhouse so as ultimately to attain about two-thirds the usual height of manhood, with knock-knees and a disproportionately large head. At twelve years old he was bound apprentice for nine years to the art, trade, mystery and occupation of a greengrocer. This was a long time to serve, and Jeffery ... ran away to Birmingham. It was his pride that though the hard labour in the factories of the 'workshop of Europe' increased the malformation of his person, it added strength to his mind; and in 1776 he returned to London with his knees and ideas knocking together much more than before. He soon afterwards formed a matrimonial connection, and had two daughters ... Miss Nancy and Miss Dinah...

From the earliest period of Sir Jeffery's life he was a friend to 'good measures' — especially those for spirituous liquors, and he never saw the inside of a pot without going to the bottom of it. This determination of character created difficulties for him... At length he made free with a few of the pots ... and suffered an imprisonment. On his liberation he returned to an occupation he had long followed, the dealing in

Sir Jeffery Dunstan, with his wig-bag over his shoulder

old wigs, and some circumstances ... seem to favour a supposition that the bag he carried had enabled him to conceal his previous 'free trade' in pots. But be that as it might, it is certain that to his armorial bearings of four wigs he added a quart pot for a crest...

On the death of Sir John Harper he issued an address to the electors, committees were formed and an active canvass was commenced at every public-house... On the day of election Sir Jeffery left London [for Garratt] in a splendid phaeton, with a body of friends in every possible description of vehicle, from a coal-wagon to a wheelbarrow drawn by dogs...

Sir Jeffery usually carried his wig-bag over his shoulder, and to avoid the charge of vagrancy vociferated as he passed along the street, 'Old wigs!' But having a person like Æsop, and a countenance and manner marked by irresistible humour, he never appeared without a train of boys and curious persons, whom he entertained by his sallies of wit ... and sharp repartees; and from whom, without begging, he collected sufficient to maintain his dignity of mayor and knight.

A Whitechapel reader contributes:

Sir Jeffery once kept an ass that had but one ear... With this poor creature, who carried the 'wigs, &c', he for many years collected a crowd... His wit and smart sayings flew about. Now the joke fell on himself and now on his one-eared ass. Then he varied the cry of 'old wigs' by mimicking another's singing-cry of 'Lily, lily, lily, lily white sand oh!' [refrain of a ribald popular song]. After the pence had well tumbled in he would retire to his favourite retreat, The Horse and Leaping Bar... Sir Jeff, in a regular manner, got 'regularly drunk'. Here he sung the London cries, recited his mock speeches on the corruptions of parliament, and, placed in an armchair on the table, nightly afforded sport to a merry company...

The wig trade: Some he disposed of privately, the rest he sold to the dealers in Rag Fair. In those days 'full bottoms' were worn by almost every person, and it was no uncommon thing to hear seafaring persons or others exposed to the cold exclaim, 'Well, winter's at hand and I must e'en go to Rosemary-lane and have a dip for a wig.' This 'dipping for wigs' was nothing more than putting your hand into a large barrel and pulling one up. If you liked it you paid your shilling. If not, you dipped again, and paid sixpence more, and so on. Then, also, the curriers used them for cleaning the waste, &c, off the leather, and I have no doubt would use them now if they could get them.

Charles Lamb tells Hone that he used to see Sir Jeffery in his declining years.
He lived in 'a wretched shed in the most beggarly purlieu of Bethnal Green'.
As for his appearance, 'no graphic art can convey an idea of the general
squalor of it'. And his wig-bag: Lamb says —

My life upon it, it contained no curls at the time I speak of. The most decayed and spiritless remnants of what was once a peruke would have scorned the filthy case... No, it was empty, or brought home bones, or a few cinders possibly.

A strong odour of burnt bones, I remember, blended with the odour of horseflesh seething into dog's meat, and only relieved a little by the breathings of a few brick kilns, made up the atmosphere of the delicate suburban spot which this great man had chosen for the last scene of his earthly vanities. The cry of 'old wigs' had ceased... His quips were silent too, and his brain was empty as his sack... If a few boys followed him, it seemed rather from habit than any expectation of fun. But it is thus that the world rewards its favourites in decay.

What faults he had, I know not. I have heard something of a peccadillo or so. But some little deviation from the precise line of rectitude might have been winked at in so tortuous and stigmatic a frame. Poor Sir Jeffery! It were well if some MPs in earnest have passed their parliamentary existence with no more offences against integrity than could be left to thy charge!

A correspondent gives an account of Sir Jeffery's death in 1797 —

His gravedigger, Thomas Michael, relates this story. Sir Jeffery had called in at the sign of The Red Lion, opposite the London Hospital [in

Whitechapel], a house where low company resorted. It was then kept by one George Float ... who supplied Sir Jeffery with liquor till he was completely *non compos*. He was then carried to the door of his house ... and there left to perish, for he was found a corpse on the same spot the next morning.

It was strongly suspected that Sir Jeffery's death was caused by resurrection men. The surgeons of the day were eager to obtain a prize [for dissection], but their hopes were disappointed... A grave ten feet deep was dug close to the north wall of the watchhouse of Saint Mary, Whitechapel, where he now lies.

Real Guys and real bonfires

THERE CANNOT BE a better representation of Guy Fawkes as he is borne about the metropolis in effigy on the fifth of November, every year, than the drawing to this article by George Cruikshank.

It is not to be expected that poor boys should be well informed as to Guy's history or be particular about his costume. With them Guy Fawkes Day, or as they as often call it, Pope Day, is a holiday, and ... this, on account of its festivous enjoyment, is the greatest holiday of the season... The guy is the last thing thought of, the bonfire the first. About this time ill is sure to betide any ill-secured fence. Stakes are extracted from hedges and branches from trees. Crack, crack goes loose paling. Deserted buildings yield up their floorings. Unbolted flip-flapping doors are released from their hinges ... and more burn-ables are deemed lawful prize than the law allows...

Then comes the making of the guy, which is easily done with straw ... an old coat, waistcoat, breeches and stockings... A barber's block for the head is 'the very thing itself'. Chalk and charcoal make capital eyes and brows... A large wig is a capital achievement. Formerly an old cocked hat was the reigning fashion for a guy, though the more strictly informed dresser of the character preferred a mock mitre. Now, however, both hat and mitre have disappeared, and a stiff paper cap, painted and knotted with paper strips in imitation of ribbon, is its substitute... Yet this neither was, nor is, a guy without a dark lantern in one hand and a spread bunch of matches in the other.

The figure thus furnished, and fastened in a chair, is carried about the streets in the manner represented in the engraving [*see next page*], the boys shouting forth the words of the motto with loud huzzas, and running up to passengers hat in hand with 'Pray remember Guy! Please to remember Guy!'

Scuffles seldom happen now, but in my youthful days 'when guy

Please to remember the fifth of November,
    Gunpowder, treason and plot.
We know no reason why gunpowder treason
    Should ever be forgot!
        Holla boys! holla boys! huzza—a—a!

A stick and a stake for King George's sake,
A stick and a stump for Guy Fawkes's rump!
        Holla boys! holla boys! huzza—a—a!

met guy — then came the tug of war!' ...Sometimes desperate bands
who omitted or were destitute of the means to make guys went forth
like Froissart's knights 'upon adventures'. An enterprise of this sort
was called 'going to *smug* a guy', that is, to steal one by force of arms,
fists and sticks...

In such times, the burning of 'a good guy' was a scene of uproar
unknown to the present day. The bonfire in Lincoln's Inn Fields was
of this superior order of disorder. It was made at the Great Queen-

street corner... Fuel came all day long, in carts properly guarded against surprise. Old people have remembered when upwards of two hundred cartloads were brought to make and feed this bonfire, and more than thirty guys were burnt upon gibbets between eight and twelve o'clock at night.

At the same period the butchers in Clare Market [south of Lincoln's Inn Fields] had a bonfire ... and they thrashed each other 'round about the wood-fire' with the strongest sinews of slaughtered bulls [their pizzles]. Large parties of butchers from all the markets paraded the streets, ringing peals from marrowbones and cleavers [their traditional noise-making], so loud as to overpower the storms of sound that came from the rocking belfries of the churches. By ten o'clock London was so lit up by bonfires and fireworks that from the suburbs it looked in one red heat. Many were the overthrows of horsemen and carriages from the discharge of hand-rockets...

This fiery zeal has gradually decreased... Boys carry about their guy with no other sentiment or knowledge respecting him than body-snatchers have of a newly-raised corpse... Their only question is how much they will get by the operation to make merry with...

A corporation notice is annually left at the house of every inhabitant in the city of London... 'In order to prevent any Tumults and Riots that may happen on the Fifth of November and the next ensuing Lord Mayor's Day, you are required to charge all your Servants and Lodgers that they neither make nor cause to be made any SQUIBS, SERPENTS, FIRE BALLOONS or other FIREWORKS, nor fire, fling nor throw them out of your House, Shop or Warehouse or in the Streets of this City, on the Penalties contained in an Act of Parliament made in the Tenth Year of the late King WILLIAM [1697]. *Note*: The Act was made perpetual, and is not expired as some ignorantly suppose.'

The fading charm of St Chad's Well

Hone has a look at a London spa, St Chad's Well, in its declining years. The site is a stone's-throw southeast of King's Cross Station.

THE MIRACULOUS WATER is aperient, and was some years ago quaffed by the bilious and other invalids who flocked thither in crowds to drink at the cost of sixpence what people of these latter days by the ingenious chemist's art can make as effectual as St Chad's virtues 'at the small price of one halfpenny'.

If anyone desires to visit this spot of ancient renown, let him descend from Holborn-bars to the very bottom of Gray's Inn-lane [now

160

'road']. On the lefthand side formerly stood a considerable hill whereon were wont to climb and browse certain mountain goats of the
metropolis, in common language called swine. The hill was the largest
heap of cinder-dust [and refuse] in the neighbourhood of London. It
was formed by the annual accumulation of some thousands of cartloads, since exported to Russia for making bricks to rebuild Moscow
after the conflagration [*of 1812; but can this story be true?*]...

On the righthand side of the road is an anglewise faded inscription:
ST CHAD'S WELL ... An elderly pair of wooden gates ... opens on a
scene which the unaccustomed eye may take for the pleasure-ground
of Giant Despair. Trees stand as if made not to vegetate ... and name-
less weeds straggle weakly... If you look upwards you perceive
painted on an octagon board, Health Restored and Preserved. Further
on towards the left stands a low, oldfashioned, comfortable-looking
large-windowed dwelling; and ten to one but there also stands, at the
open door, an ancient ailing female in a black bonnet, a clean coloured
cotton gown and a check apron, her silver hair only in part tucked
beneath the narrow border of a frilled cap, with a sedate and patient
yet somewhat inquiring look. This is The Lady of the Well.

She gratuitously informs you that 'the gardens' of St Chad's Well
are 'for circulation' by paying for the water, of which you may drink
as much, or as little, or nothing, as you please, at one guinea per year,
9s 6d quarterly, 4s 6d monthly or 1s 6d weekly. You qualify for a
single visit by paying sixpence, and a large glass tumbler full of warm
water is handed to you... You are told that 'St Chad's Well was
famous at one time'. Should you be inquisitive, the dame will instruct
you, with an earnest eye, that 'people are not what they were', 'things
are not as they used to be', and she 'can't tell what'll happen next'.
Oracles have not ceased.

While drinking St Chad's water you observe an immense copper
into which it is poured, wherein it is heated to due efficacy, and from
whence it is drawn by a cock into the glasses. You also remark, hanging on the wall, a 'tribute of gratitude' versified and inscribed on vel-
lum ... an effusion for value received from St Chad's invaluable water.

But above all there is a fullsized portrait in oil of a stout, comely
personage with a ruddy countenance, in a coat or cloak supposed
scarlet, a laced cravat falling down the breast, and a small red
nightcap carelessly placed on the head, conveying the idea that it was
painted for the likeness of some opulent butcher who flourished in the
reign of Queen Anne.

Ask the dame about it, and she refers you to 'Rhone'. This is a tall
old man, who would be taller if he were not bent by years. 'I am
ninety-four,' he will tell you, 'this present year of our Lord, one

thousand eight hundred and twenty-five.' All that he has to communicate concerning the portrait is, 'I have heard say it is the portrait of St Chad.' Should you venture to differ, he adds, 'This is the opinion of most people who come here...'

An old American loyalist, who has lived in Pentonville ever since 'the rebellion' [the American Revolution] forced him to the mother country, enters to 'totter not unseen' between the stunted hedgerows. It was the first 'place of pleasure' he came to after his arrival, and he goes nowhere besides — 'everything else is so altered'. For the same reason, a tall, spare, thinfaced man with dull grey eyes and underhung chin, from the neighbourhood of Bethnal Green, walks hither for his 'Sunday morning's exercise', to untruss a theological point with a law clerk who also attends the place, because his father, 'when he was 'prentice to Mr ——— the great law stationer in Chancery-lane in 1776, and sat writing for sixteen hours a day, received great benefit from the waters, which he came to drink fasting, once a week'...

St Chad's Well is haunted, not frequented. A few years and it will be with its water as with the water of St Pancras Well, which is enclosed in the garden of a private house near old St Pancras churchyard.

The well's name survives in St Chad's-place, a fittingly faded back street.

Croupees, puffs, squibs and flashers

Oldtime gaming houses — from the *London Mercury* of January 13, 1721.

THERE ARE it seems in the parish of Covent Garden twenty-two such houses, some of which clear sometimes £100, and seldom less than £40 a night. They have their proper officers, both civil and military, with salaries proportionable to their respective degrees and the importance they are of in the service, viz:

A commissioner or commis, who is always a proprietor of the gaming-house. He looks in once a night, and the week's account is audited by him and two others of the proprietors.

A director, who superintends the room.

The operator, the dealer at faro.

Croupees, two, who watch the card, and gather the money for the bank.

A puff, one who has money given him to play, in order to decoy others.

A clerk, who is a check upon the puff to see that he sinks none of that money.

A squib is a puff of a lower rank and has half the salary of a puff.

A flasher, one who sits by to swear how often he has seen the bank stript.

A dunner, waiter.

An attorney or solicitor.

A captain, one who is to fight any man that is peevish or out of humour at the loss of his money.

An usher, who takes care that the porter or grenadier at the door suffers none to come in but those he knows.

A porter, who at most of the gaming-houses is a soldier hired for that purpose.

A runner, to get intelligence of all the meetings of the justices of the peace, and when the constables go upon the search.

Any link-boy, coachman, chairman, drawer or other person who gives notice of the constables being upon the search has half a guinea.

Springtime at Jemmy Whittle's

AT LAURIE & WHITTLE'S printshop 'nearly opposite St Dunstan's Church, Fleet-street', or rather at Jemmy Whittle's, for he was the manager of the concern —

I cannot help calling him 'Jemmy', for I knew him afterwards in a passing way when *every*body called him Jemmy; and after his recollection failed and he dared no longer to flash his merriment at The Cock at Temple Bar and The Black Jack in Portugal-street, but stood, like a sign of himself, at his own door, unable to remember the names of his old friends, they called him '*poor* Jemmy!'

— I say, I remember at Jemmy Whittle's there was always a change of prints in springtime. Jemmy liked, as he said, to 'give the public something alive, fresh and clever, classical and correct!' One print, however, was never changed. This was 'St Dunstan and the Devil'. To any who inquired why he always had 'that *old* thing' in the window, and thought it would be better out, Jemmy answered, 'No, no, my boy! That's *my* sign — no change — church and state, you know! — no politics, you know! — I hate politics! There's the church, you know (*pointing to St Dunstan's*), and here am I, my boy! It's *my* sign, you know! No change, my boy!'

Alas, how changed: I desired to give a copy of the print on St Dunstan's day in the first volume of *The Every-Day Book*, and it could not be found at 'the old shop', nor at any printsellers I resorted to.

Another print of Jemmy Whittle's was a favourite with me as well as himself, for through every mutation of 'dressing out' his window it maintained its place with St Dunstan. It was a mezzotinto called 'The

A carnival character, he holds a rommelpot, a Dutch noisemaker

Laughing Boy'. During all seasons this print was exhibited, 'fresh and fresh'. At that time prints from the Flemish and Dutch masters, and humorous matters of all kinds, were public favourites. From my early liking to 'The Laughing Boy', and because, with the merit of good design, it is a superior specimen of popular taste at the time I speak of, a copy of it is at the service of that reader who may perhaps think with 'poor Jemmy Whittle' that an agreeable subject is always in season...

I am now speaking of five and thirty years ago, when shop windows, especially printsellers', were set out according to the season. I remember that in springtime Jemmy Whittle, and Carrington Bowles in St Paul's Churchyard, used to decorate their panes with twelve prints of flowers of 'the months', engraved after Baptiste [17th-century French artist] and coloured 'after nature' — a show almost, at that time, as gorgeous as 'Solomon's Temple in all its glory, all over nothing but gold and jewels', which a man exhibited to my wondering eyes for a halfpenny.

Spring arrives in London — and even east of Temple Bar — as early as in the country. For though there are neither hawthorns to blossom nor daisies to blow, there is scarcely a house in the city without a few flower-pots inside or outside... To the east of Temple Bar the flower-girl is the herald of spring. She cries 'Cowslips! Sweet cowslips!' till she screams 'Bowpots! Sweet and pretty bowpots!' which is the sure and certain token of full spring in London.

When *I* was a child, I got a bowpot [or beaupot, boughpot] of as many wallflowers and harebells as I could then hold in my hand, with a sprig of sweet briar at the back of the bunch, for a halfpenny — *such a handful*. But now, 'They can't make a ha'penny bowpot — there's nothing under a penny'. And the penny bowpot is not half so big as the ha'penny one, and somehow or other the flowers don't smell, to me, as they used to do. It will not do, however, to run on thus...

> To give some idea of the print trade: in Laurie & Whittle's catalogue of 1795, when Hone was a youth, 'The Laughing Boy' is one of 365 'half-sheet mezzotintos, humorous'; there are many hundreds more of other kinds and sizes; and this was just one of many printsellers.

St Dunstan and the goldsmiths

When Hone failed in his hunt for the 'St Dunstan and the Devil' print, as he says above, he got George Cruikshank to draw the scene. As Cruikshank grew up near Jemmy Whittle's shop (and did some early work for him), his version no doubt gives a good idea of the original.
Dunstan, a notable 10th-century Archbishop of Canterbury, was also credited with the goldsmithing art, and this inspired some lively fictions.

THE LEGEND of St Dunstan relates many miracles of him, the most popular of which is to this effect: that St Dunstan, as the fact really was, became expert in goldsmith's work...; that while he was busied in making a chalice, the devil annoyed him ... and tempted him, whereupon St Dunstan suddenly seized the fiend by the nose with a pair of iron tongs, burning hot, and so held him while he roared and cried until the night was far spent...

On lord mayor's day in 1687, the pageants of Sir John Shorter as lord mayor were very splendid. He was of the Company of Gold-smiths, who at their own expense provided one of the pageants... It must have been of amazing size, for it was a 'hieroglyphic of the Company' ... with forges, anvils, hammers and all instruments proper

St Dunstan, as the story goes,
Once pulled the devil by the nose
With redhot tongs, which made him roar,
That he was heard three miles or more.

for the mystery of the goldsmiths... On a rich golden chair of state sat St Dunstan, the ancient patron and tutelar guardian of the company ... in a robe of fine lawn with a cope over it of shining cloth of gold reaching to the ground. He wore a golden mitre set with precious stones, and bore in his left hand a golden crozier and in his right a pair of goldsmith's tongs...

At the steps of the prelatical throne were a goldsmith's forge and furnace, with fire, crucibles and gold, and a workman blowing the bellows. On each side was a large press [cupboard] of gold and silver plate. Towards the front were shops of artificers and jewellers all at work, with anvils, hammers and instruments for enamelling, beating out gold and silver plate. On a step below St Dunstan sat an assay-master with his trial balance and implements. There were two apartments for the processes of disgrossing, flatting and drawing gold and silver wire, and the fining, melting, smelting, refining and separating of gold and silver... Another apartment contained ... miners in canvas breeches, red waistcoats and red caps, bearing spades, pick-axes, twibills and crows for sinking shafts...

Steaming up the river to Richmond

IN THE BEGINNING OF MAY a steamboat for conveying passengers ascends the Thames in the morning from Queenhithe to Richmond, and returns the same day; and so she proceeds to and fro until the autumn... Her band on deck plays a lively tune, and 'off she goes' towards Blackfriars Bridge. From thence, leisurely walkers and holiday-wishing people on their way to business look from between the balustrades on the enviable steamer. They see her lower her chimney to pass beneath the arch, and ten to one, if they cross the road to watch her coming forth on the other side, they receive a puff from the re-elevating chimney...

If the day be fine, the passage is very pleasant. The citizen sees various places where he has enjoyed himself. He can point out the opening to Fountain-court wherein is the Coal Hole [near the Strand], the resort of his brother 'Wolves', a club of modern origin, renowned for its support of Edmund Kean. On the left bank he shows the site of Cuper's Gardens [now the southern approach to Waterloo Bridge], to which he was taken when a boy by his father's foreman... Or he has a story to tell of the Fox-under-the-Hill, near the Strand, where Dutch Sam [Sam Elias, pugilist, 1775–1816] mustered the fighting Jews and Perry's firemen who nightly assisted John Kemble's 'What d'ye want?' during the O.P. row at Covent Garden Theatre...

He will tell you of the capital porter-shops that were in Palace-yard before the old coffee-houses were pulled down, and he directs you to the high chimney of Hodges's distillery in Church-street, Lambeth. He stands erect, and looks at Cumberland-gardens as if they were his freehold — for there has he been in all his glory. And at the Red House, at Battersea, he would absolutely go ashore, if his wife and daughters had not gone so far in geography as to know that Richmond is above Battersea Bridge...

Others see other things ... the tomb of Hogarth in Chiswick churchyard; 'Brentford, town of mud', so immortalized by one of our poets, from whence runs Boston-lane wherein dwelt the good and amiable James Granger, who biographized every Englishman of whom there was a portrait [in his *Biographical History of England*, 1769]...

The aits, or osier islands, are picturesque interspersions on the Thames. Its banks are studded with neat cottages, or elegant villas crown the gentle heights. The lawns come sweeping down like carpets of green velvet to the edge of its soft-flowing waters, and the grace of the scenery improves till we are borne into the full bosom of its beauty — the village of Richmond, or as it was anciently called, Sheen.

On coming within sight of this, the most delightful scene in our seagirt isle, the band on board the steamboat plays 'The Lass of Richmond Hill' while the vessel glides on the translucent water till she curves to the bridgefoot, and the passengers disembark... A short walk through the village brings us to the top of the far-famed hill, from whence there is a sudden sight of one of the loveliest views in the world.

Here, unless an overflowing purse can command the preference of The Star and Garter [*still there*], we enter the pleasant and comfortable Roebuck Inn, which has nothing to recommend it but civil treatment and domestic conveniences. The westward room on the second floor is quiet, and one of the pleasantest in the house... Hither come ye whose hearts are saddened or whose nerves are shattered by the strife of life or the disturbances of the world. Inhale the pure air and gaze a while on a prospect more redolent of beauty than Claude or Poussin ever painted or saw... The lively French, the philosophic German, the elegant Italian, the lofty Spaniard and the Cossack of the Don pronounce the prospect from the hill the most enchanting in Europe.

> *O.P. row*: When Kemble raised the prices at the newly rebuilt theatre in 1809, performances were disrupted by 'Old Price' barrackers. He hired strong men to deal with them, but had to compromise in the end.

Islington harmony and friendship

AN ANONYMOUS correspondent obligingly enclosed and begged my acceptance of a ticket for a parish dinner at Islington on the 11th of April, 1738... As the editor was not prepared to join the guests at the great dinner 'not where they eat, but where they are eaten', he appropriates the ticket to the use for which it was intended by the donor... It would do the reader's heart good to see this ticket, printed from a copperplate ten inches high by seven inches wide — as large as a lord mayor's ticket, and looking much better, because engraved by W H Toms, a fine firm artist of 'the good old school', which taught truth as an essential and prohibited refinements not existing in nature...

First, above the invitation ... is a capital view of the *old* parish church and the churchyard wherein lie the remains of most of the company who attended the parish dinner... Let anyone who knows the new church of Islington [built 1751–4] compare it with ... the old church [15th-century] and say which church he prefers. At this time, however, the present church may be more suitable to Islington, grown or grown up to, as it is, until it is a part of London; but who would not wish it still a village, with the old edifice for its parish church?

That Islington is now more opulent and more respectable may be very true; but opulence monopolizes and respectability is often a vain show in the stead of happiness, and a mere flaunt on the ruins of comfort. The remark is, of course, general, and not of Islington in particular, all of whose opulent and respectable residents may really be so, for aught I know to the contrary...

Immediately beneath the view of the old church on the ticket follows the stewards' invitation...

You are desir'd to meet many others, NATIVES of this place, on TUESDAY, ye 11th Day of April, 1738, at Mrs ELIZ. GRIMSTEAD'S, ye ANGEL & CROWN, in ye Upper Street, about ye Hour of One; then & there wth FULL DISHES, GOOD WINE & GOOD HUMOUR, to improve & make lasting that HARMONY and FRIENDSHIP which have so long reigned among us.

> Walter Sebbon
> John Booth
> Bourchier Durell
> James Sebbon   STEWARDS

N.B. — THE DINNER will be on the Table peremptorily at Two.

Pray Pay the Bearer Five Shillings.

'Merry Islington!' — We may almost fancy we see the 'jolly companions, every one', in their best wigs, ample coats and embroidered waistcoats, at their dinner; that we hear the bells ringing out from the square tower of the old church, and the people and boys outside the door of the 'Angel and Crown, in ye Upper Street' huzzaing and rejoicing that their betters were dining 'for the good of the parish' — for so they did: read the ticket again.

A walk in search of vanishing scenes

> People methinks are better, but the scenes
> Wherein my youth delighted are no more.
> I wander out in search of them, and find
> A sad deformity in all I see.
> Strong recollections of my former pleasures
> And knowledge that they never can return
> Are causes of my sombre-mindedness:
> I pray you then, bear with my discontent.   *Hone*

A WALK OUT OF LONDON is, to me, an event. I have an *every-day* desire to bring it about, but weeks elapse before the time arrives... In my boyhood I had only to obtain parental permission and stroll in fields now no more — to scenes now deformed or that I have been wholly robbed of by 'the spirit of improvement'. Five and thirty years have altered everything — myself with the rest. I am obliged to 'ask leave to go out' of time and circumstance...

I did so yesterday. 'This is the time,' I said to an artist [George Cruikshank; May 1825], 'when we Londoners begin to get our walks. We will go to a place or two that I knew many years ago, and see how they look now; and first to Canonbury House.'

Having crossed the back Islington road [now Liverpool-road] we found ourselves in the rear of The Pied Bull. Ah! I know this spot well: this stagnant pool was a famous carp pond among boys. How dreary the place seems! The yard and pens were formerly filled with sheep and cattle for Smithfield market. Graziers and drovers were busied about them... Now all is thrown open and neglected, and not a living thing to be seen.

We went round to the front... Nobody answered to our knocking. It had been the residence of the gallant Sir Walter Raleigh, who threw down his court mantle for Queen Elizabeth to walk on ... and who finally lost his life on a scaffold for his courage and services. By a door in the rear we got into 'the best parlour'... It had been Raleigh's dining-room.

Here the arms of Sir John Miller are painted in glass in the end window, and we found Mr John Cleghorn sketching them. This gentleman, who lives in the neighbourhood, and whose talents as a draftsman and engraver are well known, was obligingly communicative, and we condoled on the decaying memorials of past greatness. On the ceiling of this room are stuccoed the five senses: Feeling in an oval centre and the other four in the scroll-work around. The chimney-piece of carved oak, painted white, represents Charity, supported by Faith on her right and Hope on her left...

We hastily passed through the other apartments and gave a last farewell look at Sir Walter's house; yet we bade not adieu to it till my accompanying friend expressed a wish that as Sir Walter, according to tradition, had there smoked the first pipe of tobacco drawn in Islington, so *he* might have been able to smoke the last whiff within the walls that would in a few weeks be levelled to the ground...

They also drank toasts to Raleigh in a negus made by Hone. The old tavern was originally an Elizabethan mansion. Long standing tradition said Raleigh had lived there. There is evidence to support this: in 1577, unruly servants of his, summoned before the Middlesex justices, are recorded as domiciled in Islington. The arms of Sir John Miller were of a later date.

The building was demolished just after Hone's visit. Until recent times there was a Pied Bull on the site; now even the name is gone.

Havoc and stench at Canonbury

MY FRIEND THE ARTIST obligingly passed the door of Canonbury Tower to take a sketch of its northeast side; not that the tower has not been taken before, but it has not been given exactly in that position. We love every look of an old friend, and this look we get after crossing the bridge of the New River, coming from The Thatched House to Canonbury Tavern. A year or so ago the short walk from the lower Islington road [now Essex-road] to this bridge was the prettiest 'bit' on the river nearest to London... Now, how changed!

My ringing at the tower gate was answered by Mr Symes, who for thirty-nine years past has been resident in the mansion, and is bailiff of the manor of Islington, under Lord Northampton. Once more ... I ranged the old rooms, and took perhaps a last look from its roof. The eye shrunk from the wide havoc below. Where new buildings had not covered the sward, it was embowelling for bricks, and kilns emitted flickering fire and sulphurous stench. Surely the dominion of the brick-and-mortar king will have no end, and cages for commercial spirits [houses for businessmen] will be instead of every green herb.

In this high tower some of our literary men frequently shut themselves up, 'far from the busy haunts of men'. Mr Symes says that his mother-in-law, Mrs Evans, who had lived there three-and-thirty years, and was wife to the former bailiff, often told him that her aunt,

Cruikshank's sketch of Canonbury Tower in 1825 (it survives)

Mrs Tapps, a seventy years inhabitant of the tower, was accustomed to talk much about Oliver Goldsmith and his apartment. It was the old oak room on the first floor. Mrs Tapps affirmed that he there wrote his *Deserted Village* [1770], and slept in a large press bedstead...

Hither have I come almost every year, and frequently in many years, and seen the changing occupancy of these apartments... It is worth while to take a room or two, were it only to hear Mr Symes's pleasant conversation about residents and residentiaries, manorial rights and boundaries, and 'things as they used to be' in his father's time ... and 'in Mrs Evans's time' or 'Mrs Tapps's time'. The grand tenantry of the tower has been in and through him and them during a hundred and forty-two years.

Canonbury Tower ... is part of an old mansion which appears to have been erected, or if erected before, much altered, about the reign of Elizabeth... [*The tower itself is pre-1570; other parts a little later.*] It was possessed by Sir John Spencer, an alderman and lord mayor of London, known by the name of 'rich Spencer'... His sole daughter and heiress, Elizabeth, was carried off in a baker's basket from Canonbury House by William, the second Lord Compton, lord president of Wales. He inherited Canonbury with the rest of Sir John Spencer's wealth at his death, and was afterwards created Earl of Northampton. In this family the manor still remains [*the heart of it does to this day*].

The present earl's rent-roll will be enormously increased by the extinction of comfort to the inhabitants of Islington and its vicinity through the covering up of the open fields and verdant spots... None who see the goings-on and ponder well will be able to foretell whether Mr Symes or the tower will enjoy benefit of survivorship.

> ...All thy pleasant fields
> Have fled, and brick-kilns, bricks and houses rise
> At his command; the air no longer yields
> A fragrance — scarcely health. The very skies
> Grow dim and townlike...   *Hone*

Bulldogs and drunken ruffians

COPENHAGEN HOUSE stands alone in the fields north of the metropolis, between Maiden-lane [now York-way], the old road to Highgate on the west, and the very ancient north road, or bridleway, called Hagbush-lane [see pages 233–7] on the east...

It is certain that Copenhagen House has been licensed for the sale of beer and wine and spirits for upwards of a century; and for such refreshments and as a teahouse, with a garden and grounds for skittles and Dutch pins, it has been greatly resorted to by Londoners. No house of the kind commands so extensive and uninterrupted a view of the metropolis and the immense western suburb, with the heights of Hampstead and Highgate and the rich intervening meadows. Those nearest London are now rapidly destroying [being destroyed] for their brick-earth, and being covered with houses...

[*In the early 1800s*] Copenhagen House was kept by one Tooth, who encouraged brutal sports for the sake of the liquors he sold. On a Sunday morning the fives-ground was filled by bulldogs and ruffians, who lounged and drank to intoxication. So many as fifty or sixty bulldogs have been seen tied up to the benches at once, while their masters boozed and made match after match, and went out and fought their dogs before the house amid the uproar of idlers... This scene lasted throughout every Sunday forenoon, and then the mob dispersed and the vicinity was annoyed by the yells of the dogs and their drunken masters on their return home. There was also a common field east of the house wherein bulls were baited; this was called the bull-field... The magistrates, after repeated warnings to Tooth, refused him a licence in 1816 and granted it to Mr Bath, the present landlord, who abated the nuisance by refusing to draw beer or afford refreshment to anyone who had a bulldog at his heels...

> Copenhagen House was demolished in 1855 to make way for a cattle market. But the site has returned to recreational use: it is now a park.

Pastures and hedgerows no more

A year later Hone walks out again to his once-loved scenes.

I PREFER WALKING where I walked when novelty was charming; where I can have the pleasure of recollecting that I formerly felt pleasure... One of my oldest and therefore one of my still-admired walks is by the way of Islington. I am partial to it because when I was eleven years old I went every evening from my father's, near Red Lion Square [Holborn], to a lodging in that village 'for a consumption' [for the sake of his lungs], and returned the following morning. I thus became acquainted with Canonbury, and The Pied Bull, and Barnsbury Park, and White Conduit House; and the intimacy has been kept up until presumptuous takings-in and enclosures and new buildings have nearly destroyed it.

He goes to see the remains of the White Conduit, a stone structure erected in the 17th century over a well that supplied the Charterhouse, Clerkenwell.

About 1810 the late celebrated William Huntington, S.S. [Sinner

Saved, as he styled himself], of Providence Chapel, who lived in a handsome house within sight, was at the expense of clearing the spring for the use of the inhabitants; but because his pulpit opinions were obnoxious some of the neighbouring vulgar threw loads of soil upon it in the night, which rendered the water impure and obstructed its channel... The building itself was in a very perfect state at that time... As the new buildings proceeded it was injured and defaced by idle labourers and boys from mere wantonness, and reduced to a mere ruin... To the buildings grown up around it might have been rendered a neat ornament by planting a few trees and enclosing the whole with an iron railing, and have stood as a monument of departed worth.

This vicinity was anciently full of springs and stone conduits... Only one has been preserved, which is notoriously deficient as a supply to the populous neighbourhood ... frequently exhausted by 3 or 4 o'clock in the afternoon. The handle of the pump is then padlocked till the next morning... It would seem as if the parochial powers in this quarter were leagued with publicans and sinners to compel the thirsty to buy deleterious beer and bowel-disturbing 'pop', or to swallow the New River water fresh with impurities from the thousands of people who daily cleanse their foul bodies in the stream...

White Conduit House [tavern and tea-gardens] has ceased to be a recreation in the good sense of the word. Its present denomination is the 'Minor Vauxhall', and its chief attraction during the passing summer [1826] has been Mrs Maria Bland [singer, born 1769; for years a star at Drury Lane]. She still has powers, and if their exercise here has been a stay and support to this sweet melodist, so far the establishment may be deemed respectable. It is a ground for balloon-flying and skittle-playing, and just maintains itself above the very lowest... There is at night a starveling show of odd company and coloured lamps, a mock orchestra with mock singing, dancing in a room which decent persons would prefer to withdraw their young folks from...

Such is the present state of a vicinage which 'in my time' was the pleasantest near spot to the north of London. The meadow of the White Conduit commanded an extensive prospect of the Hampstead and Highgate hills, over beautiful pastures and hedgerows... In a few short years London will distend its enormous bulk to the heights ... and nothing will be left to me to admire, of all that I admired.

Hone does not mention that his father was a 'sinner saved', a convert to Huntington's Calvinist church — against whose doctrines Hone rebelled as a youth into unbelief.

A pub survives on the White Conduit site, but in the early 1990s it was pointlessly renamed the Penny Farthing.On a field next the tavern, Thomas Lord founded his cricket club (it migrated to St John's Wood in 1787).

Mr Gliddon's gorgeous divan

IN THE EAST it is common to see dirty streets and poor-looking houses, and on being admitted into the interior of one of them to find yourself in a beautiful room, noble with drapery and splendid with fountains and gilded trellises. We do not mean to compare King-street, Covent Garden, with a street in Bagdad or Constantinople. We have too much respect for that eminent thoroughfare, clean in general and classical always; where you cannot turn but you meet recollections of the Drydens and the Hogarths. The hotel next to the Cigar Divan is still the same as in Hogarth's picture of the Frosty Morning...

And making due allowance for the palace of an effendi and the premises of a tradesman, a person's surprise could hardly be greater, certainly his comfort not so great, in passing from the squalidness of a Turkish street into the gorgeous but suspicious wealth of the apartment of a pasha, as in slipping out of the mud and dirt and mist and cold of an out-of-door November evening in London into the oriental and carpeted warmth of Mr Gliddon's Divan.

It is pleasant to think what a number of elegant and cheerful places lurk ... where nobody would expect them. Mr Gliddon's shop is a very respectable one, but nobody would look for the saloon behind it... You find yourself in a room like an eastern tent, the drapery festooned up around you, and views exhibited on all sides of mosques and minarets and palaces rising out of the water.

But here we are inside ourselves. What do you think of it?

B. This is a tent indeed, exactly as you have described it. It seems pitched in the middle of the Ganges or Tigris, for most of the views are in the midst of water.

I. Yes, we might fancy ourselves a party of British merchants who had purchased a little island in an eastern gulf and built themselves a tent on it to smoke in... This noble edifice on the left, touched in that delicate manner with silver (or is it rather not gold?) unites the reality of architecture built by mortal hands with the fairy lustre of a palace raised by enchantment. One has a mind to sail to it and get an adventure...

O. Well, this snug little corner for me under the bamboos. Two gigantic walking-sticks in leaf! A cup of coffee served by a pretty Hindoo would do very well here; and there is a temple to be religious in, when convenient. 'Tis pleasant to have all one's luxuries together...

C. Are you sure we are not all mussulmen? I begin to think I am a Turk under the influence of opium... We shall have the sultan upon us presently.

L. With old Ibrahim to give us the bastinado. I have no fair Persian at hand to offer him, and if I had, wouldn't do it...

E. I cannot help thinking we are the calenders [dervishes], got into the house full of ladies, and that we shall have to repent and rub our faces with ashes, crying out, '*This* is the reward of our debauchery. *This* is the reward of taking too many cups of coffee. *This* is the reward of too much girl and tobacco.'

L. But alas! in that case we should have the repentance without the lady, which is unfair. No ladies, I believe, are admitted here, Mr Gliddon?

Mr G. No, sir. It has been often observed to me by way of hint that it was a pity ladies were not admitted into English coffeehouses, as they are on the continent. But this is a smoking as well as a coffee-room. Ladies do not smoke in England, as they do in the East. And then, as extremes meet, and the most respectable creatures in the world render a place, it seems, not respectable, I was to take care how I risked my character and made my Divan too comfortable.

O. And we call ourselves a gallant nation...!

L. Women and smoking would not do together, unless we smoked perfumes and saw their eyes through a cloud of fragrance, like Venus in her ambrosial mist...

J. The next time Mr Gliddon indulges us with a new specimen of his magnificence, he must give us animate instead of inanimate scenes, and treat us with a series of subjects out of the Arabian Nights — lovers, genii and elegant festivities.

Mr G. Gentlemen, here is a little festivity at hand, not, I hope, al-together inelegant. Your coffee and cigars are ready.

C. Ah, this is the substantial picturesque...

L. It is curious to see how we identify smoking with the eastern nations, whereas it is a very modern thing among them, and was taught them from the west. One wonders what the Turks and Persians did before they took to smoking; just as the ladies and gentlemen of these nervous times wonder how their ancestors existed without tea for breakfast...

J. 'Coffee without tobacco,' quoth the Persian, as our friend's learned placard informs us, 'is like meat without salt'...

Hone quotes from Gliddon's 'learned placard' or prospectus, an early example of the advertiser's art. Here are extracts from his extract:

The recreation of smoking, which was introduced into this country in an age of great men, by one of the greatest and most accomplished men of that or any other age [Walter Raleigh], was for a long time considered an elegance and a mark of good breeding. Its very success gradually got it an ill name by rendering it too common and popular, and something became necessary to give it a new turn in its favour... Two circumstances combined to effect this desirable change.

One was the discovery of a new mode of smoking by means of rolling up the fragrant leaf itself and making it perform the office of its own pipe; the other was the long military experience in our late wars ... which, by throwing the most gallant of our gentry upon the hasty and humble recreations eagerly snatched at by all campaigners, opened their eyes to the difference between real and imaginary good breeding, and made them see that what comforted the heart of man under such grave circumstances must have qualities in it that deserved to be rescued from an ill name.

Thus arose the cigar, and with it a reputation that has been continually increasing. There is no rank in society into which it has not made its way, not excepting the very highest... George the Fourth ... has not thought it beneath his princely refinement to give the cigar his countenance.

The art of smoking is a contemplative art, and being naturally allied to other arts meditative, hath an attachment to a book and a newspaper. Books and newspapers are accordingly found at the Cigar Divan, the latter consisting of the principal daily papers, and the former of a PROFUSE COLLECTION OF THE MOST ENTERTAINING PERIODICALS...

A fine time for publicans and poets

Anti-Napoleonic fervour of 1803 is recalled by 'A City Volunteer' in 1827.

I DO NOT TRAVEL out of the road to take the 'eleven City regiments' into my battalion, nor do I call for the aid of the 'Gray's Inn Sharpshooters' (as lawyers are) and other gents of the 'sword and sash' who then emulated their brethren in scarlet and blue. Erecting my canteen at Moorgate, I hint to other quilldrivers to extend *their* forces when and where their memories serve. Inkshed, not bloodshed, is my only danger — my greatest failing is a propensity, I fear, to digress...

Moorfields, alas! has no fields. Where the Beth'lem Hospital raised its magnificent but gloomy front, with old Caius Gabriel Cibber's statues of Raving and Melancholy Madness siding the centre entrance, no vestiges remain, except the church and parts of London Wall leading from Broker-row to the Albion Chapel, commonly called the Plumcake. Who that knew the crossing from Finsbury-square to Broad-street remembers not the open-barred window at which Mad Molly daily appeared, singing, and talking inconsistencies of love, confinement and starvation? Who that stood before that massive building heard not the tones of agony, and felt not deep pity for the poor reasonless creatures?

In Moorfields, when Buonaparte threatened this country with invasion [in 1803], the beat of drum and the shrillings of the fife brought corps of gentlemen volunteers into rank and file to show how much a 'nation of shopkeepers' could do. Ladies in clusters assembled here to witness the feats of their soldier-like heroes...

The 'Bank gentlemen', distinguished by their long gaiters, and therefore called blacklegs, went further off and exercised before bank hours in the tenter-ground beyond the Vinegar-yard. The East India Company's three regiments (the best soldiers next to the foot-guards) drilled in a field which lay in the way on the one side to The Rosemary Branch, noted for a water-party or fives match [*a pub of this name survives, beside the Grand Union Canal*], and the White Lead Mills, whose wind-sails are removed by the steam Quixotes of the day. On the other side skirted the once pleasant path leading from The Shepherd & Shepherdess across the meadow either to Queen's Head lane, The Britannia or the almshouses near The Barley Mow, Islington. The East India field is now divided into gardens and snug arbours, let to the admirers of flowers and retreats...

Moorfields gathered more regiments than any other spot excepting the Park [Hyde Park], in which reviews and sham-fights concentrated the corporate forces on field-days. Wimbledon Common became also an occasional scene of busy parade and preparation: baggage long drawn out, multitudes of friends, sweethearts and wives... Many a white handkerchief dried the parting tear... Salutes [kisses] given behind the counter or snatched in the passage affected the sensibilities like last meetings...

Sermons were preached in and out of the establishment to 'soldiers'. Representations were given at the theatres to 'soldiers'. The shop-windows presented tokens of courage and love to 'soldiers'. Not a concert was held, not a 'free and easy' passed, without songs and melodies to 'soldiers'. It was a fine time for publicans and poets. Abraham Newland's promises [banknotes with the signature of the Bank of England chief cashier] kept army clothiers, gunmakers, Hounslow powder-mills and William Pitt's affairs in action... And Charles Dibdin [popular songwriter] and Joseph Grimaldi [the clown] — wicked wags! — satirized the fashion of 'playing at soldiers'...

Maidstone, Colchester and Rochester were select places for trying the shopkeeping volunteers. They were on duty for weeks, and returned with the honours of the barracks. Things taking a more peaceful aspect, or rather the alarm of invasion having subsided, the regimentals were put by, and scarcely a relic is now seen to remind the rising generation of the deeds of their fathers...

Cibber's statues (created 1780) do survive, at Bethlehem Royal Hospital museum, Beckenham. They and other items can be seen (telephone first).

A New Matrimonial Plan

THIS IS THE TITLE of a bill printed and distributed four or five years ago, and now before me [*Hone writes*], advertising 'an establishment where persons of all classes who are anxious to sweeten life by repairing to the *altar of Hymen* have an opportunity of meeting proper partners... Their personal attendance is not absolutely necessary. A statement of facts is all that is required at first.'

The method is simply this: for the parties to become subscribers, the amount to be regulated according to circumstances, and that they should be arranged in classes in the following order:

Ladies

1st Class I am twenty years of age, heiress to an estate in the county of Essex of the value of £30,000, well educated and of domestic habits; of an agreeable, lively disposition and genteel figure. Religion that of my future husband.

2d Class I am thirty years of age, a widow, in the grocery line in London — have children. Of middle stature, full made, fair complexion and hair, temper agreeable, worth £3,000.

3d Class I am tall and thin, a little lame in the hip, of a lively disposition, conversible, twenty years of age, live with my father, who if I marry with his consent will give me £1,000.

4th Class I am twenty years of age; mild disposition and manners; allowed to be personable.

5th Class I am sixty years of age; income limited; active and rather agreeable.

Gentlemen

1st Class A young gentleman with dark eyes and hair, stout made, well educated; have an estate of £500 per annum in the county of Kent, besides £10,000 in the three per cent consolidated annuities; am of an affable disposition and very affectionate.

2d Class I am forty years of age, tall and slender, fair complexion and hair, well tempered and of sober habits; have a situation in the Excise of £300 per annum, and a small estate in Wales of the annual value of £150.

3d Class A tradesman in the city of Bristol in a ready-money business, turning £150 per week at a profit of £10 per cent; pretty well tempered, lively and fond of home.

4th Class I am fifty-eight years of age, a widower without encumbrance, retired from business upon a small income; healthy constitution and of domestic habits.

5th Class I am twenty-five years of age, a mechanic, of sober habits, industrious, and of respectable connections.

It is presumed that the public will not find any difficulty in describing themselves. If they should, they will have the assistance of the managers, who will be in attendance at the office, No 5 Great St Helens, Bishopsgate-street, on Mondays, Wednesdays and Fridays between the hours of eleven and three o'clock. Please to inquire for Mr Jameson, up one pair of stairs. All letters to be post-paid.

The subscribers are to be furnished with a list of descriptions, and when one occurs likely to suit, the parties may correspond; and if mutually approved, the interview may be afterwards arranged. Further particulars may be had as above.

Such a strange device in our own time for catching would-be lovers seems incredible, and yet here is the printed plan with the name and address of the matchmaking gentleman ... 'up one pair of stairs'.

Brickfields invade the groves

Hone returns once again, in 1831, to a topic that grieves him, London's unstoppable swallowing-up of the green fields.

THE GROVES ROUND LONDON within a few years have been nearly destroyed by the speculating builders... The grove best known perhaps to the inhabitants of London is that at Camberwell — a spacious roadway and fine walks above half a mile in length, between rows of stately trees, from the beginning of the village and ascending the hill to its summit, from whence there is, or rather was, the finest burst of scenery the eye can look upon within the same distance from London. The view is partially obstructed by new buildings, and the character of the grove itself has been gradually injured by the breaking up of the adjacent grounds and meadows into brickfields, and the flanking of its sides with town-like houses...

Hampstead, however, is the 'place of groves'. How long it may remain so is a secret in the bosom of speculators and builders. Its first grove, townward, is the noble private avenue from the Hampstead-road to Belsize House, in the valley between Primrose Hill and the hill whereon the church stands...

In the neighbourhood of Hampstead church, and between that edifice and the heath, there are several old groves. Winding southwardly from the heath there is a charming little grove in Well Walk, with a bench at the end, whereon I last saw poor Keats, the poet of 'The Pot of Basil', sitting and sobbing his dying breath into a handkerchief — gleaning parting looks towards the quiet landscape he had delighted in — musing as in his 'Ode to a Nightingale':

> My heart aches, and a drowsy numbness pains
> My sense, as though of hemlock I had drunk...

Hone quotes 30 lines.

A real *Every-Day* English dialogue

A (advancing) How d'ye do, Brooks?
B Very well, thank'ee. How do *you* do?
A Very well, thank'ee. Is Mrs Brooks well?
B Very well, I'm much obliged t'ye. Mrs Adams and the children are well, I hope?
A Quite well, thank'ee. *(A pause)*
B Rather pleasant weather today.
A Yes, but it was cold in the morning.
B Yes, but we must expect that at this time o' year.
   (Another pause — neckcloth twitched and switch twirled)
A Seen Smith lately?
B No — I can't say I have — but I have seen Thompson.
A Indeed — how is he?
B Very well, thank'ee.
A I'm glad of it. Well — good morning.
B Good morning.

Here it is always observed that the speakers, having taken leave, walk faster than usual for some hundred yards.

> *This London dialogue (borrowed by Hone from* The Examiner, *1825) inspired a double caricature, 'French Salutation : English Salutation'. Two showy, gesticulating Frenchmen overflow with charm and compliment. Brown and Smith, with their hands under strict British control...*

...have dialogue nearly the same as the above, ending with,
'Going to business?' 'Yes, where are you going, eh?'

Eating, drinking, keeping well

AUTUMN

Laden with richest products of the earth,
Its choicest fruits, enchanting to the eye,
Grateful to taste and courting appetite.

182

Lively ladies of the oyster-cellar

IF A DESCRIPTION of Scottish manners printed about fifty years ago, *Letters from Edinburgh* [by Major Edward Topham, 1776], may be relied on, it was then a fashion with females at Edinburgh to frequent a sort of public-house... The writer says:

January 15, 1775. — A few evenings ago I had the pleasure of being asked to one of these entertainments by a lady. At that time I was not acquainted with this scene of 'high life below stairs', and therefore when she mentioned the word 'oyster-cellar' I imagined I must have mistaken the place of invitation. She repeated it, however, and I found it was not my business to make objections, so agreed immediately...

I had the pleasure of being ushered in ... to a large and brilliant company of both sexes, most of whom I had the honour of being acquainted with. The large table round which they were seated was covered with dishes full of oysters and pots of porter. For a long time I could not suppose that this was the only entertainment we were to have, and I sat waiting in expectation of a repast that was never to make its appearance. The table was cleared, and glasses introduced. The ladies were now asked whether they would choose brandy or rum punch. I thought this question an odd one, but I was soon informed by the gentleman who sat next me that no wine was sold here but that punch was quite 'the thing'; and a large bowl was immediately introduced.

The conversation ... now became general and lively. The women, who to do them justice are much more entertaining than their neighbours in England, discovered [displayed] a great deal of vivacity and fondness for repartee. A thousand things were hazarded, and met with applause, to which the oddity of the scene gave propriety, and which could have been produced in no other place. The general ease with which they conducted themselves, the innocent freedom of their manners and their unaffected good nature all conspired to make us forget that we were regaling in a cellar... They began to dance reels, their favourite dance, which they performed with great agility and perseverance...

The ladies found it time to retire. The coaches were therefore called, and away they went, and with them all our mirth. The company were now reduced to a party of gentlemen. Pipes and politics were introduced: I took my hat and wished them goodnight. The bill for entertaining half a dozen very fashionable women amounted only to two shillings apiece. If you will not allow the entertainment an elegant one, you must at least confess that it was cheap.

A good fire, hot tea, buttered toast

Quoting from Leigh Hunt in his magazine *The Indicator*, 1825:

HERE IT IS ready laid. Imprimis, tea and coffee; secondly, dry toast; thirdly, butter; fourthly, eggs; fifthly, ham; sixthly, something potted; seventhly, bread, salt, mustard, knives and forks, &c. One of the first things that belong to a breakfast is a good fire. There is a delightful mixture of the lively and the snug in coming down into one's break-fast-room of a cold morning and seeing everything prepared for us: a blazing grate, a clean tablecloth and tea-things, the newly-washed faces and combed heads of a set of good-humoured urchins, and the sole empty chair at its accustomed corner, ready for occupation.

When we lived alone we could not help reading at meals, and it is certainly a delicious thing to resume an entertaining book at a particularly interesting passage, with a hot cup of tea at one's elbow and a piece of buttered toast in one's hand. The first look at the page, accompanied by a coexistent bite of the toast, comes under the head of intensities.

Bonbons for all in Paris

IN PARIS on new year's day, which is called *le jour d'étrennes*, parents bestow portions on their children, brothers on their sisters, and hus-bands make presents to their wives. Carriages may be seen rolling through the streets with cargoes of *bonbons*, *souvenirs* and the variety of etceteras with which little children and grown-up children are bribed into good humour; and here and there pastrycooks are to be met with carrying upon boards enormous temples, pagodas, churches and playhouses made of fine flour and sugar and the embellishments which render French pastry so inviting.

But there is one street in Paris to which a new year's day is a whole year's fortune. This is the Rue des Lombards, where the wholesale confectioners reside, for in Paris every trade and profession has its peculiar quarter. For several days preceding the 1st of January this street is completely blocked up by carts and wagons laden with cases of sweetmeats for the provinces. These are of every form and description which the most singular fancy could imagine: bunches of carrots, green peas, boots and shoes, lobsters and crabs, hats, books, musical instruments, gridirons, frying-pans and saucepans, all made of sugar and coloured to imitate reality, and all made with a hollow within to hold the *bonbons*.

The most prevailing device is what is called a *cornet*, that is, a little cone ornamented in different ways, with a bag to draw over the large end and close it up. In these things, the prices of which vary from one franc (tenpence) to fifty, the *bonbons* are presented by those who choose to be at the expense of them; and by those who do not, they are only wrapped in a piece of paper; but *bonbons* in some way or other must be presented.

It would not perhaps be an exaggeration to state that the amount expended for presents on new year's day in Paris, for sweetmeats alone, exceeds 500,000 francs or £20,000. Jewellery is also sold to a very large amount... No person able to give must on this day pay a visit empty-handed. Everybody accepts, and every man gives according to the means which he possesses. Females alone are excepted from the charge of giving. A pretty woman, respectably connected, may reckon her new year's presents at something considerable. Gowns, jewellery, gloves, stockings and artificial flowers fill her drawing-room, for in Paris it is the custom to display all the gifts in order to excite emulation...

New year's day in London is not observed by any public festivity, but little social dining parties are frequently formed amongst friends, and convivial persons may be found at taverns and in publicans' parlours... The only open demonstration of joy in the metropolis is the ringing of merry peals from the belfries ... late on the eve of the new year, and until the chimes of the clock have sounded its last hour.

An innkeeper's gastronomic opulence

BRISTOL has now attained to so great wealth and prosperity as to provide inns of importance equal perhaps to any in the kingdom. A friend who sojourned there at the undermentioned date hands me a printed document which he received from his landlord, Mr John Weeks. It is so great a curiosity, as bespeaking the opulence of the ancient city and the spirit of its great innkeeper, that I cannot refrain from recording it.

Bush Tavern
BILL OF FARE FOR CHRISTMAS, 1800

1 bustard, red game, black game, 1 turtle (120lb), 1 land tortoise

72 pots turtle [soup], vermicelli soup, British turtle, giblet soup, pease soup, gravy soup, soup santé, soup bouillie, mutton broth, barley broth

3 turbots, 4 cods, 2 brills, 2 pipers, 12 dories, 2 haddocks, 14 rock-fish, 18 carp, 12 perch, 4 salmon, 12 plaice, 17 herrings, sprats, 122 eels, salt fish, 78

roach, 98 gudgeons, 1 dried salmon, crawfish, pickled salmon, sturgeon, pickled oysters, oysters stewed and colloped, lobsters, 52 barrels Pyfleet & Colchester oysters, Milford & Tenby oysters

1 haunch hevior venison [of a gelded deer], 5 haunches doe, 5 necks, 10 breasts, 10 shoulders

42 hares, 17 pheasants, 41 partridges, 87 wild ducks, 17 wild geese, 37 teal, 31 widgeon, 16 bald coots, 2 sea pheasants, 3 mews, 4 moorhens, 2 water drabs, 7 curlews, 2 bitterns, 81 woodcocks, 149 snipes, 17 wild turkeys, 18 golden plovers, 1 swan, 5 quists, 2 land rails, 13 galenas, 4 peahens, 1 peacock, 1 cuckoo, 116 pigeons, 121 larks, 1 sea magpie, 127 stares, 208 small birds, 44 turkeys, 8 capons, 19 ducks, 10 geese, 2 owls, 61 chickens, 4 ducklings, potted partridges

11 rabbits, 3 pork griskins, 11 veal burrs [sweetbreads], 1 roasting pig, hogs' puddings, ragout'd feet and ears, scotched collops [minced beef], veal cutlets, haricot'd mutton, Maintenon chops, pork chops, mutton chops, rump steaks, joint steaks, pinbone steaks, sausages, Hambro [Hamburg] sausages, tripe, cow heels and knotlings [chitterlings], 5 house lambs

3 veal legs & loins, 2 breasts & shoulders, 2 heads

5 beef rumps, 3 sirloins, 5 rounds, 2 pieces of 5 ribs each, 7 pinbones, Dutch & Hambro'd beef [hamburger]

8 mutton haunches, 8 legs, 8 necks, 11 loins, 6 saddles, 6 chines, 5 shoulders

4 pork legs, 4 loins, 4 chines, spare-ribs, half a porket

(*Cold*) 1 boar's head, 1 baron beef, 2 hams, 4 tongues, 6 chickens, hogs' feet & ears, 7 collars brawn, 2 rounds beef, collared veal [rolled and tied], collared beef, collared mutton, collared eels, collared pig's head, Dutch tongues, Bologna sausages, Paraguay pies, French pies, mutton pies, pigeon pies, venison pasty, sulks [a sort of pie?]

430 mince pies, 13 tarts, jellies, 4 pineapples.

Could our ancestors take a peep from their graves at this bill of fare, we may conceive what would be their astonishment at so great a variety and abundance of provision for travellers at a single inn...

It is not out of the way to observe that the old inns of the metropolis are daily undergoing alterations that will soon destroy their original character... There are specimens of this inn-architecture [with ancient galleried courtyards] still remaining to be observed at The Belle Sauvage, Ludgate-hill; The Saracen's Head, Snow-hill; The George and The Ram in Smithfield; The Bull & Mouth [Aldersgate-street]; The Swan With Two Necks [Gresham-street]; The Green Dragon, Bishops-gate, and a few others; not forgetting The Talbot Inn in the Borough [Southwark], from whence Chaucer's pilgrims set out...

All these inns vanished during the 19th century. A sole London survivor with a galleried courtyard is The George, Southwark.

The capriciousness of gout

THE CONTEST among medical men for the most proper mode of curing this complaint cannot but produce a smile when we recollect that the afflicted have recourse to various and opposite remedies with success. We have heard of a man who would find his pains alleviated by drinking a wineglass full of verjuice [from unripe fruit], while a tablespoonful of wine would torture him almost to distraction.

There were two counsellors some years ago who generally cured themselves in a very pleasant manner. One, who was accustomed to drink water constantly, would cure himself by drinking wine, and the other, who took his bottle or more of wine a day, was constantly cured by the use of water.

Others, by living on a milk diet only, have entirely cured themselves.

Some years ago there was a man in Italy who was particularly successful in the cure of the gout: his mode was to make his patients sweat profusely by obliging them to go up and down stairs, though with much pain to themselves.

A quack in France acquired great reputation for the cure of this malady by the use of a medicine he called Tincture of the Moon, of which he administered some drops every morning in a basin of broth. It was never used by any but the richest persons, for the price of a bottleful, not larger than a common-sized smelling-bottle, was eighty louis d'or. Antoine Furetière [1619–88, French author] mentions this quack and says he possessed many valuable secrets. He adds that the surprising cures, to which he was witness, by the Tincture of the Moon astonished all the faculty at Paris...

A choice of Oxford night-caps

IN THE EVENINGS of this cold and dreary season 'the dead of winter', a comfortable potation strengthens the heart of the healthy and cheers the spirits of the feeble... To begin, resort is now made to *Oxford Night-Caps* [1827], 'a collection of recipes for making various beverages used in the university'...

Egg-posset, alias *Egg-flip*
Otherwise, in college language, 'rum booze'

Beat up well the yolks of eight eggs with refined sugar pulverized and a nutmeg grated. Then extract the juice from the rind of a lemon by rubbing loaf sugar upon it, and put the sugar, with a piece of cinnamon and a bottle of wine, into a saucepan. Place it on the fire, and when it boils take it off, then add a single glass of cold white wine. Put the liquor into a spouted jug and pour it gradually among the yolks of eggs, &c. All must be kept well stirred with a spoon while the liquor is pouring in. If it be not sweet enough, add loaf sugar. And lastly, pour the mixture as swiftly as possible from one vessel to another until it yields a fine froth.

Half a pint of rum is sometimes added, but it is then very intoxicating and consequently pernicious. Port wine is sometimes used instead of white, but is not generally so palatable.

This beverage should be drunk about bedtime, out of wine-glasses, and while it is quite hot.

Observe that if the wine be poured boiling hot among the eggs the mixture will curdle and the posset be spoiled.

Rum Fustian

is a night-cap made precisely in the same way as the preceding, with the yolks of twelve eggs, a quart of strong home-brewed beer, a bottle of white wine, half a pint of gin, a grated nutmeg, the juice from the peel of a lemon, a small quantity of cinnamon, and sugar sufficient to sweeten it. [*Note that in old slang, 'rum' meant good, strong, etc.*]

Beer Flip

This night-cap is prepared in the same way and with the same materials as egg flip, excepting that a quart of strong home-brewed beer is substituted for the wine. A glass of gin is sometimes added, but it is better omitted.

Bishop

Make incisions in the rind of a lemon, stick cloves in the incisions and roast the lemon by a slow fire. Put small but equal quantities of cinnamon, cloves, mace and allspice, and a race of ginger, into a saucepan with half a pint of water. Let it boil until it is reduced to half. Boil a bottle of port wine, and by applying a lighted paper to the saucepan, burn a portion of the spirit out of it. Add the roasted lemon and spice unto the wine, stir all well together and let it stand near the fire ten minutes.

Rub some knobs [of sugar] on the rind of a lemon, put the sugar into a bowl or jug with the juice of half a lemon not roasted. Pour the wine upon this mixture, grate nutmeg into it, sweeten all to your taste, and you have a bishop. Serve it up with the lemon and spice floating in it. In your Oxford bishop oranges are not used; but the true London way of making a bishop is to use oranges instead of lemons.

Then come three higher-ranking variants of bishop 'which owe their origin to some Brasenose bacchanalians':

Lawn Sleeves

Proceed ... as with bishop, only substituting madeira or sherry for port wine, and adding three glasses of hot calves-feet jelly.

Cardinal

ranks higher than bishop, being made in all respects the same except that claret is substituted for port wine.

Pope

Make a bishop with champagne instead of port, and you have a pope.

How to make the genuine swig

ON ST DAVID'S DAY an immense silver-gilt bowl containing ten gallons, which was presented to Jesus College, Oxford, by Sir Watkin Williams Wynn in 1732, is filled with 'swig'...

Put into a bowl half a pound of Lisbon sugar. Pour on it a pint of warm beer. Grate into it a nutmeg and some ginger. Add four glasses of sherry and five additional pints of beer. Stir it well. Sweeten it to your taste. Let it stand covered up two or three hours, then put into it three or four slices of bread cut thin and toasted brown, and it is fit for use. A couple or three slices of lemon, and a few lumps of sugar rubbed on the peeling of a lemon, may be introduced.

Bottle the liquor, and in a few days it may be drunk in a state of effervescence.

Another pleasant tipple at Oxford is said to derive its name from one of the fair sex, a bedmaker, who invariably recommended the potation to Oxonians who availed themselves of her care...

Brown Betty

Dissolve a pound of brown sugar in a pint of water; slice a lemon into it; let it stand a quarter of an hour; then add a small quantity of powdered cloves and cinnamon, half a pint of brandy and a quart of good strong ale. Stir all well together, put into the mixture a couple of slices of toasted bread, grate some nutmeg and ginger on the toast, and you have a Brown Betty. Ice it, and you will find it excellent in summer; warm it, and it will be right comfortable in winter.

> The bowl at Jesus College is still a treasured possession, but the Saint David's swigging died out long ago. The bowl is occasionally used for other purposes; for example, as a christening font.

Air and exercise for ladies

THERE IS a notion that air spoils the complexion. It is possible that an exposure to all weathers might do so; though if a gypsy beauty is to be said to have a bad complexion, it is one we are very much inclined to be in love with. A russeton apple has its beauty as well as a peach. At all events, a spoilt complexion of this sort is accompanied with none of the melancholy attending the bad complexions that arise from late hours, and spleen, and plodding, and indolence, and indigestion. Fresh air puts a wine in the blood that lasts from morning to night and not merely for an hour or two after dinner. If ladies would not carry buttered toast in their cheeks [its colour] instead of roses they must shake the blood in their veins till it spins clear. Cheerfulness itself helps to make good blood, and air and exercise make cheerfulness.

When it is said that air spoils the complexion, it is not meant that breathing it does so, but exposure to it. We are convinced it is altogether a fallacy, and that nothing but a constant exposure to the extremes of heat and cold has any such effect. The not breathing the fresh air is confessedly injurious… We find, by repeated experiments, that we can write better and longer with the admission of air into our study. We have learnt also, by the same experience, to prefer a large study to a small one; and here the rich, it must be confessed, have another advantage over us. They pass their days in large airy rooms — in apartments that are field and champaign compared to the closets that we dignify with the name of parlours and drawing-rooms.

A gypsy and they are in this respect, and in many others, more on a footing, and the gypsy beauty and the park beauty enjoy themselves accordingly. Can we look at that extraordinary race of persons — we mean the gypsies — and not recognize the wonderful physical perfection to which they are brought solely by their exemption from some of our most inveterate notions and by dint of living constantly in the fresh air! Read any of the accounts that are given of them, even by writers the most opposed to their way of life, and you will find these very writers refuting themselves and their proposed ameliorations by confessing that no human being can be better formed or healthier or happier than the gypsies, so long as they are kept out of the way of towns and their sophistications. A suicide is not known among them… A gypsy with an eye fit for a genius it is not difficult to meet with; but where shall we find a genius, or even a fundholder, with the cheek and health of a gypsy…?

It is common with persons who inherit a good stock of health from their ancestors to argue that they take no particular pains to preserve it, and yet are well… It does not follow … that a neglect of the rational means of retaining health will ultimately be good for anybody. Healthy people may live a good while upon their stock... Nature does indeed provide liberally for abuses; but the abuse will be felt at last. It is generally felt a long while before it is acknowledged. Then comes age, with all its train of regrets and superstitions... Many a real sufferer, who is haunted by a regret or takes himself for the most ill-used of bilious old gentlemen, might trace the loftiest of his woes to no better origin than a series of ham-pies, or a want of proper use of his boots and umbrella.

From *The New Monthly Magazine.*

Gymnastics for pale Londoners

A leading figure in the revival of gymnastics in England was a German, Carl Voelker, disciple of Friedrich Jahn, who had established a gymnasium (Turnhalle) in Berlin. In the 1820s Voelker opened one near Regent's Park and another in Finsbury-square. Fees were £1 a month or less. (A Turnhalle built by his German Gymnastic Society in 1865 at St Pancras was threatened at time of writing by tracklaying plans for the Eurostar service.)
    A contributor writes in 1825:

AN INHABITANT of London need only look out of his own window to see practical illustrations of the necessity of these exercises. How often do we see a young man with an intelligent but very pale countenance, whose legs have hardly strength to support the weight of his bent and emaciated body. He once probably was a strong and active boy, but he came to London, shut himself up in an office, took no exercise because he was not obliged to take any; grew nervous and bilious; took a great deal of medical advice and physic; took everything in fact but the remedy, exercise...

Give us pure air and we can exist with comparatively little exercise; but bad air and no exercise at all are poisons...

These exercises are so contrived that they exert equally every part of the body without straining or tiring any... After two hours' practice in Professor Voelker's gymnasium, opposite Marylebone Church in the new Paddington road, I am not more fatigued than when I entered it, and feel an agreeable glow of body and flow of spirits which walking or riding does not create. I as well as some other pupils have two or three miles to walk to the gymnasium ... and we do not find that the walk and two hours of the exercises before breakfast fatigue us or incapacitate us in the slightest degree...

First, preliminary exercises of the hands and legs which give force and agility ... and prepare the body for the other exercises.

Secondly, horizontal parallel bars, from three to five feet high according to the size of the pupil, on which he raises his body by the arms and swings his legs over in a variety of directions. This exercise opens the chest and gives great strength to the muscles of the arms and body.

Thirdly, the horizontal round pole supported by posts from five to eight feet high... An endless variety of exercises may be performed on this pole, such as raising the body by the arms, going from one end to the other by the hands alone, vaulting, swinging the body over in all directions, &c, &c.

Fourthly, the horse, a large wooden block shaped like the body of a horse. The pupils jump upon and over this much-enduring animal...

Fifthly, leaping in height and distance with and without poles.

Sixthly, climbing masts, ropes and ladders of various heights.

Seventhly, throwing lances, running with celerity and for a length of time, hopping, &c, &c, &c...

The improvement which the gentlemen ... experience in health, not to mention strength, agility and grace, is very considerable, and altogether wonderful in several who have entered in a feeble and sickly state...

Voelker's pupils in action 'opposite Marylebone Church in the new Paddington road', sketched by George Cruikshank

Enough to feed the ploughmen

IT IS THE CUSTOM in the North Riding of Yorkshire, when a new tenant enters on a farm, for his neighbours to give him what is called a plough-day; that is, the use of all their ploughs and the labour of all their ploughmen and ploughshares, on a fixed day, to prepare the ground for sowing the grain. The following provision ... was actually made for such an occasion by a farmer's wife near Guisborough in 1808.

Twelve bushels of wheat were ground and made into seventeen white loaves and fifty-one dumplings. In the dumplings were forty-two pounds of currants and fourteen pounds of raisins. Seven pounds of sugar, with a proportionate quantity of vinegar and melted butter, composed the sauce for the dumplings. One hundred and ninety-six pounds of beef ... succeeded the dumplings, and to this was added two large hams and fourteen pounds of peas made into puddings.

Three large Cheshire cheeses and two home-made ones weighing twenty-eight pounds each concluded this mighty repast, which was washed down with ninety-nine gallons of ale and two of rum.

At this ploughing there were about eighty ploughs.

One-a-penny, two-a-penny

GOOD FRIDAY. A holiday at all the Public Offices.

This and Christmas Day are the only two close holidays now observed throughout London by the general shutting up of shops and the opening of all the churches. The dawn is awakened by a cry in the streets of 'Hot-cross-buns, one-a-penny buns, two-a-penny buns, one-a-penny, two-a-penny, hot-cross-buns!' This proceeds from some peep-o'-day boy willing to take the 'top of the morning' before the rest of his compeers. He carries his covered buns in a basket hanging on one arm, while his other hand is straightened like an open door at the side of his mouth to let forth his childish voice... Scarcely has he departed before others come; 'another and another still succeeds', and at last the whole street is in one 'common cry of *buns*'...

The bun-vendors who eclipse the rest in voice and activity are young women who drove fruit-barrows — barrows, by the by, are no more, but of them by-and-by [*see next page*]. A couple of these ex-barrow-women trip along, carrying a wicker clothes-basket between them, in which the hot-cross-buns are covered, first by a clean flannel or green baize, and outwardly by a clean white cloth, which coverings are slowly and partially removed, for fear of letting the buns cool, when a customer stops to buy or calls them to the door... These scenes and sounds continue till church-time, and resume in the afternoon...

Some thirty or forty years ago pastrycooks and bakers vied with each other for excellence in making hot-cross-buns. The demand has decreased, and so has the quality of the buns. But the great place of attraction for bun-eaters at that time was Chelsea, for *there* were the two '*royal* bun-houses'... Several hundreds of square black tins, with dozens of hot buns in each tin, were disposed of in every hour from a little after six in the morning till after the same period in the evening of Good Friday. Those who knew what was good ... gave the preference to the 'old *original* royal bun-house' [*in the fields of Pimlico; demolished 1839*], which had been a bun-house 'ever since it was a house' and at which 'the king himself once stopped', and who could say as much for the other?

Cherries! Rare ripe cherries!

It is July 1825...

THIS IS CHERRY SEASON, but it is not to me as cherry seasons were. I like a great deal that *is*, but I have an affection for what *was*.. Bygone days seem to have been more fair than these... I have lived through the extremity of one age into the beginning of another, and I believe a better; yet the former has been too much detracted. Everything new is not therefore good, nor was everything old, bad.

When I was a boy, I speak of just after the French revolution broke out, my admiration and taste were pure and natural, and one of my favourites at all times, and in cherry-time especially, was the London barrow-woman. There are no barrow-women now. They are quite 'gone out', or rather they have been put down, and by many they are not even missed. Look around: there is not one to be seen.

In those days there were *women* on the earth: finely grown, every way well-proportioned, handsome, and in stature like Mrs Sarah Sid-dons [the actress]. I speak of London women. Let not the ladies of the metropolis conceive offence if I maintain that some of their mothers, and more among their grandmothers, were taller and more robust than they... They have declined in personal elevation as they have increased in moral elevation.

At that time lived the London barrow-woman... On her legs were 'women's blacks', or in dry sunny weather ... stockings of white cotton, with black high-heeled shoes and a pair of bright sparkling buckles. Tight lacing distended her hips, which were further enlarged by her flowered cotton or chintz gown being drawn through the

pocket-holes to balloon out behind, and display a quilted glazed petticoat of black or pink stuff, terminating about four inches above the
ankles. She wore on her bosom, which was not so confined as to injure
its fullness, a light gauze or muslin kerchief. This was her full dress as
she rolled through the street and cried —

> Round and sound,
> Twopence a pound,
> Cherries! Rare ripe cherries!

'Green and ripe gooseberries! Amber-berries! Ripe amber-berries!
Currants! Rare ripe currants!' Ending as she began with cherries —

> Cherries a ha'penny a stick!
> Come and pick, come and pick!
> Cherries big as plums!
> Who comes? Who comes?

Each side of her well-laden barrow was dressed nearly halfway along
with a row of sticks having cherries tied on them. To assist in retailing
her other fruit, there lay before her a 'full alehouse measure' of clean
pewter and a pair of shining brass scales with thick turn-over

Mr George Cruikshank ... whose close observation of
passing manners is unrivalled by any artist of the day,
has sketched the barrow-woman for *The Every-Day
Book* from his own recollection of her, aided somewhat
by my own. It is engraved on wood by Mr Henry White.

rims and leaden weights, for the 'real black-hearts' that dyed the white cloth they lay on with purple stains.

If she had an infant, she was sometimes met with it at a particular spot for her to suckle. She was then a study for a painter. Her hearty caresses of her child while she hastily sat down on the arm of her barrow and bared her bountiful bosom to give it nourishment; the frolic with which she tickled it; the tenderness with which she looked into its young upturned eyes while the bland fluid overflowed its laughing mouth; her smothering kisses upon its crowing lips after its nurture; and her loud affectionate 'God bless it!' when it was carried away, were indescribably beautiful...

With the rolling year she rolled round to us its successive fruits, but cherry-time was the meridian of her glory. Her clear and confident cry was then listened for, in the distance, with as much anxiety to hear it as the proclamation of a herald... 'What can keep the barrow-woman so long? — Surely she has not gone another way! — Hush! There she is, I hear her!' ...Good housewives and servants came to the doors with basins and dishes... As she slowly trundled her barrow along the pavement, what doting looks were cast upon its delicacies by boys with ever-ready appetites! How he who had nothing to lay out envied him whom a halfpenny entitled to a perplexing choice...!

Before barrow-women quite 'went out', the poor things were sadly used. If they stopped to rest or pitched their seat of custom where customers were likely to pass, street-keepers, authorized by orders unauthorized by law, drove them off, or beadles overthrew their fruit into the road. At last an act of parliament [1817] made it penal to roll a wheel or keep a stand for the sale of any articles upon the pavement...

Fruit-stalls are not wholly extinct. A few, very few, still exist by mere sufferance... Ah! what a goodly sight was Holborn-hill in '*my* time'. Then there was a comely row of fruit-stalls skirting the edge of the pavement from opposite the steps of St Andrew's Church to the corner of Shoe-lane. The fruit stood on tables covered with white cloths and placed end to end in one long line. In autumn it was a lovely sight...

First, of the pears, came the 'ripe Kat'er'nes'. These were succeeded by 'fine Windsors' and 'real bergamys'. Apples came in with 'green codlins'; then followed golden rennets, golden pippins and ripe nonpareils. These were the common street-fruits. Such golden pippins as were then sold three and four for a halfpenny are now worth pence apiece, and the true golden rennet can only be heard of at great fruiterers. The decrease in the growth of this delightful apple is one of the 'signs of the times'!

The finest apples in Covent Garden market come from Kent.

Growers in that county, by leaving only a few branches upon the tree, produce the most delicious kinds, of a surprisingly large size. For these they demand and obtain very high prices. But instead of London in general being supplied, as it was formerly, with the best apples, little else is seen except swine-feed, or French or American apples. The importations of this fruit are very large, and under the almost total disappearance of some of our finest sorts, very thankful we are to get inferior ones of foreign growth.

Englishmen at their full pots

FROM THE WASSAIL we derive perhaps a feature by which we are distinguished. An Englishman eats no more than a Frenchman, but he makes yuletide of all the year. In virtue of his forefathers he is given to strong drink. He is a beer-drinker, an enjoyer of 'fat ale', a lover of the best London porter and double-XX, and discontented unless he can get stout. He is a sitter withal. Put an Englishman 'behind a pipe' and a full pot and he will sit on until he cannot stand.

At first he is silent, but as his liquor gets towards the bottom he inclines towards conversation. As he replenishes, his coldness thaws and he is conversational. The oftener he calls to 'fill again' the more talkative he becomes; and when thoroughly liquefied, his loquacity is deluging. He is thus in public-house parlours; he is in parties some-what higher much the same. The business of dinner draws on the greater business of drinking, and the potations are strong and fiery: full-bodied port, hot sherry and ardent spirits. The occupation consumes five or six hours and sometimes more after dining. There is no rising from it but to toss off the glass and 'huzza' after the 'hip! hip! hip!' of the toast-giver.

A calculation of the number who customarily 'dine out' in this manner would be very amusing, if it were illustrated by portraits of some of the indulgers. It might be further, and more usefully, though not so agreeably, illustrated by the reports of physicians, wives and nurses, and the bills of apothecaries. Habitual sitting to drink is the besetting sin of Englishmen — the creator of their gout and palsy, the embitterer of their enjoyments, the impoverisher of their property, the widow-maker of their wives.

By continuing the wassail of our ancestors we attempt to cultivate the body as they did, but we are other beings, cultivated in other ways, with faculties and powers of mind that would have astonished their generations more than their robust frames, if they could appear, would astonish ours. Their employment was in hunting their forests for food, or battling in armour with risk of life and limb. They had no counting-houses, no ledgers, no commerce, no Christmas bills, no letter-writing, no printing, no engraving, no bending over the desk, no 'wasting of the midnight oil' and the brain together, no financing, not a hundredth part of the relationships in society nor of the cares that *we* have, who wassail as they did, and wonder we are not so strong as they were…

And a Scot at work on his port

A legal wonder, found in Robert Chambers's *Traditions of Edinburgh*, 1825:

THE LATE LORD NEWTON was one of the ablest lawyers, and profoundest drinkers, of his day. He had a body of immense breadth, width and depth, which could hold (without affecting in the least degree the broad, wide and deep head attached to it) six bottles of port. He was never so able to do business as after drinking that enormous quantity of liquor. Upon one occasion, after having dined with two friends and, to use his own phrase, drunk them both under the table, he dictated to his clerk a law-paper of sixty pages, which that gentleman has since declared to be one of the ablest and clearest he had ever known his lordship to produce.

Where drunkards go

A Scotch pastor recognized one of his female parishioners sitting by the side of the road, a little fuddled. 'Will you just help me up with my bundle, gude mon?' said she as he stopped.

'Fie, fie, Janet,' cried the pastor, 'to see the like o' you in sic a plight. Do you know where all drunkards *go*?'

'Ay, sure,' said Janet, 'they just go whar a drop o' gude drink is to be got.'

To sleep well in cold weather

OBTAIN a free circulation of the blood by walking or other wholesome exercise so as to procure a gentle glow over the entire surface of the body. Hasten to your chamber, undress yourself quickly and jump into bed without suffering its temperature to be heightened by the machine called a warming-pan. Your bed will be warmed by your own heat, and if you have not eaten a meat supper or drunk spirits you will sleep well and warm all night.

DECEMBER

While I have a home and can do as I will,
December may rage over ocean and hill
And batter my door — as he does once a year.
I laugh at his storming and give him good cheer.

Derry down, &c —

I've a trencher and cup, and something to ask
A friend to sit down to, and then a good flask.
The best of all methods to make winter smile
Is living as I do — in old English style.

Derry down, &c —

Now whoever regards a comfortable fire in an oldfashioned cottage as
a pleasant sight will be pleased by this sketch as a cheerful illustration
of the dreary season... The artist who drew and engraved it is Mr
Samuel Williams. [*The song is by Hone.*]

Burns's douce couthie tavern

Just before a noted Edinburgh tavern, Johnnie Dowie's, was demolished in 1831, a drawing of it by the artist Walter Geikie (1795–1837) was sent to Hone by an Edinburgh man, with some memories:

I HAVE SENT YOU a sketch of a tavern which, for the last quarter of the last century, was the resort of all the revelling wits of our Gude Town. Robert Burns was one of its constant — poor fellow, too constant — frequenters; so much so that when he died his name was assumed as its distinguishing and alluring cognomen. Until it was finally closed lately, previous to being taken down (it being immediately in the line of the new South Bridge), it was visited nightly by many a party of jolly fellows, whose admiration of the poet, or more probably, whose predilection for the 'gusty viver' [tasty food] and exhilarating potions which were ministered to them, drew them, nothing loth, to its 'douce couthie cosy canty ingles'.

Few strangers omitted to call in to gaze at the *coffin* of the bard — this was a small dark room which could barely accommodate, even by squeezing, half a dozen, but in which Burns used to sit. Here he composed one or two or his best songs, and here were preserved to the last the identical seats and table which had accommodated him...

Long gone: Dowie's Tavern, in a steep lane called Libberton's Wynd

Turning to Robert Chambers's Traditions of Edinburgh, *1825, Hone adds*: Dowie's was one of the most popular taverns of its day, and much resorted to by the Lords of Session... The ale was Younger's. That brewer, together with John Gray, city-clerk of Edinburgh; Mr John Buchan, writer to the Signet; David Martin [1736–98], the celebrated portrait-painter and the master of Sir Henry Raeburn, and some others instituted a club here...

Johnnie Dowie was the sleekest and kindest of landlords. Nothing could equal the benignity of his smile when he brought in a bottle of 'the ale' to a company of well-known and friendly customers. It was a perfect treat to see his formality in drawing the cork, his precision in filling the glasses, his regularity in drinking the healths of all present in the first glass (which he always did, and in every successive bottle) and then his *douce* civility in withdrawing. Johnnie lived till within the last few years, and with laudable attachment to the old costume always wore a cocked hat and buckles at knees and shoes, as well as a cane with a cross top, somewhat like an implement called by Scottish gardeners 'a dibble'.

Of the Edinburgh brewing clan, it was Archibald Campbell Younger (1757–1819) who about 1778 developed a strong ale which the benign Johnnie Dowie did much to promote. Other notable drinkers at the tavern were Raeburn himself, Adam Smith and the song-collector David Herd. The renaming of the tavern was in fact only after Dowie died in 1817.

Christmas doughs, pies and porridge

YULE-DOUGH, or *dow*, a kind of baby or little image of paste, was formerly baked at Christmas and presented by bakers to their customers, in the same manner as the chandlers gave Christmas candles. They are called yule cakes in the county of Durham...

Anciently, 'at Rome on the vigil of the nativity *sweetmeats* were presented to the fathers in the Vatican, and all kinds of little images ... were to be found in the confectioners' shops'. John Brand, who mentions these usages, thinks 'there is the greatest probability that we have had from thence both our yule-doughs, plum-porridge and mince-pies, the latter of which are still in common use...'

According to John Selden's *Table Talk*, the coffin shape of our Christmas pies is in imitation of the *cratch* or manger wherein the infant Jesus was laid... In Henri Misson's *Travels in England* , he says, 'Every family against Christmas makes a famous pie, which they call Christmas pie. It is a great nostrum. The composition of this pasty is a most learned mixture of neat's-tongues, chicken, eggs, sugar, raisins, lemon and orange peel, various kinds of spicery, &c.' The most notably familiar poet of our seasonable customs [Robert Herrick] interests himself for its safety:

> Come guard this night the Christmas pie
> That the thief, though ne'er so sly,
> With his flesh-hooks don't come nigh
>> To catch it

> From him who all alone sits there,
> Having his eyes still in his ear
> And a deal of nightly fear
>> To watch it.

Mr Brand observes of his own knowledge that 'in the north of England a goose is always the chief ingredient in the composition of a Christmas pie'; and to illustrate the usage 'further north', he quotes that the Scottish poet Allan Ramsay, in his 'Elegy on Lucky Wood' [an alehouse keeper], tells us that among other baits by which the good alewife drew customers to her house, she never failed to tempt them at Yule with *a bra goose pie* ...

Misson adds of our predecessors in his time [late 17th century] that besides the 'famous pie' at Christmas 'they also make a sort of soup with plums which is not at all inferior to the pie, which is in their language called plum-porridge'.

Lastly, Mr Brand makes this important note... 'Memorandum: I dined at the chaplain's table at St James's [Palace] on Christmas day, 1801, and partook of the first thing served and eaten on that festival at that table, *i.e.* a tureen full of rich luscious plum-porridge. I do not know that the custom is anywhere else retained.'

Blackbirds, and more, baked in a pie

THE FOLLOWING appeared in *The Newcastle Chronicle*, 6th Jan. 1770:

Monday last was brought from Howick to Berwick, to be shipp'd for London for Sir Hen. Grey, Bart, a pie, the contents whereof are as follows: viz 2 bushels of flour, 20 lbs of butter, 4 geese, 2 turkeys, 2 rabbits, 4 wild ducks, 2 woodcocks, 6 snipes, 4 partridges, 2 neats' tongues, 2 curlews, 7 blackbirds and 6 pigeons.

It is supposed a very great curiosity; was made by Mrs Dorothy Patterson, housekeeper at Howick [*still the Grey estate*]. It was near nine feet in circumference at bottom, weighs about twelve stones [168lb, 76 kilograms], will take two men to present it to table. It is neatly fitted with a case, and four small wheels to facilitate its use to every guest that inclines to partake of its contents at table.

Mighty boars for Christmas

Now was the last loud squeaking roar
Of many a mighty forest boar,
Whose head, when came the Christmas days,
Was crowned with rosemary and bays,
And so brought in with shoutings long,
And minstrelsy and choral song.

Hone

In search of
the country

SUMMER

Now cometh welcome summer with great strength,
    Joyously smiling in high lustihood,
Conferring on us days of longest length
    For rest or labour, in town, field or wood;
Offering to our gathering richest stores
    Of varied herbage, corn, cool fruits, and flowers...
    To fill our homesteads, and to deck our bowers.   *Hone*

A walk into another air

It is May 1827. Hone, confined for debt, is granted enough liberty from the King's Bench Prison to set off from Southwark with his chief artist, engraver and friend, Samuel Williams, into what was then the green countryside of Penge, Beckenham, West Wickham and Hayes.

A COACHMAN hailed us from the box of a Dulwich stage. We gave him an assenting nod and mounted the roof [cheaper seats there], and after a brisk drive through Walworth and Camberwell, which are now no other way distinguishable from the metropolis than by the irregular forms and sizes of the houses and the bits of sickly grass and bottle-green poplars that further diversify them, we attained to the sight of the first out-of-town-looking trees and verdure on the ascent towards Herne Hill. Here we began to feel another air; and during the calm drive down the hill into Dulwich — the prettiest of all the village entrances in the environs of London — we had glimpses between the elms and sycamores of pleasant lawns and blooming gardens, with bursts of the fine distances...

Beyond Dulwich, they walk: We reached the summit of the hill and found a direction-post that pointed us to a choice of several roads. We strolled into one leading to Penge Common through enclosed woodlands. Our ears were charmed by throngs of sweet singing birds. We were in a cathedral of the feathered tribes...

> Chiefs of the choir, and highest in the heavens,
> As emulous to join the angels' songs,
> Were soaring larks, and some had dared so far
> They seem'd like atoms sailing in the light.
> Their voices and themselves were scarce discern'd
> Above their comrades, who in lower air
> Hung buoyant, brooding melody, that fell
> Streaming and gushing on our thirsty ears.... *Anonymous*

A gate in the road was opened to us by a poor woman... She had the care of collecting the toll from horsemen and carriage-drivers. We were foot-passengers, and credited our tailors for the civility [*although mere pedestrians, they were decently dressed*]. At a few yards beyond this turnpike we stopped to read a dictatorial intimation: 'All trespassers on these woods will be prosecuted, and the constables have orders to take them into custody.' ...The land had been open to all till spoliation deprived the commoners of their ancient right and annexed the common soil to a neighbouring domain...

I look around, and cottages have disappeared, and there are villas instead; and the workhouses are enlarged, and instead of labour, treadmills are provided. According to a political economist of ancient times, 'There is much food in the tillage of the poor,' and 'He that maketh haste to be rich shall not be innocent.' To whom of old was it said, 'The spoil of the poor is in your houses'?

We lingered on our way, and passed a bridge over the [Croydon] canal towards a well-looking public-house called The Old Crooked Billet... The landlord and his family were at dinner in a commodious, respectable bar... We found from his notable dame that we could have eggs and bacon, and spinach put into the pot from the garden, in a few minutes. Nothing could have been suggested more suitable to our inclination, and we had the pleasure of being smiled into a comfortable parlour with a bow-window view of the common... The house affords as 'good accommodation for man and horse' as can be found in any retired spot so near London. Our stroll to it was delightful...

The Old Crooked Billet (replaced by a new building
in 1840, but the inn's name survives)

Sylvan reverie by a stickleback brook

ON OUR WAY from Penge, Williams thought this object worth sketching. He occupied himself with his pencil, and I amused myself with dropping grains of dust among a fleet of tadpoles on the yellow sands, and watching their motions. A few inches from them, in a clearer shallow, lay a shoal of sticklebacks as on their Dogger Bank. A thread and a bloodworm, and the absence of my friend and of certain feelings on behalf of the worms, would have afforded me excellent sport...

I fell into a reverie on Wilson's magnificent painting of the falls of Niagara, in Mr Landseer's painting-room. While I seated myself by the wayside and, among ground-ivy and periwinkle discriminating the diminutive forms of trees in the varied mosses of an old bank, I recollected descriptions I had read of transatlantic scenery, and the gigantic vegetation on the Ohio and the Mississippi.

A labourer told us that this little brook is called Chaffinch's River and that it springs from 'the Alders' near Croydon, and runs into the Ravensbourne. [*The bridge is long gone; the brook survives*.]

A rustic cage, a 'beautified' church

THE PARISH of Beckenham ... according to the last census contains 196 houses and 1,180 inhabitants. The living is a rectory valued in the king's books at £6 18s 9d...

Beyond Chaffinch's River there is an enticing fieldpath to Beckenham, but occasional sights of noble trees kept us along the high road, till the ring of the blacksmith's hammer signalled that we were close upon the village ... two or three old farmlike-looking houses, rudely encroached upon by a number of irregularly built dwellings, and a couple of inns... We soon came to an edifice which ... startles the feelings of the passenger in this as in almost every other parish, and

The church 'pinnacling this pleasant grove' (demolished 1885)

has perhaps a greater tendency to harden than reform the rustic offender — the 'cage' [*for publicly exposing lawbreakers*], with its accessory, the pound. An angular turn of the road from these lodgings for men and cattle when they go astray afforded us a sudden and delightful view of

> The decent church that tops the neighb'ring hill.

On the right, an old, broad, high wall flanked with thick buttresses and belted with magnificent trees climbs the steep, to enclose the domain of I know not whom. On the opposite side, the branches from a plantation arch beyond the footpath. At the summit of the ascent is the village church with its whitened spire, crowning and pinnacling this pleasant grove, pointing from amidst the graves — like man's last only hope — towards heaven...

The woman 'who has the care of the church' ... gladly accompanied us, with the keys clinking, through the mournful yewtree grove and threw open the great south doors of the church. It is an old edifice — despoiled of its ancient font — deprived by former beautifyings of carvings and tombs that in these times would have been remarkable... [*The font, removed by a churchwarden, was seen by Hone in the garden of The Old Crooked Billet, Penge.*]

Fixed against the northern corner of the west end is a plate of copper bearing an inscription to this import:

> Mary Wragg of St John's, Westminster, bequeathed £15 per annum forever to the curate of Beckenham in trust for the following uses, viz, a guinea to himself for his trouble in taking care that her family vault should be kept in good repair; a guinea to be expended in a dinner for himself, the clerk and parish officers; £12 10s to defray the expenses of such repairs; if in any year the vault should not require repair, the money to be laid out in eighteen pennyworth of good bread, five shillings worth of coals and 4s 6d in money, to be given to each of twenty of the poorest inhabitants of the parish. If repairs should be required, the money left to be laid out in like manner...

Her vault in the churchyard is properly maintained, and distribution made of beef, bread and money every 28th of January... As many as please go down into the vault, and the parochial authorities of Beckenham have a holiday and 'keep wassel'...

Hone and Williams visit the key-keeper, a widow aged over eighty:

Finding she brewed her own beer with the common utensils and fireplace of her little room, we asked her to describe her method. A tin kettle is her boiler, she mashes in a common butter-firkin, runs off the liquor in a 'crock' and tuns it in a small-beer barrel. She is of opinion that 'poor people might do a great deal for themselves if they knew how. *But,*' says she, 'where there's a *will*, there's a *way*.'

Ancient lichgate, ancient yews

Beyond the lichgate stand ten ancient yews,
Branching so high they seem like giant mutes
With plumes, awaiting rich men's funerals
And poor men's buryings — stretching over all
An arch of triumph for Death's victories.   *Hone*

OVER THE WICKETS to many of the churchyards in Kent is a shed or covered way, of ancient structure, used as a resting-place for funerals and for the shelter of the corpse until the minister arrives to commence the service for the dead. This at Beckenham is the most perfect in the county. The footway beyond to the great entrance-door of the church is canopied by a grove of trees, 'sad sociate to graves'.

These old churchyard buildings, now only seen in villages, were formerly called lichgates, and the paths to them were called lichlanes or lichways. The word lich signified a corpse. Hence the death-owl was anciently called the lich-owl... [*The lichgate and yews survive.*]

An unlucky baptismal slop-basin

FROM BECKENHAM CHURCH we walked about two miles along a nearly straight road ... till we reached West Wickham... The manor-house [Wickham Court] and church are distant from the village about half a mile, with an intervening valley beautifully pleasant, in which is a road from Hayes Common to Addington and Croydon...

[In the church] are many ancient figured tiles sadly neglected, loose in the pavement, some displaced and lying one upon the other. Worst of all ... the ancient stone font, which is in all respects perfect, has been removed from its original situation and is thrown into a corner. In its place, at the west end, from a nick (not a niche) between the seats a little trivet-like iron bracket swings in and out, and upon it is a wooden hand-bowl such as scullions use in a kitchen sink, and in this hand-bowl of about twelve inches diameter, called a font, I found a common blue-and-white Staffordshire-ware halfpint basin. It might be there still; but while inveighing to my friend Williams against the deprivation of the fine old font and the substitution of such a paltry modicum, in my vehemence I fractured the crockery... Perhaps I sinned; but I made restitution beyond the extent that would replace the baptismal slop-basin.

The fragments of old painted glass in the windows of this church are really fine. The best are St Anne teaching the virgin to read; whole-lengths of St Christopher wading, with the infant Saviour bearing the globe in his hand; an elderly female saint, very good; and a skeleton with armour before him... [The glass survives.]

Wildlife for weather forecasting

It was in the 1850s that public forecasts made a modest start. Even with our present wide-reaching service, some of these hints may be locally useful.

WHEN THE RAVEN is observed early in the morning at a great height in the air, soaring round and round and uttering a hoarse croaking sound, we may be sure the day will be fine...

The loud and clamorous quackling of ducks, geese and other water-fowl is a sign of rain. Before rain, swine appear very uneasy and rub in the dust, as do cocks and hens.

Before storms, kine and also sheep assemble at one corner of the field and are observed to turn all their heads toward the quarter from whence the wind doth not blow...

In fine weather the bat is observed to continue flying about very late of an evening...

The clamorous croaking of frogs indicates rainy weather.

The appearance of beetles flying about of an evening in summer indicates that the next day will be fair.

Before rain, dogs are apt to grow very sleepy and dull, and to lie all day before the fire... Moles throw up the earth more than usual...

When spiders are seen crawling on the walls more than usual, rain will probably ensue.

The much barking of dogs in the night frequently indicates a change in the weather.

When the trees and hedges are very full of berries it indicates a hard winter.

The abundance of woodsear ['cuckoo-spit'] and honeydew on herbs indicates fair weather, as does floating gossamer.

It is said in Wiltshire that the dunpickles or moor buzzards alight in great numbers on the downs before rain.

Before storms the missel-thrush is observed to sing particularly loud and to continue so till the commencement of the rain... It is in some places called the stormcock.

It is a sign of rain when pigeons return slowly to the dovehouses.

When bees do not go out as usual but keep in or about their hives, rain may be expected.

Before wind, swine run squeaking about as though they were mad, which has given rise to the notion that pigs can see the wind.

Before rain the pintados called come-backs [guinea-fowl] squall more than usual; as do peacocks...

When the dew lies plenteously upon the grass in the evening, the next day will probably be fine; when there is little or no dew, probably wet.

Spiders' gossamer barometers

IF THE WEATHER is likely to become windy or in other respects disagreeable, spiders fix the terminating filaments, on which the whole web is suspended, unusually short. If the terminating filaments are made uncommonly long the weather will be serene, and continue so at least for ten or twelve days.

If spiders be totally indolent, rain generally succeeds; though their activity during rain is certain proof that it will be only of short duration and followed by fair and constant weather.

Spiders usually make some alterations in their webs every twenty-four hours. If these changes take place between the hours of six and seven in the evening they indicate a clear and pleasant night.

Flowers to tempt the maid

APRIL

With thee all nature finds a voice
And hums a waking song.
The lover views thy welcome hours
And thinks of summer come,
And takes the maid thy early flowers
To tempt her steps from home.

John Clare, *The Shepherd's Calendar*

Over lovers' stiles to sweet fieldpaths

A contribution from 'a respected friend':

I LOVE our real old English footpaths. I love those rustic and picturesque stiles, opening their pleasant escapes from frequented places
and dusty highways into the solitudes of nature. It is delightful to
catch a glimpse of one on the village green, under the old elder-tree by
some ancient cottage, or half-hidden by the overhanging boughs of a
wood. I love to see the smooth dry track winding away in easy curves
along some green slope to the churchyard, to the embosomed cottage
or to the forest grange.

It is to me an object of certain inspiration. It seems to invite one
from noise and publicity into the heart of solitude and of rural
delights. It beckons the imagination on, through green and whispering
cornfields, through the short but verdant pasture, the flowery
mowing-grass, the odorous and sunny hayfield, the festivity of
harvest; from lovely farm to farm; from village to village, by clear and
mossy wells, by tinkling brooks and deep wood-skirted streams; to
crofts where the daffodil is rejoicing in spring, or meadows where the
large blue geranium embellishes the summer wayside; to heaths, with
their warm, elastic sward and crimson bells, the chithering of grass-
hoppers, the foxglove, and the old gnarled oak; in short, to all the
solitary haunts after which the city-pent lover of nature pants as 'the
hart panteth after the water-brooks'.

What is there so truly English? What is so linked with our rural
tastes, our sweetest memories and our sweetest poetry as stiles and
fieldpaths? Goldsmith, Thomson and Milton have adorned them with
some of their richest wreaths. They have consecrated them to poetry
and love. It is along the footpath in secluded fields — upon the stile in
the embowered lane — where the wild rose and the honeysuckle are
lavishing their beauty and their fragrance, that we delight to picture
to ourselves rural lovers, breathing, in the dewy sweetness of a
summer evening, vows still sweeter. It is there that the poet, seated,
sends back his soul into the freshness of his youth among attach-
ments since withered by neglect, rendered painful by absence or
broken by death...

Again I say, I love fieldpaths and stiles of all species — ay, even the
most inaccessible piece of rustic erection ever set up in defiance of age,
laziness and obesity. How many scenes of frolic and merry confusion
have I seen at a clumsy stile! What exclamations, and charming
blushes, and fine eventual vaulting on the part of the ladies, and what
an opportunity does it afford to beaux of exhibiting a variety of gallant

and delicate attentions. I consider a rude stile as anything but an impediment in the course of a rural courtship.

Those good old turnstiles too — can I ever forget them? The hours I have spun round upon them when a boy; or those in which I have almost laughed myself to death at the remembrance of my village pedagogue's disaster! Methinks I see him now. The time a sultry day; the dominie a godly person of some eighteen or twenty stone; the scene a footpath sentinelled with turnstiles, one of which held him fast, as in utter amazement at his bulk. Never shall I forget his efforts and agonies to extricate himself, nor his lion-like roars, which brought some labourers to his assistance, who when they had recovered from their convulsions of laughter knocked off the top and let him go...

But, without a jest, stiles and footpaths are vanishing everywhere. There is nothing upon which the advance of wealth and population has made so serious an inroad. As land has increased in value, wastes and heaths have been parcelled out and enclosed, but seldom have footpaths been left. The poet and the naturalist, who before had perhaps the greatest *real* property on them, have had no allotment... Nor is this all. Goldsmith complained in his day [*Deserted Village*, 1770] —

> The man of wealth and pride
> Takes up a space that many poor supplied;
> Space for his lake, his park's extended bounds;
> Space for his horses, equipage and hounds.
> The robe that wraps his limbs in silken sloth
> Has robbed the neighbouring fields of half their growth;
> His seat, where solitary sports are seen,
> Indignant spurns the cottage from the green.

And it is but too true that 'the pressure of contiguous pride' has driven farther and farther, from that day to this, the public from the rich man's lands... Even the quiet and picturesque footpath that led across his lawn or stole along his woodside, giving to the poor man with his burden a cooler and a nearer cut to the village, is become a nuisance. One would have thought that the rustic labourer with his scythe on his shoulder or his billhook and hedging mittens in his hand, the cottage dame in her black bonnet and scarlet cloak, the bonny village maiden in the sweetness of health and simplicity, or the boy strolling along full of life and curiosity, might have had sufficient interest in themselves, for a cultivated taste, passing occasionally at a distance across the park or lawn, not only to be tolerated but even to be welcomed as objects agreeably enlivening the stately solitude of the hall. But they have not.

And what is more, *they* are commonly the most jealous of pedestrian trespassers who seldom visit their own estates... How often have

I myself been arrested in some long-frequented dale ... by a board exhibiting, in giant characters, *Stopped by an order of Sessions*! and denouncing the terms of the law upon trespassers. This is a little too much. I would not be querulous for the poor against the rich. I would not teach them to look with an envious and covetous eye upon their villas, lawns, cattle and equipage; but when the path of immemorial usage is closed, when the little streak, almost as fine as a mathematical line, along the wealthy man's ample field is grudgingly erased, it is impossible not to feel indignation at the pitiful monopoly.

Is there no village champion to be found bold enough to put in his protest against these encroachments, to assert this public right — for a right it is, as authentic as that by which the land itself is held, and as clearly acknowledged by the laws? Is there no local 'Hampden with dauntless breast' to 'withstand the little tyrant of the fields' and to save our good old footpaths? If not, we shall in a few years be doomed to the highways and the hedges... Already the stranger, if he lose his way, is in jeopardy of falling into the horrid fangs of a steel-trap; the botanist enters a wood to gather a flower and is shot with a spring-gun; death haunts our dells and copses...

Exactly in the same proportion as our population and commercial habits gain upon us do we need all possible opportunities to keep alive in us the spirit of nature.

> The world is too much with us. Late and soon,
> Getting and spending, we lay waste our powers.
> Little there is in nature that is ours.   *Wordsworth*

...Whenever, therefore, I behold one of our old fieldpaths closed, I regard it as another link in the chain which Mammon is winding around us...

steel-traps and spring-guns: deadly devices planted by landowners at the edge of their estates to deter poachers; banned in 1828 after a long struggle.

Miseries of travel: steam v coach

Steam disasters were in the news. A contributor calling himself Gaspard puts them in perspective — opening with lines from Byron's *Don Juan*:

> *Now there is nothing gives a man such spirits,*
> *Leavening his blood as cayenne doth a curry,*
> *As going at full speed ————*

IF THE NUMBER of persons who have been killed, maimed and disfigured for life in consequence of stagecoach *mishaps* could be ascertained, since the first establishment of steam-packets in this country, and on the other hand the number who have been similarly unfortunate by steam-boilers bursting, we should find that the stage-coach proportion would be in the ratio of ten to one! A solitary 'blow-up' of a steam-packet is noised and proclaimed from the Land's End to the other extremity of the island; while hundreds of coach accidents, and many of them fatal, occur which are never heard of beyond the village near to which the casualty takes place, or the neighbouring alehouse.

These affairs it is to the interest of the proprietors to hush up... Should a poor man have a leg or an arm broken through the careless-ness of a drunken coachman ... an arrangement between him and the proprietors is easily effected, the unfortunate fellow rather receiving fifty or a hundred pounds 'hush money' than bring his action, when perhaps from some technical informality in the proceedings (should he find a lawyer willing to act for him, being *poor*) he would be nonsuited, with all the costs of both parties on his own shoulders...

These remarks were suggested by reading an American work some time since on the above subject, from which I have extracted the following —

Stagecoach Adventures

INSIDE   Crammed full of passengers — three fat, fusty old men — a young mother and sick child — a cross old maid — a poll-parrot — a bag of red herrings — double-barrelled gun (which you are afraid is loaded) — and a snarling lapdog, in addition to yourself. — Awaking out of a sound nap with the cramp in one leg and the other in a lady's band-box — pay the damage (four or five shillings) for 'gallantry's sake'. — Getting out in the dark at the halfway house [for change of coaches] — in the hurry stepping into the return coach and finding yourself the next morning at the very spot you had started from the evening before — Not a breath of air — asthmatic old man, and child with the measles — windows closed in consequence — unpleasant smell —shoes filled with warm water — look up and find it's the child — obliged to bear it — no appeal — shut your eyes and scold the dog — pretend sleep, and pinch the child — mistake, pinch the dog, and get bit — execrate the child in return — black looks, 'no gentleman'. — Pay the coachman and drop a piece of gold in the straw — not to be found... Get laughed at — lose your temper — turn sulky — and turned over in a horse-pond.

OUTSIDE [on top of the coach]   Your eye cut out by the lash of a clumsy coachman's whip — hat blown off into a pond by a sudden gust of wind. — Seated between two apprehended murderers and a noted sheep-stealer in irons who are being conveyed to jail. — A drunken fellow, half asleep, falls off the coach, and in attempting to save himself drags you along with him into the mud. — Musical guard, and driver 'horn mad'. — Turned over — one leg under a bale of cotton, the other under the coach — hands in breeches pockets, head in a hamper of wine... Send for surgeon — wounds dressed — lotion and lint four dollars — take postchaise — get home — lie down — and laid up...

A springtime walk to the Surrey hills

A poetic reader in Southwark describes an early April excursion.

A FEW MORNINGS AGO, taking with me a certain talisman with his majesty's head thereon, I bent my steps through the now populous town of Walworth ... through Camberwell... [and then to Herne Hill], the Elysium of many of our merchants and traders, whose dwellings look the abodes of happy mortals...

> O how blest is he who here
> Can calmly end life's wild career...
> Losing in this peaceful spot
> Memory of his former lot.
> And O, how happy were it mine
> To build me here, ere life decline,
> A cot 'mid these sequestered grounds,
> With every year three hundred pounds.

Gentlemen of Herne Hill, I envy you — but I am not a money-getting man, so it is useless to wish for such a treasure...

I wind down the southern declivity of this lovely Olympus... On the left a quiet green lane, such as Byron would have loved, leads to Dulwich, famous for its college and the well-paid and well-fed inhabitants thereof, and its gallery of pictures... Descending further, green fields and still greener hedges are on each side of me, studded with various wild flowers. At every step I hear the rich music of nature. The skylark is above me singing, heedless if the gled [hawk] be in the blue cloud; and at least a score of robins with their full bright eyes and red bosoms hopping about me... There is a mixture of cheerfulness and melancholy in their song which to me is pleasing: now loud and shrill, and now a long rolling sound like the rising of the wind.

Advancing, I come in sight of the new church of Norwood with its unsightly steeple. Ichabod! the glory of the church has departed. I never observe the new churches on the Surrey side of the river without imagining their long bodies and short steeples look, from a distance, like the rudders of so many sailing barges. Where is the grand oriel? the square tower? What have we in their stead? A common granary casement and a shapeless spire.

I again move onward, rather tired, and turning to the left, after a short uphill journey with a charming view on all sides, arrive at The Woodman, where the talisman I spoke of showed its power by instantly procuring me good eating and other refreshing solace... Here I repose —

> Inhaling, as the news I read,
> The fragrance of the Indian weed.

You [Hone] are, I have heard, no smoker; yet there is 'a something' in a pipe which produces that tranquillity of mind you so much need. If alone, it is a companion, bringing quiet thoughts and pleasing visions. It is a good friend if not abused, and is, above all, a promoter of digestion — no bad quality.

Below me, yet wearing its livery of brown, lies the wood, the shadowy haunt of the gypsy tribe ere magisterial authority drove them away. Many a pleasant hour have I spent in my younger days with its Cassandras [fortune-tellers], listening to their prophetic voices and looking at their dark eyes.

> O the dusky hands are ne'er forgot
>   That my palm trac'd,
> Of her I clasp'd, in that calm spot,
>   Around the waist.
>   I feel the thrill
>   Of her fingers still.
> Her dark eyes on me beam.
> O what joyous thoughts my bosom fill
>   Of that sweet dream...

Sydenham lies before me. Beyond it in softened distance, Beckenham and Bromley meet the eye, with Dulwich below — and half-hidden and afar off is smoky London, with the Abbey towers and St Paul's dome looking gloomily grand. In the foreground lies a rich variety of upland and dale, studded with snow-white dwellings. Leaving the wood on my left, I reach the reservoir of the canal and read no less than three boards threatening with the severest penalties all intruders. Again I am surrounded with skylarks... Pacing slowly up a quiet lane to the left of the canal, I arrive at a few delightful cottages on the brow of the hill. Below them to the south —

> A lovely prospect opens wide,
> Wave-like hills on every side,
> By human hands diversified...

Turning to the left I view Forest Hill, the sweetest haunt of my poetic hours, but here, as at every other desirable spot for meditation, frowns the warning board, placed by the hand of envious monopoly —

'The law will punish all who enter here.'

Nunhead Hill, the favourite resort of smoke-dried artisans and other Londoners, is taken from them, and a narrow path is all that remains for their Sunday promenade. Ruminating on the change, I move on, and espying a gap in the hedge, enter a field, where, reclining on the long grass, I muse... I listen! It is the music of heaven — numerous skylarks tower aloft, the best I have yet heard. Ye that wish for good ones, catch them here...

Hark! It is the titlark [pipit], the harbinger of the nightingale. He is just come over, and the other will quickly follow. He drops from the tallest tree, and sings till earth receives him. His song is short but very sweet. Nothing can equal his rising 'weet—weet—weet—weet— weet—weet —weet' and dying 'feer—feer—feer—feer—feer—feer— feer' and his lengthened 'snee————jug—jug—jug'. It is from him that the best notes of your canaries are obtained...

About the fifteenth [of April] the fowler will go out, and the nightingale will sell his freedom for a mealworm. How many of us mortals do the same to gratify our appetites! ...I bend my course through Peckham, and again enter the busy haunts of men...

How to cage larks and nightingales

A friend writes about a hobby that leaves Hone in two minds:

AS THE TIME has arrived [in May] for taking the young from the feathered tribe, it may not be amiss to say a few words by way of advice to the unitiated concerning the rearing and training of these amusing creatures, who repay our care with their rich melody.

We may now get chaffinches, goldfinches, linnets, larks, &c in the streets or at the different shops at a very small expense, either singly or by the nest according to their ages, but I should recommend all who wish to purchase young birds to go to a regular dealer, who will sell them quite as cheap, and warrant them cocks...

For linnets, goldfinches and chaffinches mix rapeseed, bruised, and bread steeped in boiling water ... putting it into their mouths from the end of a stick about every two hours. Water they will not require, the food being sufficiently moist for them. When you find them peck at the stick and take their food eagerly from it, which they will do at about a fortnight old, place some food about the cage with clean dry gravel, scattering among it some dry seed bruised. They will pick it up and so be weaned off the moist food... Place water in the pot... If your fancy runs on soft-billed birds such as the skylark, woodlark, nightingale or robin, you must feed them with egg, and bread moistened with water, or beef raw or cooked; changing it, as they grow and begin to feed themselves, to dry egg chopped small and crumbled bread, throwing in with it German paste until you find them contented with the latter. All these birds will live healthy and sing stout on this food, except the nightingale; he *must* have beef and egg...

When a month old, cage them off in their proper cages... Squirt a mouthful of water over your birds now and then... It will much assist

Now, through the furrows where the skylarks build
Or by the hedgerows green, the fowler strays
Seeking the infant bird.

them in their moulting and make them throw their feathers faster, particularly larks, nightingales and robins. The latter may have their water-pans to fix inside the cage so that they can dabble in them when they like. This will save the trouble of taking them out to clean their feet. Larks *must* be taken out once a week or their claws will become clogged with dirt, and rot off. The cleaning their feet is but very little trouble: dip them in warm water and rub the dirt gently off with your thumb and finger.

As these innocent creatures delight you with the beauty of their feathers and sweetness of their song, too much cannot be done for their comfort...

> Hone adds some uneasy comments. He regrets that he cannot 'persuade those who think they have vested rights in the bodies of certain of the airy race to open their cages and set the prisoners free'. Of the water-squirting suggestion, he ventures to ask 'whether to *syringe* a little may not be as beneficial as to *squirt a mouthful*'. And finally: 'He agrees that a nightingale — a *caged* nightingale, alas! — "*must* have beef and egg" and that "larks *must* be taken out once a week"; and — he may be wrong — if they fly away, so much the better. He is strongly of opinion that birds are like himself — they cannot bear confinement and be happy.'
>
> The following year, though, he prints another piece from the same man:

In praise of the 'linnet fancy'

'LINNET FANCY!' I think I hear some taker-up of *The Table Book* say. 'What's in a linnet? Rubbish —

> 'A bird that when caught
> May be had for a groat.'

Music! I answer —— melody, unrivalled melody equal to Philomel's, that ever *she*-bird of the poets. I wish they would call things by their proper names, for after all it is a cock. Hens never make harmonious sounds.

The fancy is possessed but by a few, and those generally of the 'lower orders' — the weavers and cobblers of Whitechapel and Spitalfields, for instance. A good bird has been known to fetch ten sovereigns. I have frequently seen three or four given for one...

From what I have heard the titlark and skylark do, I incline to believe that a good deal of theirs is in the song of the linnet. This song consists of a number of *jerks*, as they are called, some of which a bird will dwell on and time with the most beautiful exactness: this is termed 'a *weighed* bird'. Others rattle through it in a hurried manner, and take to what is termed *battling*; these are birds often 'sung' against others... These *jerks* are as under. Old fanciers remember more... I have heard some of them say that even larks are not so good as they were forty years ago.

He lists forty-four jerks. Here are a few for bird-lovers to consider:

> Tuck tuck fear – ic quake-e-weet
> Tuck tuck tuck tuck joey – tolloc cha, ic quake-e-weet
> Tuck tuck wizzey – tyr tyr tyr cher – wye wye cher
> Tolloc ejup er – weet weet weet
> Tolloc tolloc cha – ic ic ic ic quake – ic ic
> Tolloc tolloc er – weet weet weet cheer – tolloc cha – ejup
> Tolloc tolloc er ——ejup – pipe pipe pipe
> Lug lug echow – lug ic ic quake-e-weet
> Ic quake-e-pipe – tolloc ic – tolloc ic – tolloc ic – er cher
> Pipe pipe pipe pipe – ejup ejup ejup...

Get a good bird. As soon as *nestlings* can be had, purchase four or even six... [*Here he explains feeding and caging.*] Some persons prefer *branchers* to nestlings; these are birds caught about July. When they are just able to fly among the trees they are in some cases better than the others; and invariably so if they take your old bird's song, being stronger and steadier. Nestlings lose half their time in playing about the cage...

To render your birds tame, and free in song, move them about. Tie them in handkerchiefs and put them on the table, or anywhere that you safely can. Only let their usual place of hanging be out of sight of each other. Their seeing one another makes them fretful...

The man who keeps birds *should* pay attention to them. They cannot speak, but their motions will often tell him that something is wrong, and it will then be his business to discover what. He who confines birds and neglects them deserves to be confined himself; they merit all we can do for them, and are grateful. What a fluttering of wings — what a stretching of necks and legs — what tappings with the bill against the wires of their cages have I heard when coming down to breakfast! What a burst of song, as much as to say, 'Here's master!'

Should anyone be induced ... to become a fancier, let him be careful *with whom* and *how* he deals, or he will assuredly be taken in. In choosing a bird, let him see that it stands up on its perch boldly; let it be snake-headed, its feathers smooth and sleek, its temper good. This you may know by the state of its tail: a bad-tempered bird generally rubs his tail down to a mere bunch of rags. Hear the bird sing, and be sure to keep the seller at a distance from him; a motion of his master's hand, a turn of his head, may stop a bird when about to do something bad. Let him go through with his song uninterrupted; you will then discover his faults...

Nightingales coming to town

This enthusiast does also delight in hearing uncaged nightingales. In April 1831 he contributes this:

FRIEND HONE – As you are, like me, fond of the song of Philomel, and may have as little leisure to go far to hear it, I give you notice that the nightingale was heard this year on the 17th of March at Dartford, and may now be heard in full song near London.

On Monday morning at daybreak I walked in company with a *catcher* (!) from Dartford to New Cross. He had been out for his third and last trip and had sixteen with him, making forty-three birds caught since the 9th. All the way, on each side of the road, he called and they answered him, so that I think at least twenty must have sung. They are *now* laired and not worth catching, so the lovers of song may have a treat. There is one at the end of the [Royal Naval] College, Blackheath Corner, the best I ever heard, and I suppose by this time they are to be found in Kensington Gardens, for they appear to be travelling westward. The birds the catcher had were very lean.

Those who wish to hear nightingales in the *day* time may be gratified by going to Champion Hill, leading to Lordship-lane [East Dulwich]: I heard four yesterday at 2 o'clock. There is a beautiful view over Norwood, Dulwich, &c, from that spot: the sight of the green trees and rich grass, and the hearing of those birds, with the song of a good robin and some few chaffinches, joined to the warble of a fine lark, is worth the while of anyone who has 'music in his soul' and an eye for the beauties of nature.

An inn where you sit at your ease

A further instalment of Hone's Kentish trip with Samuel Williams.

IF A DELIGHTFUL two hours' lounging walk from Bromley be desired, take the turning from The Swan at Bromley to Beckenham church, go through the churchyard over a stile, keep the meadow footpath, cross the Wickham road and wander by hedgerow elms as your will and the country-folk direct you till you arrive at Hayes Common. Then make for the lower or lefthand side of the common, and leaving the mill on the right, get into the cottaged lane. At a few hundred yards past the sheepwash, formed in a little dell by the Ravensbourne, at the end of the open rise stands Keston Cross.

Before reaching this place on my first visit to it, the country people had indiscriminately called it Keston *Cross* and Keston *Mark*... I puzzled myself with conjectures as to whether it was the site of a cross of memorial, a market cross, a preaching cross or what other kind of cross. It was somewhat of a disappointment to me when, in an angle of a crossroad, instead of some ancient vestige there appeared a commodious, respectable and comfortable-looking house of accommodation for man and horse, and, swinging high in air, its sign, the red cross ... which I take to be a forgotten memorial of some old boundary stone or landmark. [The present inn is called Keston Mark.]

Keston Cross I call 'headquarters', because in this house you will find yourself 'at home'. You may sparkle forth to many remarkable spots in the vicinage and then return and take your 'corporal refection'

The Keston Cross ostler, William Blake, at his stable door

and go in and out at will ... or you may sit at your ease and do nothing but contemplate in quiet... The house itself is not one of your bold-looking inns that if you enter you assure yourself of paying toll at, in regard of its roystering appearance ... and you will *not* find any article presented to you of an inferior quality...

To this pleasant house there is attached a delightful little flower and fruit-garden, with paddocks, poultry-yard, outhouses and every re-quisite... The stabling is under the management of an ostler of long service... The rooms in the house are marked by its owner's attachment to horses and field-sports. In the common parlour ... is a coloured print of the burial of a huntsman, the attendants in 'full cry' over the grave... A parlour for the accommodation of private parties has an oil painting of the old Duke of Bolton, capitally mounted in the yard of his mansion, going out attended by his huntsman and dogs...

The ostler of Keston Cross is the most remarkable of its obliging humble servants. The poor fellow has lost an eye and is like 'the high-mettled racer' in his decline [a racehorse in a popular song] — except that he is well-used. While looking about me I missed W[illiams], and found he had deemed him a picturesque subject, and that he was in the act of sketching him from behind the door of the stable yard while he leaned against the stable door with his corn-sieve in his hand.

I know not why the portrait should not come into a new edition of Henry Bromley's *Catalogue of Engraved British Portraits* [1793] or an appendix to James Granger. Sure I am that many far less estimable persons figure in the *Biographical History of England*... I craved my friend W to engrave him on a woodblock. I have no other excuse to offer for presenting an impression of it than the intrinsic worth of the industrious original, and the merit of the likeness.

Wildfowl shooting in Picardy

A 'sporting friend' reports from Abbeville, November 1825:

EVERY LABOURING MAN in France has a right to sport [*forbidden under British game laws*], and keeps a gun... From the middle of October or the beginning of this month, vast quantities of wildfowl are annually shot in and about the fens of Picardy... To allure them from their heights, two or three tame ducks, properly secured to stones near the sportsmen's huts, keep up an incessant quacking during the greater part of the night. The huts are sufficiently large to admit two men and a dog. One man keeps watch while his companion sleeps half the night... The huts are formed in the following manner: a piece of ground is raised sufficiently high to protect the fowlers from the wet ground, upon which is placed the frame ... mostly made of ozier, firmly interwoven... This frame is covered with dry reeds and well plastered with mud or clay to the thickness of about four inches, upon which are placed, very neatly, layers of turf, so that the whole at a little distance looks like a mound of verdant earth.

Three holes about four inches in diameter, for the men inside to see and fire through, are neatly cut. One is in the front, and one on each side. Very frequently there is a fourth at the top. This is for the purpose of firing from at the wildfowl as they pass over. The fowlers, lying upon their backs, discharge guess shots at the birds, who are only heard by the noise of their wings... Fowlers with quick ears attain considerable expertness in this guess-firing. The numbers that are shot in this way are incredible...

For myself, though for the sake of variety I have now and then crept into a fowler's hut and shot in ambuscade, I prefer open warfare... I will just mention the birds I have shot here within the last three weeks. [Seven varieties of godwit, seven of sandpiper, two of curlew, three of heron, ten of duck.]

If you were here you should have a 'gentleman's recreation' of the most delightful kind... Confound all 'black letter' [Hone's old books], say I, if it keeps a man from such delightful scenes as I have enjoyed every hour since I came here. As for picture-loving, come and see *these* pictures [the landscape], which never tire by looking at. I like a good picture though myself, and shall pick up some prints at Paris... You may be certain therefore of my collecting something for you, after the birds have left — especially woodcuts... In my next you shall have something about lark-shooting, which in England is nothing compared with what the north of France affords.

Six dozen larks before breakfast

Another dispatch from Abbeville some weeks later:

PARTRIDGE AND QUAIL shooting cease in this delightful part of the world about the middle of October, for by that time the partridges are so very wild and wary that there is no getting near them. The reason of this is that our fields here are all open without either hedge or ditch, and when the corn and hemp are off, the stubble is pulled up so close by the poor people for fuel that there is no cover for partridges. As to the quails, they are all either 'killed off' or take their departure for a milder climate. And then there is nothing left for the French gentry to amuse themselves with but lark-shooting.

These birds are attracted to any given spot in great numbers by a singular contrivance called a *miroir*. This is a small machine made of a piece of mahogany shaped like a chapeau-bras and highly polished, or else it is made with common wood inlaid with small bits of looking-glass so as to reflect the sun's rays upwards. It is fixed on the top of a thin iron rod or upright spindle, dropped through an iron loop or ring attached to a piece of wood to drive into the ground... By pulling a string fastened to the spindle, the *miroir* twirls, and the reflected light unaccountably attracts the larks, who hover over it and become a target for the sportsman. In this way I have had capital sport. A friend of mine actually shot six dozen before breakfast. While he sat on the ground he pulled the twirler himself, and his dogs fetched the birds as they dropped...

Ladies often partake in the amusement on a cold dry morning, not by shooting but by watching the sport. So many as ten or a dozen parties are sometimes out together, firing at a distance of about five hundred yards apart, and in this way the larks are constantly kept on the wing. The most favourable mornings are when there is a gentle light frost, with little or no wind and a clear sky, for when there are clouds the larks will not approach... The fascination of the twirler is so strong as to rob them of the usual 'fruits of experience'. After being

The seated boy pulls the twirler string; shot larks lie on the ground

fired at several times they return to the twirler and form again into groups above it. Some of them even fly down and settle on the ground within a yard or two of the astonishing instrument, looking at it 'this way and that way and all ways together' as if nothing had happened.

Larks in France fetch from three to four sous a piece... Were you here at the season, to eat larks in their perfection and dressed as we dress them, I think your praise of the cooking would give me the laugh against you if you ever afterwards ventured to declaim against the use of the gun, which next to my pencil is my greatest hobby. I send you a sketch of the sport, with the boy at the twirler...

Hone points a moral in verse —

As far-off islanders,
Innocent of trade, unskilled in commerce,
To whom a glass or toy unknown before
Is wonderful, give freely flocks and fruits
To gain mere baubles; so these silly birds
Attracted by the glisten of the twirler
Hover above the passing strange decoy,
Intent to gaze, and fall the gunner's prey.

A week later Hone learns that 'our ingenious neighbours the French are rivalled by the lark-catchers of Dunstable', for a reader there writes:

PERHAPS you are not aware that in many parts of England a similar instrument is employed for catching the lark... Persons go out with what is called a larking-glass ... made somewhat in the shape of a cucumber. This invention is hollow and has holes cut round it, in which bits of looking-glass are fitted. It is fixed on a pole and has a sort of reel from which a line runs [to twirl it]. The larks ... come headlong down to it, a net is thrown over them, and thus many are taken, deceived like ourselves with glittering semblances. Yes! Lords as we deem ourselves of the creation, we are as easily lured by those who bait our passions or propensities as those poor birds...

Over the moors to the Lakes

A Yorkshire reader contributes 'Notes on a Tour, chiefly Pedestrian, from Skipton in Craven, Yorkshire, to Keswick in Cumberland':

JULY 14, 1827. Left Skipton for Keswick. The road from Skipton to Burnsall exhibits some romantic scenery, which the muse of Wordsworth has made classic ground. About half a mile from Rilston, on the right-hand side of the road, are the ruins of Norton tower, one of the principal scenes in the poem of 'The White Doe of Rylstone'...

15th, Sunday. ...While attending divine service [at Burnsall], one or two things struck me as remarkable. The church has an organ, on which two voluntaries were played, one after the psalms for the day and the other after the second lesson; but during the singing of the metrical psalms the organ was silent. Instead of it, two or three strange-looking countrymen in the organ gallery raised an inharmonious noise with a small fiddle, a flute and a clarinet. Why do the churchwardens allow this? The gallery of the church should not be allowed to resemble the interior of an alehouse at a village feast. [*Soon churches barred such players, thus discouraging village music-making*.]

The church would have looked better had it been cleaner: the pew wherein I sat was covered with cobwebs. The business of the churchwardens seemed to me to consist rather in thumping the heads of naughty boys than in looking after the state of the church.

Afternoon, same day. At Linton, about two miles up the river, arrived during the time of service. This church has suffered much from the 'beautifiers', who amongst other equally judicious improvements have placed a *Venetian* window over the altar of the *Gothic* edifice... The altar rails were covered with garlands made of artificial flowers. Church garlands were formerly made of real flowers. They are borne before the corpses of unmarried young women. I have heard an old woman in Durham sing the following stanza, which evidently alludes to the custom:

> When I am dead, before I be buried,
>> Hearken ye maidens fair, this must ye do —
> Make me a garland of marjoram and lemon thyme
>> Mixed with the pansy, rosemary and rue.

The practice of bearing the garlands is still very common in the country churches in Craven.

In the churchyard is the following inscription on a stone, date 1825. The march of intellect [a current phrase] is surely here proceeding at a rapid pace!

> Remember, man that passeth by,
> As thou is now, so once was I
> And as I is, so must thou be.
> Prepare thyself to follow me.

Someone had written beneath,

> To follow you's not my intent
> Unless I knew which way you went.

July 16. Went from Linton over the moors to Clapham, passed through Skirethorns, over Skirethorns moor, by Malham Water [Tarn], by the

side of Penyghent, through Great and Little Stainforth, over ———
moor, through Wharfe and Austwick. Malham Water is a beautiful
lake ... supposed to be the source of the River Aire [*it is*]... About a
mile from it is the famous chasm Gordale... Above the village of Little
Stainforth is a sublime view of mountain scenery in which Penyghent
is a principal object. No traveller should pass through Little Stainforth
without seeing the waterfall below the bridge [Stainforth Force]...
From the waterfall the bridge appears to great advantage...

July 17, 18. Kirkby Lonsdale. This town is on the banks of the Lune,
which here winds through a finely wooded valley. It has an elegant
old bridge... The church is a handsome structure... At the west end is
a fine Norman doorway, a considerable sufferer by 'beautifying'... A
walk extending from the north gate of the churchyard along the banks
of the Lune affords a delightul prospect of the county...

July 19. [Windermere] Bowness is to the inhabitants of Kendal what
Hornsey is to the Cockneys, and during the summer months gypsying
excursions are very frequent. On the evening that I arrived some
Oxonians were 'astonishing the natives': they seemed to think that as
they were from college they had a right to give themselves airs. The
inhabitants appeared to regard them with mingled pity and derision.

July 20. Left Bowness for Grasmere, through Ambleside and Rydal. At
the last place I turned aside to see Rydal Mount, the residence of the
celebrated poet, Wordsworth... The approach is shaded by beautiful
laurels — proper trees for the residence of Wordsworth! While recon-
noitring I was caught in a heavy thunder-shower and should have
been drenched had not a pretty servant girl invited me into the
kitchen... On the dresser, in a large wicker cage, were two turtle
doves. These, I learnt, were great favourites, or rather *pets* (that was
the word) with the bard. The shower having ceased, I obtained Mrs
Wordsworth's leave to walk through the garden. From the mount in it
I gained an excellent view of the front part of the house.

I had scarcely reached the village of Rydal when another shower
drove me into a cottage, from the door of which I had my first view of
the author of the Lyrical Ballads. He is rather tall, apparently about
fifty years of age [*he was 57*]. He was dressed in a hair cap, plaid coat
and white trousers. It was gratifying to hear how the Rydal people
spoke of this good man. One said he was kind to the poor; another,
that he was very religious; another, that he had no pride and would
speak to anybody: all were loud in his praise.

At Rydal is a neat gothic church, lately erected [1824] at the sole
cost of Lady le Fleming. I have not seen any new church that pleased
me so much as this. The east end is finely conceived, and both the

exterior and interior reflect the highest credit on the taste and talent of the artist, Mr [George] Webster of Kendal. I wished Mr Hone had seen it with me, for I know he would have been delighted with it... Rydal lake is small but very romantic. On some of the surrounding hills I observed those rude erections of loose stones which the country boys are in the habit of building, and which they call *men*... A few of these 'men', being provided with arms, resemble crosses, and transport the imagination of the beholder to catholic countries...

July 21. Grasmere... This is a most lovely village... The church door was open, and I discovered that the villagers were strewing the floors with fresh rushes. I learnt from the old clerk that according to annual custom the rushbearing procession would be in the evening. I asked the clerk if there were any dissenters in the neighbourhood. He said no, not nearer than Keswick, where there were some that called themselves Presbyterians, but he did not know what they were, he believed them to be a kind of *papishes*. (The only instance of dissent I heard of betwixt Kendal and Keswick was a private Unitarian chapel at a gentleman's seat near Bowness. At Kendal and Keswick the dissenters are very numerous.)

During the whole of this day I observed the children busily employed in preparing garlands of such wild flowers as the beautiful valley produces, for the evening procession, which commenced at nine... The children, chiefly girls, holding these garlands, paraded through the village, preceded by the Union Band (thanks to the great drum for this information). They then entered the church, where the three largest garlands were placed on the altar... (By the by, the beautifiers have placed an ugly window above the altar, of the nondescript order of architecture.) In the procession I observed the Opium Eater [Thomas De Quincey] ... Mr and Mrs Wordsworth, Miss Wordsworth and Miss Dora Wordsworth. Wordsworth is the chief supporter of these rustic ceremonies...

The party adjourned to the ballroom, a hayloft at my worthy friend Mr Bell's [the innkeeper], where the country lads and lasses tripped it merrily and *heavily*. They called the amusement *dancing*, but I called it *thumping*, for he who could make the greatest noise seemed to be esteemed the best dancer... Billy Dawson, the fiddler, boasted to me of having been the officiating minstrel at this ceremony for the last six and forty years. He made grievous complaints of the outlandish tunes which the 'Union Band chaps' introduce. In the procession of this evening they annoyed Billy by playing 'the Hunters' Chorus in Friskits'. 'Who,' said Billy, 'can keep time with such a queer thing?'

Amongst the gentlemen dancers was one Dan Burkitt. He introduced himself to me by seizing my coat collar in a mode that would have given a Burlington Arcade lounger the hysterics [*thinking he was being seized for debt*], and saying, 'I'm old Dan Burkitt of Wytheburn, sixty-six years old — not a better jigger in Westmorland.' No, thought I, nor a greater tosspot.

On my relating this to an old man present, he told me not to judge of Westmorland manners by Dan's — 'for,' said he, 'you see, sir, he is a *statesman* and has been at Lunnon, and so takes liberties'. In Westmorland, farmers residing on their own estate are called statesmen.

The dance was kept up till a quarter to twelve, when a livery servant entered and delivered the following verbal message to Billy: 'Master's respects, and will thank you to lend him the fiddlestick.' Billy took the hint; the sabbath morn was at hand, and the pastor of the parish had adopted this gentle mode of apprizing the assembled revellers that they ought to cease their revelry. The servant departed with the fiddlestick, the chandelier was removed, and when the village clock struck twelve not an individual was to be seen out of doors... No disturbance of any kind interrupted the dance. Dan Burkitt was the only person at all 'How came you so?' and he was *non se ipse* before the jollity commenced. He told me he was 'seldom sober', and I believed what he said.

The rushbearing is now, I believe, almost entirely confined to Westmorland [*but see page 138*]. It was once customary in Craven... Billy remembered when the lasses bore the rushes in the evening procession, and strewed the church floor at the same time as they decorated the church with garlands. Now the rushes are laid in the morning by the ringer and clerk... I do not like old customs to change, for, like mortals, they change before they die altogether...

July 24. Walked to Keswick ... a neat town. The Greta runs through it; but alas! its once pure waters have become polluted by the filthy factories now on its banks...

FARMERS	
IN	
1722	1822
Man to the plough	Man tally-ho
Wife to the cow	Miss, piano
Girl to the sow	Wife silk and satin
Boy to the mow	Boy Greek and Latin
And your rents will be netted.	And you'll all be *Gazetted*.*
From *The Times*	*As bankrupts

Spoilers abroad in Hagbush-lane

We have seen Hone roving southwards from the metropolis into Kent. But his heart lay in the other direction, where he had gone as a boy 'to frolic in the newmown hay and listen to the songs of the birds'. By the 1820s new streets were covering many of the fields, and a green lane he loved was vanishing too: ancient Hagbush-lane, which wound its way up through the western parts of Islington and on towards Highgate. Hone reports in June 1825:

HAGBUSH-LANE, though now wholly disused, and in many parts destroyed, was the old, or rather the *oldest*, north road or ancient bridleway to and from London... The wild onion, clown's-wound-wort, wake-robin and abundance of other simples, lovely in their form and of high medicinal repute in our old herbals ... take root and seed and flower here in great variety. How long beneath the tall elms and pollard oaks and the luxuriant beauties on the banks the infirm may be suffered to seek health, and the healthy to recreate, who shall say? Spoilers are abroad... Bargains and sales have been made ... and the public road thrown bit by bit into private fields...

Building, or what may more properly be termed the tumbling up of tumble-down houses, to the north of London is so rapidly increasing that in a year or two there will scarcely be a green spot for the resort of the inhabitants. Against covering of private ground in this way there is no resistance; but against its evil consequences to health some remedy should be provided by the setting apart of open spaces...

Though persons from the country smile at Londoners when they talk of being 'rural' at a distance of a few miles from town, a country-man would find it difficult to name any lane in his own county more sequestered or of greater beauty.

In this lane, Hone learns of a human drama — a fight for survival by a poor man, William Corrall. The lane and the man become a united cause to which he devotes many pages. What follows is a much-condensed account:

An aged and almost decayed labouring man, a native of Cheshunt in Hertfordshire, with his wife and child, lay out every night upon the roadside of Hagbush-lane under what of bough and branch they could creep for shelter, till winter's cold came on, and then he erected this 'mud edifice' [*pictured in next page*]. He had worked for some great landholders and owners in Islington, and still jobbed about. Like them he was, to this extent of building, a speculator; and to eke out his insufficient means he profited, in his humble abode, by the sale of small beer to stragglers and rustic wayfarers.

His cottage stood between the lands of two rich men, not upon the

'Just such a scene as Morland would have coveted to sketch'
— drawn by Joseph Fussell, an Islington artist

land of either, but partly on the disused road and partly on the waste of the manor. Deeming him by no means a respectable neighbour for their cattle, they warned him off. He, not choosing to be houseless, nor conceiving that their domains could be injured by his little enclosure between the banks of the road, refused to accept this notice. For this offence, one of them caused his labourers to level the miserable dwelling to the earth...

Corrall is assured that the destruction is unlawful; begins another hut; 'wealth again made war upon poverty'; he is turned away at the workhouse, and builds yet another hut —

— wherein he dwells, and sells his small beer to people who choose to sit and drink it on the turf seat against the wall of his cottage. It is chiefly in request, however, among the brickmakers in the neighbourhood and the labourers on the new road cutting across Hagbush-lane from Holloway to the Kentish Town road... For the present he remains almost unmolested in his almost sequestered nook, and the place and himself are worth seeing, for they are perhaps the nearest specimens to London of the old country labourer and his dwelling...

*Hone thinks he has done with Hagbush-lane and 'the tale of the poor
man's wrongs'; but two years later a reader writes to tell him of 'the final
destruction of this sample of rusticity':*

SIR — Never, since reading your interesting narrative and description, have I strolled that way without passing through Hagbush-
lane... Last week I was sadly astonished... The cottage, with its
garden-rails and benches, had disappeared, and the garden was
entirely laid waste. Trees, bushes and vegetables rudely torn up by the
roots lay withering where they had flourished. Upon the site of the
demolished dwelling stood the poor old man, bent by affliction as
much as by age, leaning on his stick... He declared, with a tear, that 'it
had ruined him forever and would be the death of him'...

*Further up the lane he manages with some boards and old canvas to make
a shelter, 'a most wretched sty'. Hone obtains more details:*

His story was short... So early as five in the morning, some men
brought a ladder, a barrow and a pickaxe, and ascending the ladder
began to untile the roof while the old man and his wife were in bed.
He hastily rose. They demanded of him to unlock the door. On his
refusing they burst it open with the pickaxe, and having thus forced
an entrance, compelled his wife to get up. They then wantonly threw
out and broke the few household utensils, and hewed down the walls
of the dwelling.

In the little garden they rooted up and destroyed every tree, shrub
and vegetable. And finally they levelled all vestiges which could mark
the place as having been used or cultivated for the abode and sus-
tenance of human beings. Some of the less destructible requisites of
the cottage they trundled in the barrow up the lane ... whither the old
man and his wife followed, and were left with the few remnants of
their miserable property by the housebreakers. On that spot they put
together their present hut... The old man represents the 'ringleader',
as he calls him, in this last work of ruin, to be the foreman of a great
cowkeeping landholder and speculator [developer]...

In the summer of 1825 I heard it said that their cottage was the
resort and drinking-place of idle and disorderly persons... It is quite
true that I saw persons there whom I preferred not to sit down with,
because their manners and habits were different from my own; yet I
not unfrequently took a cup of the old man's beer among them, and
silently watched them, and sometimes talked with them... They were
quite as honourable and moral as persons of more refined language
and dress who frequent respectable coffeehouses...

On the hedge side of the cottage was a small low lean-to, wherein the old man kept a pig to fatten. At the front end was an enclosure of a few feet of ground with domestic fowls... In the rear of the cottage was a rod [16^1/2 ft, 5 metres] or two of ground banked off and well planted with potatoes, cabbages and other garden stuff... Between his vegetables and his livestock and his few customers he had enough to do, and I never saw him idle...

There I have seen a brickmaker or two with their wives and daughters sitting and regaling, as much at home, and as sober and innocent, as parties of French ladies and gentlemen at Chedron's in Leicester-square... There I have seen a comfortably dressed man, in a clean shirt and a coat and hat as good as a Fleet-street tradesman's, with a jug of '*small* entire' before him, leisurely at work on a pair of shoes, joining in the homely conversation and in choruses of old English songs raised by his compeers. There too I have heard a company of merry-hearted labourers and holiday-making journey-men, who had straggled away from their smithies and furnaces in the lanes of London to breathe the fresh air, pealing out loud laughter, while the birds whistled over their heads from the slender branches of the green elms...

The private wrong he has sustained is in the nature of a public wrong, and it is open to everyone to consider of the means by which these repeated breaches of the peace may be prevented and redress be obtained...

On a bleak November day, Hone and a church almoner go to find out what has become of the Corralls. They have somehow found lodgings.

The overseers would have taken them into the workhouse, but the old man and his wife refused because, according to the workhouse rules, had they entered they would have been separated. In the form of solemnization of matrimony it is enjoined ... 'Those whom God hath joined together, let no man put asunder'; and though this prescription is of the highest order of law, yet it is constantly violated by parochial authority...

They purpose endeavouring to pick up a living by selling ready dressed meat and small beer to labouring people. Their child, a girl about seven years of age, seems destined to a vagabond and lawless life unless means can be devised to take her off the old people's hands and put her to school...Mr S [the almoner] left his address, that when they get settled they may apply to him...

This notice will terminate all remark on Hagbush-lane: but I reiterate that since it ceased to be used as the common highway from the north of England into London, it became a green lane, affording lovely walks to lovers of rural scenery, which lawless encroachments have despoiled... Some who retain portions of Hagbush-lane ... hold their possessions by open seizure ... which were it exercised on the personalties of passengers would infallibly subject successful claimants to the inconvenience of taking either a long voyage to New South Wales or perhaps a short walk without the walls of Newgate, there to receive the highest reward the sheriff's substitute can bestow [*they would be either transported or hanged*].

Had I a cottage here

At an earlier date, sitting 'beneath the tall elms and pollard oaks', Hone was moved to compose these 'Lines Written in Hagbush-lane':

> A scene like this
> Would woo the careworn wise
> To moralize,
> And courting lovers court to tell their bliss.

> Had I a cottage here
> I'd be content, for where
> I have my books
> I have old friends,
> Whose cheering looks
> Make me amends
> For coldnesses in men: and so
> With them departed long ago,
> And with wild-flowers and trees
> And with the living breeze
> And with the 'still small voice'
> Within, I would rejoice,
> And converse hold while breath
> Held me, and then — come Death!

The beneficence of birds

'A distinguished naturalist' contributes some good advice, and also a record of the arrival times of birds during the 1760s–1820s:

A NOTION PREVAILS that birds do great injury in gardens and fields, and hence rewards are frequently offered to induce boys and others to kill them in spring. The notion and the practice are erroneous. A gentleman of long experience in horticulture has ascertained that birds, in general, do more good by destroying vermin than they do harm by the little fruit and grain they consume. An entire district in Germany was once nearly deprived of its corn harvest by an order to kill all the rooks having been generally obeyed. [*Mao Tse-tung caused similar havoc in China by ordering the destruction of all sparrows.*]

SPRING BIRDS: Table of the average terms of their arrival, deduced from a journal of natural history kept during nearly sixty years.

Least willow wren [now chiffchaff]	March 31
Stone curlew	March 27
Nightingale	April 14
Chimney swallow [common swallow]	April 15
Yellow willow wren [willow warbler]	April 15
Pied flycatcher	April 15
Redstart	April 16
Grasshopper lark [grasshopper warbler]	April 16
Blackcap	April 17
Martlet [house martin]	April 20
Spotted flycatcher	April 20
Cuckoo	April 21
Lesser reed sparrow [sedge warbler]	April 23
Sand martin	April 25
Black martin	May 9
Swift	May 14
Fern owl [nightjar]	May 20

Another naturalist sends Hone, 'from a twenty years' journal', similar dates, except for 'smallest willow wren', April 3. He also has common willow wren, April 10; First Cuckoo Day in Sussex, April 14; sand swallow, Hirundo riparia, April 19.

Rob Hume, editor of *Birds*, journal of the Royal Society for the Protection of Birds, has kindly provided some modern names [bracketed]. He thinks 'black martin' must be the all-dark swift. He notes the following slight variations in arrival times:

Stone curlew, most a little later; grasshopper warbler, now around April 20; blackcap, about as shown, except that increased numbers from central Europe now come in winter; house martin, now expected April 10–12; spotted flycatcher, often mid- or even late May; cuckoo, usually April 10–13; sand martin, mid-March; swift, end April/beginning May.

Sheepshearing and rustic merriment

A 'constant reader' contributes from Cumberland:

A FEW DAYS previous to the 'clipping' or shearing of the sheep, they are washed at a beck or small river not far from the mountain on which they are kept. The clippings that I have witnessed have generally been in St John's Vale [near Keswick]. Several farmers wash their sheep at the same place, and by that means greatly assist each other. The scene is most amusing.

Imagine to yourself several hundred sheep scattered about in various directions, some of them enclosed in pens by the waterside; four or five men in the water rolling those about that are thrown in to

JUNE

Then come the tying, clipping, tarring, bleating;
The shearers' final shout, and dance, and eating.
From hence the old engravers sometimes made
This lovely month a shearer at his trade...

them; the dames and the pretty maidens supplying the 'mountain dew' very plentifully to the people assembled, particularly those that have got themselves well ducked; the boys pushing each other into the river, splashing the men and raising tremendous shouts.

Add to these a fine day in the beginning of June, and a beautiful landscape composed of mountains, woods, cultivated lands and a small meandering stream; the farmers and their wives, children and servants, with hearty faces and as merry as summer and good cheer can make them; and I am sure, sir, that you, who are a lover of nature in all her forms, could not wish a more delightful scene.

I will now proceed to the clipping itself. Early in the forenoon of the appointed day the friends and relatives of the farmer assemble at his house, for they always assist each other, and after having regaled themselves with hung-beef, curds and home-brewed ale, they proceed briskly to business. The men seat themselves on their stools with shears in their hands, and the younger part of the company supply them with sheep from the fold; which after having been sheared have the private mark of the farmer stamped upon them with pitch.

In the meantime the lasses are fluttering about, playing numerous tricks, for which, by the by, they get paid with interest by kisses; and the housewife may be seen busy preparing the supper, which generally comprises all that the season affords.

After the clipping is over and the sheep driven on to the fells (mountains), they adjourn in a body to the house, and then begins a scene of rustic merriment which those who have not witnessed it can have no conception of. The evening is spent in drinking home-brewed ale, and singing. Their songs generally bear some allusion to the subject in question, and are always rural.

But what heightens the pleasure is that there is no quarrelling, and the night passes on in the utmost harmony. I have attended many of them, and never saw the slightest symptoms of anger... They seldom break up till daylight...

A health unto our miaster

Thirty-year-old William Barnes, long before making his name as a Dorset poet, sends Hone in 1831 this vivid picture of a harvest supper:

SOME YEARS AGO the harvest home in my native county, Dorset, was kept up with good old English hospitality. When the last load was ricked, the labourers, male and female, the swarthy reaper and the sunburnt haymaker, the saucy boy who had not seen twelve summers and the stiff horny-handed old mower who had borne the toil of fifty, all made a happy group and went with singing and loud laughing to the harvest-home supper at the farmhouse, where they were expected by the good mistress dressed in a quilted petticoat and a linsey-wolsey apron, with shoes fastened by large silver buckles which extended over her feet like a pack-saddle on a donkey.

The dame and her husband welcomed them to a supper of good wholesome food — a round of beef and a piece of bacon, and perhaps the host and hostess had gone so far as to kill a fowl or two, or stick a turkey which had fattened in the wheat-yard. This plain English fare was eaten from wooden trenchers, by the side of which were put little cups of horn filled with beer or cider. When the cloth was removed, one of the men, putting forth his hand like the gauntlet of an armed knight, would grasp his horn of beer, and standing on a pair of legs which had long outgrown the largest holes of the village stocks, and with a voice which, if he had not been speaking a dialect of the English language, you might have thought came from the deep-seated lungs of a lion, he would propose the health of the farmer in the following lines:

> Here's a health unto our miaster,
>   The founder of the feast,
> And I hope to God wi' all my heart
>   His soul in heaven mid rest.   *might*
> That every thing mid prosper
>   That ever he tiak in hand,
> Vor we be all his sarvants
>   And all at his command.

After this would follow a course of jokes, anecdotes and songs, in some of which the whole company joined, without attention to the technicalities of counterpoint, bass, tenor and treble, common chords and major thirds, but each singing the air and pitching in at the key that best fitted his voice, making a medley of big and little sounds like the lowings of oxen and the low bleatings of old ewes mixed up with the shrill pipings of the lambs at a fair.

The conversation commonly turned on the incidents of the summer: how the haymakers overtook the mowers, or how the rain kept the labour back; how they all crept in a heap under the wagon in a thunderstorm; how nearly some of them were crushed under the load that was upset; who was the best mower or reaper in the village; which field yielded the best crop; and which stack was most likely to heat...

The mower now gives labour o'er

JULY

The mower now gives labour o'er
And on his bench beside the door
Sits down to see his children play,
Smoking a leisure hour away,
While from her cage the blackbird sings
That on the woodbine arbour hings.

John Clare, *The Shepherd's Calendar*

Small earners, big earners

Then came old January, wrappèd well
In many weeds to keep the cold away;
Yet did he quake and quiver like to quell
And blowe his nayles to warme them if he may,
For they were numb'd with holding all the day
An hatchet keene with which he fellèd wood...

Spenser, *The Faery Queene*, VII, vii

'Yo'll find me yarn it, sur'

A Birmingham man, W Pare, writes about 'statute' fairs, a term that goes back to the annual public setting of labourers' and servants' wages by statute from the 14th century onwards.

ALL that is at present understood by 'statutes' or, as the vulgar call them, 'mops', is the assembling of masters and servants, the former to seek the latter, and the latter to obtain employment of the former... The statute I first attended was held at Studley in Warwickshire at the latter end of September... Towards three o'clock there must have been many thousands present. The appearance of the whole may be pretty accurately portrayed to the mind of those who have witnessed a country fair. The sides of the road were occupied with stalls for gingerbread, cakes, &c, general assortments of hardware, japanned goods, wagoners' frocks and an endless variety of wearing apparel suitable to every class, from the farm bailiff or dapper footman to the unassuming ploughboy or day-labourer.

The public-houses were thoroughly full... The scene out-of-doors was enlivened here and there by some wandering minstrel or fiddler, round whom stood a crowd of men and boys, who at intervals eagerly joined to swell the chorus of the song...

The servants were for the most part bedecked in their best church-going clothes. The men also wore clean white frocks and carried in their hats some emblem or insignia ... for instance, a wagoner or ploughboy had a piece of whipcord in his hat, some of it ingeniously plaited in a variety of ways and entwined round the hatband; a cow-man, after the same manner, had some cow-hair ... a shepherd had wool, a gardener had flowers, &c, &c.

The girls wishing to be hired were in a spot apart from the men and boys, and all stood not unlike cattle at a fair waiting for dealers. Some of them had their hands before them, with one knee protruding (like soldiers standing at ease), and never spoke save when catechized and examined by a master or mistress as to the work they had been accustomed to; and then you would scarce suppose they had learned to say anything but 'Ees, sur' or 'No, sur'...

Others, on the contrary, exercised no small degree of self-sufficient loquacity concerning their abilities, which not unusually consisted of a good proportion of main strength, or being able to drive or follow a variety of kinds of plough... They appeared to require a certain sum for wages, without reference to any combination of circumstances or the state of the times; and however exorbitant, they rarely seemed disposed to meet the master by proposing something lower. They would stand for some time and hear reasons why wages should be more moderate, and at the conclusion ... the usual answer was, 'Yo'll find me yarn [earn] it, sur,' or 'I conna gue for less'...

When a bargain is concluded ... it is the custom to ratify it ... by the master presenting to the servant what is termed 'earnest money', which is usually one shilling... Many farmers are wary enough to hire their servants for fifty-one weeks only, which prevents them having any claim upon that particular parish in case of distress, &c...

When the hiring is over, the emblems in the hats are exchanged for ribbons of almost every hue. Some retire to the neighbouring grounds to have games at bowls, skittles or pitching, &c, &c, whilst the more unwary are fleeced of their money by the itinerant Greeks [sharpers] and blacklegs with EO [even–odd] tables, pricking in the garter, the three thimbles, &c, &c. These tricksters seldom fail to reap abundant harvests at the statutes.

Towards evening each lad seeks his lass and they hurry off to spend the night at the public-houses or, as is the case in some small villages, at private houses which on these occasions are licensed for the time being... The statutes I have visited ... are Studley, Shipston-on-Stour and Aston-Cantlow, all in Warwickshire... Studley was by far the largest. At Stratford-on-Avon and some other places there is bull-roasting, &c...

Hone adds: Even in London, bricklayers and other house-labourers still carry their respective implements to the places where they stand for hire... They assemble in great numbers in Cheapside and at Charing Cross every morning at five or six o'clock.

And then to a dancing-room

Another reader describes the hirings for farmers' servants at Whitsuntide and Martinmas in Cumberland:

THOSE WHO COME to be hired stand in a body in the market-place, and to distinguish themselves hold a bit of straw or green sprig in their mouths.

When the market is over the girls begin to file off and gently pace the streets with a view of gaining admirers, whilst the young men with similar designs follow them; and having 'eyed the lasses', each picks up a sweetheart, conducts her to a dancing-room and treats her with punch, wine and cake. Here they spend their afternoon, and part of their half-year's wages, in drinking and dancing, unless, as it frequently happens, a girl becomes the subject of contention ... when the candidates for her love settle the dispute by blows...

At fairs as well as at hirings, it is customary for all the young people in the neighbourhood to assemble and dance at the inns and alehouses... Disputes frequently arise and are generally terminated by blows. During these combats the weaker portion of the company, with the minstrels, get on the benches or cluster in corners, whilst the rest support the combatants. Even the lasses will often assist in the battle in support of their relations or lovers, and in the last cases they are desperate. When the affray is over the bruised pugilists retire to wash and the tattered nymphs readjust their garments. Fresh company arrives, the fiddles strike up, the dancing proceeds as before, and the skirmish, which had commenced without malice, is rarely remembered.

Brisk trading and a merry neet

A Westmorland reader, WHH, reports on the spring fair at Brough:

THIS FAIR is held always on the second Thursday in March. It is a good one for cattle, and in consequence of the great show the inhab-itants are obliged to shut up their windows, for the cattle and the drivers are stationed in all parts of the town... From five to six o'clock the preceding evening, carts, chiefly belonging to Yorkshire clothiers, begin to arrive, and continue coming in until the morning, when at about eight or nine the cattle fair begins...

Previously to any article being sold, the fair is proclaimed in a manner depicted tolerably well in the sketch [*opposite*]. At ten, two individuals named Matthew Horn and John Deighton, having fur-nished themselves with a fiddle and clarinet, walk through the different avenues of the town three times, playing as they walk chiefly 'God Save the King'. At the end of this some verses are repeated [by which] the venders are authorized to commence selling. After it is reported through the different stalls that 'they've walked the fair', business usually commences in a very brisk manner.

Mat Horn has the best cake booth in the fair and takes a con-siderable deal more money than any 'spice wife' (as women are called who attend to these dainties). Jack Deighton is a shoemaker, and a tolerably good musician...

At the close of the cattle fair the town is swept clean, and lasses walk about with their sweethearts, and the fair puts on another appearance. 'Cheap John's here the day', with his knives, combs, bracelets, &c &c. The 'great Tom Mathews' with his gallanty show generally contrives to pick up a pretty bit of money by his droll ways. Then 'Here's spice Harry, gingerbread Harry — Harry — Harry!' from

Overture to the fair: Mat Horn and Jack Deighton on fiddle and clarinet

Richmond [Yorkshire], with his five-and-twenty lumps of gingerbread for sixpence. Harry stands in a cart with his boxes of 'spice'…

There are a few shows, viz, Scott's sleight of hand, horse performances, &c, &c; and considering the size of the town it has really a very merry-spent fair. At six o'clock dancing begins in nearly all the public-houses, and lasts the whole of 'a merry neet'. Jack Deighton mostly plays at the greatest dance, namely at the Swan Inn, and his companion Horn at one of the others. The dances are merely jigs, three reels and four reels, and country dances, and no more than three sets can dance at a time. It is a matter of course to give the fiddler a penny or twopence each dance; sometimes however another set slips in after the tune's begun and thus tricks the player.

By this time nearly all the stalls are cleared away, and the 'merry neet' is the only place to resort to for amusement. The fiddle and clarinet are to be heard everywhere, and it is astonishing what money is taken by the fiddlers. Some of the spice wives, too … go round with their cakes at intervals, which they often sell more of than before…

Bankrupted by 'women's blacks'

Working women generally wore black worsted stockings, known as
women's blacks, until cheaper cotton made 'white cottons' fashionable.
Hone tells of a victim of new textile technology:

ONE OF the greatest wholesale dealers in women's blacks in a
manufacturing town was celebrated for the largeness of his stock. His
means enabled him to purchase all that were offered to him for sale,
and it was his favourite article. He was an oldfashioned man, and
while the servant-maids were leaving them off he was unconscious of
the change, because he could not believe it. He insisted it was
impossible that household work could be done in 'white cottons'.

Offers of quantities were made to him at reduced prices, which he
bought. His immense capital became locked up in his favourite
women's blacks. Whenever their price in the market lowered, he could
not make his mind up to be quite low enough. His warehouses were
filled with them. When he determined to sell, the demand had wholly
ceased … and becoming bankrupt, he literally died of a broken heart
— from an excessive and unrequited attachment to women's blacks.

Bradford parades the Golden Fleece

Woollen-workers in many parts of England used to hold festivals every
seven years on February 3, the day of Saint Blaise, an obscure martyr
whom they adopted as patron because his image showed an instrument
resembling that used by woolcombers. By the early 19th century his fame
was in decline, but the wool town of Bradford still did him proud in 1825.

TO THE WOOLCOMBERS this saint is indebted for the maintenance
of his reputation in England, for no other trade or persons have an
interest in remembering his existence; and this popularity with a body
of so much consequence may have been the reason … for the retention
of his name in the church calendar at the Reformation.

A report from the Leeds Mercury —

Celebration of Bishop Blaise's Festival
at Bradford, 3d February, 1825

The septennial festival held in honour of Bishop Blaise and of the
invention of woolcombing attributed to that personage was on this
day celebrated at Bradford with great gaiety and rejoicing.

There is no place in the kingdom where the bishop is so splendidly
commemorated as at Bradford. In 1811, 1818 and at previous septen-

nial periods the occasion was celebrated with great pomp and festivity... The celebration of 1825 eclipsed all hitherto seen, and it is most gratifying to know that this is owing to the high prosperity of the worsted and woollen manufacturers, which are constantly adding fresh streets and suburban villages to the town.

The different trades began to assemble at eight o'clock in the morning, but it was near ten o'clock before they all were arranged in marching order in Westgate. The arrangements were actively superintended by Matthew Thompson, Esq. The morning was brilliantly beautiful. As early as seven o'clock strangers poured into Bradford ... in such numbers as to line the roads in every direction, and almost all the vehicles within twenty miles were in requisition. Bradford was never before known to be so crowded with strangers. Many thousands of individuals must have come to witness the scene. About ten o'clock the procession was drawn up in the following order:

Herald bearing a flag

Woolstaplers on horseback, each horse caparisoned with a fleece

Worsted spinners and *manufacturers* on horseback, in white stuff waistcoats, with each a sliver over the shoulder and a white stuff sash, the horses' necks covered with nets made of thick yarn

Merchants on horseback, with coloured sashes

Three guards — Masters' colours — Three guards

Apprentices and masters' sons, on horseback, with ornamented caps, scarlet stuff coats, white stuff waistcoats and blue pantaloons

Bradford and *Keighley bands*

Macebearer, on foot

Six guards — KING — QUEEN — Six guards

Guards — JASON — PRINCESS MEDEA — Guards

Bishop's chaplain

BISHOP BLAISE

Shepherd and shepherdess

Shepherd swains

Woolsorters, on horseback, with ornamented caps and various coloured slivers

Combmakers

Charcoal-burners

Combers' colours

Band

Woolcombers, with wool wigs, &c

Band

Dyers, with red cockades, blue aprons and crossed slivers of red and blue

The following were the numbers of the different bodies, as nearly as could be estimated: 24 woolstaplers, 38 spinners and manufacturers, 6 merchants, 56 apprentices and masters' sons, 160 woolsorters, 30 combmakers, 470 woolcombers and 40 dyers.

The KING, on this occasion, was an old man named Wm Clough, of Darlington, who had filled the regal station at four previous celebrations. JASON (the celebrated legend of the Golden Fleece of Colchis is interwoven with the commemoration of the bishop) was personated by John Smith; and the fair MEDEA, to whom he was indebted for his spoils, rode by his side. BISHOP BLAISE was a personage of very becoming gravity, also named John Smith, and he had enjoyed his pontificate several previous commemorations...

The ornaments of the spinners and manufacturers had a neat and even elegant appearance from the delicate and glossy whiteness of the finely combed wool which they wore. The apprentices and masters' sons, however, formed the most showy part of the procession, their caps being richly adorned with ostrich feathers, flowers and knots of various coloured yarn, and their stuff garments being of the gayest colours. Some of these dresses, we understand, were very costly, from the profusion of their decorations.

The shepherd, shepherdess and swains were attired in light green. The woolsorters, from their number and the height of their plumes of feathers ... formed in the shape of *fleur-de-lis*, had a dashing appearance. The combmakers carried before them the instruments here so much celebrated, raised on standards, together with golden fleeces, rams' heads with gilded horns, and other emblems...

Several well-painted flags were displayed, one of which represented on one side the venerable bishop *in full robes*, and on the other a shepherd and shepherdess under a tree. Another had a painting of Medea *giving up the Golden Fleece* to Jason...

When the procession was ready to move, Richard Fawcett, Esq, on horseback at the head of the spinners, pronounced, uncovered, and with great animation, the following lines, which it has long been customary to repeat on these occasions. [*Eighteen of the 32 lines* —]

> We boast no gems or costly garments vain
> Borrow'd from India or the coast of Spain.
> Our native soil with wool our trade supplies,
> While foreign countries envy us the prize.
> No foreign broil our common good annoys.
> Our country's product all our art employs.
> Our fleecy flocks abound in every vale,
> Our bleating lambs proclaim the joyful tale,
> So let not Spain with us attempt to vie,

> Nor India's wealth pretend to soar so high;
> Nor Jason pride him in his Colchian spoil,
> By hardships gain'd and enterprising toil,
> Since Britons all with ease attain the prize
> And every hill resounds with golden cries.
> To celebrate our founder's great renown
> Our shepherd and our shepherdess we crown.
> For England's commerce, and for George's sway,
> Each loyal subject give a loud HUZZA.

These lines were afterwards several times repeated in the principal streets and roads through which the cavalcade passed...

This proved to be the last such splendid celebration at Bradford. With industrialization, many workers had less reason to show pride in their craft. The next year a correspondent writes:

Since the introduction of machinery by Arkwright and others, very little cloth is manufactured by hand. The woolcomber's greasy and oily wooden horse, the 'hobby' of his livelihood, with the long teeth and pair of cards, are rarely seen. When scribblers, carders, billies and spinning jennies came into use, the wheel no longer turned at the cottage door, but a revolution among the working classes gave occasion for soldiers to protect the mills [*from the threat of machine-breakers*]. Time, however, has ended this strife with wool and begun another with cotton.

> Blaise was remembered in other ways. Charity balls were held in his name; and at the opening of Bradford town hall in 1873 a Blaise trophy was in the procession, with a banner — 'Hail to Bishop Blaize, our Patron Saint.'

The weary newsman's friendless life

THE NEWSMAN is a lone person... All the year round, and every day in the year, the newsman must rise soon after four o'clock and be at the newspaper offices to procure a few of the first morning papers allotted to him, at extra charges, for particular orders, and dispatch them by the early coaches. Afterwards he has to wait for his share of the regular publication of each paper, and he allots these as well as he can among some of the most urgent of his town orders. The next publication at a later hour is devoted to his remaining customers; and he sends off his boys with different portions...

The late arrival of foreign journals, a parliamentary debate unexpectedly protracted, or an article of importance in one paper exclusively, retard the printing and defer the newsman... He is often chid for delay when he should have been praised for speed... He hears at one house that 'Master has waited for the paper this two hours'; at another, 'Master's gone out, and says if you can't bring the paper earlier he won't have it at all'...

Besides buyers, every newsman has readers at so much each paper per hour. One class stipulates for a journal always at breakfast; another, that it is to be delivered exactly at such a time; a third, at any time, so that it is left the full hour... Though the newsman delivers, and allows the use of his paper, and fetches it, for a stipend not half equal to the lowest-paid porter's price for letter-carrying in London [ninepence a mile], yet he finds some with whom he covenanted objecting when it is called for — 'I've not had my breakfast' — 'The paper did not come at the proper time' — 'I've not had leisure to look at it yet' — 'It has not been left an hour' — or any other pretence equally futile or untrue, which were he to allow would prevent him from serving his readers in rotation, or at all...

Soon after three in the afternoon the newsman and some of his boys must be at the offices of the evening papers... He must wait till the newsmen of the Royal Exchange have received theirs for the use of the merchants on 'Change. Some of the first he gets are hurried off to coffeehouse and tavern keepers. When he has procured his full quantity he supplies the remainder of his town customers... Then comes the hasty folding and directing of his reserves for the country, and the forwarding of them to the post-office in Lombard-street or in parcels for the mails, and to other coach-offices. The [London] *Gazette* nights, every Tuesday and Friday, add to his labours. The publication of second and third editions of the evening papers is a super-addition.

On what he calls a 'regular day' he is fortunate if he find himself settled within his own door by seven o'clock, after fifteen hours of running to and fro. It is now only that he can review the business of the day, enter his fresh orders, ascertain how many of each paper he will require on the morrow, arrange his accounts, provide for the money he may have occasion for, eat the only quiet meal he could reckon upon since that of the evening before, and 'steal a few hours from the night' for needful rest...

The newsman desires no work but his own to prove 'Sunday no Sabbath', for on him and his brethren devolves the circulation of upwards of fifty thousand Sunday papers in the course of the forenoon. His Sunday dinner is the only meal he can ensure with his family, and the short remainder of the day the only time he can enjoy in their society with certainty...

In all weather, hail, rain, wind and snow, he is daily constrained to the way and the fare of a wayfaring man. He walks, or rather runs, to distribute information concerning all sorts of circumstances and

A housemaid takes in the paper. A passer-by has just bought one.

persons, except his own. He is unable to allow himself, or others, time for intimacy, and therefore unless he had formed friendships before he took to his servitude, he has not the chance of cultivating them, save with persons of the same calling... In London scarcely anyone knows the newsman but a newsman.

His customers know him least of all... If he dies, the servant receives the paper from his successor, and says when she carries it upstairs, 'If you please, the newsman's dead.' They scarcely ask where he lived; or his fall occasions a pun — 'We always said he *was*, and now we have proof that he *is*, the *late* newsman.'

Once a year a printed 'copy of verses' reminds every newspaper reader that the hand that bore it is open to a small boon. 'The Newsman's Address to his Customers, 1826' deploringly adverts to the general distress [*there was a slump*], patriotically predicts better times and seasonably intimates that in the height of annual festivities he too has a heart capable of joy…

> While at the social board friend joins with friend
> And smiles and jokes and salutations blend,
> Your Newsman wishes to be social too
> And would enjoy the opening year with you.
> Grant him your annual gift: he will not fail
> To drink your health once more with Christmas ale.
> Long may you live to share your Christmas cheer,
> And he still wish you many a happy year!

The sooty tribe's flaunty show

HERE THEY ARE! The sweeps are come! Here is the garland, and the lord and lady! Poor fellows! This is their great festival [*on May Day*]. Their garland is a large cone of holly and ivy framed upon hoops … whereon is sometimes a floral crown, knots of ribbons or bunches of flowers. Its sides are decorated in like manner; and within it is a man who walks wholly unseen, and hence the garland has the semblance of a moving hillock of evergreens.

The chimney-sweepers' jackets and hats are bedizened with gilt-embossed paper. Sometimes they wear coronals of flowers on their heads. Their black faces and legs are grotesquely coloured with Dutch-pink; their shovels are scored with this crimson pigment, interlaced with white chalk. Their lord and lady are magnificent indeed.

The lord is always the tallest of the party, and selected from some other profession to play this distinguished character. He wears a huge cocked hat fringed with yellow or red feathers or laced with gold paper. His coat is between that of the full court dress and the laced coat of the footman of quality. In the breast he carries an immense bunch of flowers. His waistcoat is embroidered; his frill is enormous; his 'shorts' [breeches] are satin, with paste knee-buckles; his stockings silk with figured clocks. His shoes are dancing pumps with large tawdry buckles. His hair is powdered, with a bag and rosette. He carries in his right hand a high cane with a shining metal knob, and in his left a handkerchief held by one corner, and of a colour once white.

His lady is sometimes a strapping girl, though usually a boy in female attire, indescribably flaunty and gaudy: her head in full dress, in her right hand a brass ladle, in her left a handkerchief like to my lord's. When the garland stops, my lord and lady exhibit their graces in a minuet *de la cour* or some other grave movement. In a minute or two they quicken into a dance which enables my lord to picture his conception of elegance. The curvilinear elevation of his arm, with his cane between his finger and thumb, is a courtly grace corresponding with the stiff thrown-back position of his head and the straight fall of the handkerchief in the other hand. My lady answers these inviting positions by equal dignity. They twirl and whirl in sight of each other, though on opposite sides of the dancing garland, to the continued clatter of the shovel and brush held by each capering member of the sooty tribe.

The dance concluded, my lord and my lady interchange a bow and curtsy. My lord flings up his cane arm, displaces his magnificent hat with the other hand and courteously bends, with imploring looks, to spectators at the adjacent windows or in the street. The little sootikins hold up their shovels, my lady with outstretched arm presents the bowl of her ladle and 'the smallest donations are thankfully received' by all the sable fraternity. This is the chimney-sweepers' London pageant on May Day 1825; but for the first time there was this year added a clown, à la Grimaldi, to one or two of the sweeping processions. He grimaces with all his might, walks before Jack-in-the-Green on his hands or his feet as may be most convenient, and practises every antic and trick that his ingenuity can devise...

It is understood, however, that ... masters share a certain portion of their apprentices' profits from the holiday; others take the whole of the first two days' receipts and leave to the worn-out, helpless objects by whom they profit all the year round no more than the scanty gleanings of the third day's performance.

The sweeps find kindly champions

Hone takes up the boys' cause; first by quoting from an essay by his friend Charles Lamb, whose nom-de-plume is Elia:

ELIA, the noble heart of Elia, responds to these humble claimants upon humanity. They cry and have none to help them; he is happy that a personal misfortune to himself can make one of them laugh... He conceives no degradation by supping with them in public at 'Bartlemy Fair'. Kind feelings and honesty make poets and philosophers. Listen to what Elia says:

I have a kindly yearning toward these dim specks — poor blots — innocent blacknesses. I reverence these young Africans of our own growth — these almost clergy imps, who sport their cloth without assumption, and from their little pulpits (the tops of chimneys), in the nipping air of a December morning, preach a lesson of patience to mankind. When a child, what a mysterious pleasure it was to witness their operation! To see a chit no bigger than oneself enter, one knew not by what process, into what seemed the *fauces Averni* — to pursue him in imagination as he went sounding on through so many dark, stifling caverns, horrid shades! To shudder with the idea that 'now, surely, he must be lost forever' — to revive at hearing his feeble shout of discovered daylight — and then (O fullness of delight) running out of doors, to come just in time to see the sable phenomenon emerge in safety, the brandished weapon of his art victorious like some flag waved over a conquered citadel...!

Reader, if thou meetest one of these small gentry in thy early rambles, it is good to give him a penny. It is better to give him twopence...

I am by nature extremely susceptible of street affronts, the jeers and taunts of the populace, the lowbred triumph they display over the casual trip or splashed stocking of a gentleman. Yet can I endure the jocularity of a young sweep with something more than forgiveness...

Pacing along Cheapside with my accustomed precipitation when I walk westward [*away from his work at East India House*], a treacherous slide brought me upon my back in an instant. I scrambled up with pain and shame enough, yet outwardly trying to face it down as if nothing had happened, when the roguish grin of one of these young wits encountered me. There he stood, pointing me out with his dusky finger to the mob ... till the tears for the exquisiteness of the fun (so he thought it) worked themselves out at the corners of his poor red eyes, red from many a previous weeping, and soot-inflamed, yet twinkling through all with such a joy snatched out of desolation ... with such a maximum of glee and minimum of mischief in his mirth ... that I could have been content, if the honour of a gentleman might endure it, to have remained his butt and his mockery till midnight...

Years before, Elia had helped a friend, Jem White, to lay on an annual feast of 'sizzling sausages' for the boy sweeps at the time of Bartholomew Fair; but Jem is dead. So too is Mrs Elizabeth Montagu (hostess of the original bluestocking salons), who every May Day gave the boys 'roast beef and plum-pudding and a shilling each' at her grand house in Portman-square, 'and they danced after their dinner'.
Now the boys 'want a "next friend" to cheer them once a year', Hone says. He prints a letter from Sheffield, 'a reproach to us of the metropolis', telling of an annual dinner given there for the climbing-boys. It is from James Montgomery — poet, editor of the *Sheffield Iris*, and publisher of *The Chimney-Sweeper's Friend and Climbing-Boy's Album*:

'This we have done for about eighteen years in succession. From twenty-four to twenty-six attend; and their appearance, behaviour and *acquirements* (I may say) do credit to their masters. They are a much better generation to look upon than they were when we first took them by the hand.

'On last Easter Monday, out of the twenty-four present, there were only two who did not attend Sunday schools; which, in whatever estimation these institutions may be held, shows that once at least every week these poor children looked like other people's children and associated with them, being clean washed, decently dressed, and employed in reading, and learning to read. Many of them could *write*. Something of the kind is projected at Leeds. A benevolent lady at Derby has this year raised friends, and a fund, for an annual dinner to the climbing-boys there on Easter Monday.'

The aim of *The Chimney-Sweeper's Friend* is 'the gradual abolition of this home slave-trade in little children'. Hone quotes from an appeal Montgomery made to various authors to contribute to the album:

'May I entreat your aid to this humble cause? Were you to see all the climbing-boys in the kingdom (and climbing-*girls*, too, for we have known parents who have employed their own daughters in this hideous way) assembled in one place, you would meet a spectacle of deformed, degraded and depraved humanity, in its very age of innocence ... which would so affect your heart that we should be sure of your hand.'

Not one being of humanity can read the statements in Mr Montgomery's volume with a dry eye — not one but before he has half perused it will resolve never to let a climbing-boy enter his chimney again... Fathers and mothers of England, read the book!

The master sweeps fight back

The boys' employers, troubled by public protests, form a United Society of Master Chimney Sweepers, and on May Day 1826 they treat the boys (and then themselves) at a tavern in St John's Wood. Hone quotes *The Times*:

TWO HUNDRED of their apprentices proceeded in great regularity through the principal streets and squares of the west end of the town, accompanied by an excellent band of music. The clean and wholesome appearance of the lads certainly reflected much credit on their masters... The boys were regaled with a substantial repast of roast beef and plum-pudding; after which the masters themselves sat down to a very excellent dinner...

The chairman addressed his brother tradesmen, congratulating them on the formation of a society that was calculated to do such essential service to the trade in general. It would be the means of promoting the welfare of their apprentices ... who, instead of being permitted to loiter and dance about the streets on the first of May, dressed up in tawdry apparel and soliciting money, should in future be regaled with substantial fare...

Mr Bennett of Welbeck-street addressed the company on the subject of cleansing chimneys with the machine [*the Scandiscope, by which a large brush was sent up the chimneys*], the introduction of which he was confident would never answer the intended purposes...

There were, he admitted, a few solitary instances of accidents happening in their trade, as well as in every other. He now only wished that their opponents might have the opportunity of witnessing the healthy and cheerful state in which their apprentices were.

A master chimney-sweeper, with great vehemence of action and manner, said, 'I am convinced, Mr Chairman, that it is a thing impossible to do away with our climbing boys. For instance, look at the Duke of York's fifty-one new chimneys. Let me ask any one of you, is it possible a machine could be poked up any one of them? I say no, and for this reason — that most of them run in a horizontal line and then abruptly turn up, so that you see a machine would be no more use than if you were to thrust up an old broomstick...

'When I look round the table, and see such respectable gentlemen on my right and on my left and in front of me, who dares to say that the United Society of Master Chimney Sweepers are not as respectable a body of tradesmen as any in London? — and although, if I may be excused the expression, there is not a gentleman now present that has not made his way in the profession by climbing up chimneys.' There was a universal nod of assent...

Hone is not moved by the masters' public-relations exercise:

On the first of May, 1807, the slave trade in the West Indies was proscribed by the British parliament, and we see by the proceedings at the Eyre Tavern, St John's Wood, that on the first of May, 1826, an effort was made to continue the more cruel black slavery of white infants...

A universal admission by all the gentlemen present that they had climbed to respectability by climbing up chimneys is of very little weight with those who observe and know that willing slaves become the greatest and most effective oppressors. And as to the Duke of York's new chimneys, it is not credible his royal highness can be informed that the present construction of his chimneys necessarily dooms unborn infants to the certain fate of having the flesh torn from their joints before they can sweep such chimneys. The scandalous default of a surveyor has subjected the Duke of York to the odium of being quoted as an authority in opposition to a society for abolishing a cruel and useless trade...

The names of the machine chimney-sweepers in different parts of London may be obtained from Mr Wilt, secretary of the Society for Superseding the Necessity of Climbing Boys [founded 1803]... Any person may become a member and acquaint himself with the easy methods by which the machine is adopted to almost any chimney...

> After a long rearguard action by the masters, the climbing of chimneys by anyone under 21 was made illegal in 1842. In the same year, female workers were banned in the mines — but boys of 10 could still work there.

The great fair of Stourbridge

Founded in medieval times, this fair became 'the greatest in the whole nation' (Daniel Defoe in his *Tour through the Island of Great Britain*, 1723). Traders dealt in a vast range of goods. Its three-week run in September was proclaimed by the aldermen and other dignitaries of Cambridge, who rode to the site in a grand procession. By the end of the 18th century it was past its peak, one cause of decline probably being the national growth of turnpike roads and canals. In a Cambridge pamphlet of 1806, quoted by Hone, an account of the fair is partly in the past tense —

THIS FAIR, which was allowed some years ago to be the largest in Europe, is kept in a cornfield about half a mile square, the River Cam running on the north side and the rivulet called the Stour (from which, and the bridge which crosses it, the fair received its name) on the east side. It is about two miles from Cambridge market-place...

The chief diversions at the fair were drolls, rope-dancing, sometimes a music-booth, and plays performed. And though there is an act of parliament which prohibits the acting of plays within ten miles of Cambridge, the Norwich company have permission to perform there every night during the fair...

The shops or booths were built in rows like streets, having each their name, as Garlick-row, Booksellers'-row, Cook-row, &c, and every commodity had its proper place, as the cheese-fair, hop-fair, wool-fair, &c. In these streets ... were all kinds of tradesmen who sell by wholesale or retail, as goldsmiths, toymen, braziers, turners, milliners, haberdashers, hatters, mercers, drapers, pewterers ... in short, most trades that could be found in London, from whence many of them came. There were also taverns, coffeehouses and eating-houses in great plenty ... in any of which (except the coffeehouse booths) you might be accommodated with hot or cold roast goose, roast or boiled pork, &c...

At the south end of Garlick-row ... was a square formed of the
largest booths, called the Duddery, the area of which was from two
hundred and forty to three hundred feet, chiefly taken up with
woollen drapers, wholesale tailors, sellers of secondhand clothes,
&c... In this duddery only, it is said that £100,000 worth of woollen
manufacture has been sold in less than a week, exclusive of the trade
carried on here by the wholesale tailors from London and other parts
of England who transacted their business wholly with their pocketbooks, and meeting with their chapmen here from all parts of the
country, make up their accounts, receive money and take further
orders. These, it is said, exceed the sale of goods actually brought to
the fair... It was frequently known that the London wholesale-men
have carried back orders from their dealers for £10,000 worth of
goods, and some a great deal more...

The 14th of September was the horse-fair day ... always the busiest
day... Colchester oysters and fresh herrings were in great request,
particularly by those who lived in the inland parts of the kingdom.

The fair was like a well-governed city... Here was a court of justice,
open from morning till night, where the mayor or his deputy always
attended to determine all controversies... He had eight servants to
attend him, called *redcoats*, who were employed as constables, and if
any dispute arose between buyer and seller, &c, upon calling out
'redcoat!' there was one of them immediately at hand. And if the
dispute was not quickly decided, the offenders were taken to the said
court and the case determined in a summary way (as was practised in
those called piepowder courts in other fairs), and from which there
was no appeal.

Old Nimble Heels remembers

A man who attended Stourbridge fair as a youth in the 1760s, when it was
flourishing, contributes his memories in 1827:

I AM a septuagenarian, and the following are my personal recollections of more than sixty years ago concerning the once vast fair at
Stourbridge, or Stirbitch...

The clamour of trumpets, deep-sounding drums, screaming of toy
trumpets and din of a thousand discordant voices assailed the ear. The
first booths ... were occupied by the customary shows of wild beasts
and wild men, conjurors, tumblers and rope-dancers... There was a
large theatrical booth occupied by a respectable company of comedians from Norwich... Walnuts being in full perfection, the vendors
continually strolled up and down the fair, bawling every moment in

your ear — 'Twenty a penny walnuts! Walnuts twenty a penny! Crack 'um awoy — crack 'um awoy here!'

Garlick-row, down the centre, was a street of booths ordered by speciality:

...The range of booths No 1 was generally appropriated to furniture-sellers, ironmongers, silversmiths, jewellers, japanners and fine cutlery dealers; the range No 2 to silk mercers, dealers in muslin, toys and millinery; No 3 to dealers in Norwich and Yorkshire manufactures, mercery, lace, hose, fine-made shoes, boots, clogs and pattens; No 4 to furs, fans, toys and to dealers in the various articles of fashionable wares from London; No 5 was occupied by oilmen and dealers in paints, pickles and preserves... My father, who kept the fair [had a booth] forty years and upwards, usually brought home £1,000 or more for goods sold and paid for, besides selling to half that amount on credit to reputable dealers and farmers.

At the end of the row, close to the little inn, stood the dealers in glassware, looking-glasses and small articles of mahogany furniture. Then the inn itself ... was the common resort of the horse-dealers. In this house sat the *pied-poudre* court ... having a pair of stocks and a whipping-post in front and a strongroom [cell] underneath.

Close adjoining northward was the oyster fair. The oysters brought from [King's] Lynn were very large, about the size of a horse's hoof... The more delicate, from Colchester and Whitstable, were very small. In the meadow adjoining were the coal fair, pottery fair and Staffordshireware dealers. The greater part of these articles were delivered up from on board vessels which drew up close to the bank of the river... [At the horse-fair] the show of beautiful animals ... was perhaps unrivalled, unless in Yorkshire: the finest racers and hunters from Yorkshire, the most bony and muscular draught horses from Suffolk... Higher up ... was Ironmonger's-row, with booths occupied by manufacturers from Sheffield, Birmingham, Wolverhampton... Booths for slop-sellers and dealers in haubergs or wagoners' frocks, jackets, half-boots... Then followed the Hatter's-row, close to which was a very respectable coffeehouse and tavern ... kept by the proprietor of Dockrell's coffeehouse in Cambridge, famed for excellent milk punch. There were likewise a number of suttling booths where plain and substantial dinners were served up...

Anyone trading at the fair for the first time had to undergo an initiation or 'christening' at the Robin Hood suttling booth:

Two sponsors having been chosen for him, he was placed in an armed-chair, his head uncovered and his shoes off. Two vergers holding staves and lighted candles assisted the officiator, who was vested in a Cantab's gown and cap, with a bell in one hand and a book in the other. He commenced the ceremony by asking, 'Is this an infidel?'

R Yes.

Q What does he require?

R Instruction...

Q Where are the sponsors? Let them stand forward.

A bowl of punch or bottle of wine was placed on the table handy for the officiator, who then chanted the following doggerel:

> Over thy head I ring this bell
> Because thou art an infidel
> And I know thee by thy smell —
> CHORUS *With a hoccius proxius mandamus*...

[*And after two more stanzas* —]

> This child now to Stirbitch fair is come.
> He may wish to kiss a pretty wench ere he returns home,
> But let him be advised and not to Barnwell roam —
> CHORUS *For a hoccius*, &c...

Q Who names this child? R We do.

The sponsors then called him 'Nimble Heels' — 'Stupid Stephen' — 'Tommy Simper' or other ludicrous names. The officiator then drank and gave the novice a full bumper.

> Nimble Heels henceforward shall be his name,
> Which to confess let him not feel shame
> Whether 'fore master, miss or dame —
> CHORUS *— With a hoccius*, &c.

> This child first having paid his dues
> Is welcome then to put on his shoes
> And sing a song or tell a merry tale, as he may choose —
> CHORUS *— About a hoccius*, &c.

A verse which memory can afford to forget [*something unprintably rude*] intervenes before the next.

> Then hand the can unto our jolly friar,
> And laugh and sing as we sit round the fire,
> And when our wine is out let all to bed retire —
> CHORUS *— With a hoccius*, &c...

Supper was then brought in ... good substantial fair-keeping fare such as roast goose, fowls, pork, vegetables, fruit pies and bread, which altogether were charged at the moderate price of one shilling a head. Malt liquor, punch and wine might be had *ad libitum*...

[*Signed*] NIMBLE HEELS
The name given me at Stourbridge fair sixty-five years ago
Somers Town [London], *13th Sept 1827*

Young lambs to sell!

Young lambs to sell! Young lambs to sell!
If I'd as much money as I could tell
I'd not come here with lambs to sell!
Dolly and Molly, Richard and Nell,
Buy my young lambs and I'll use you well.

THIS IS a 'London cry' at the present time [1827]. The engraving represents the crier, William Liston, from a drawing for which he purposely *stood*. This public character was born in the Gallowgate in the city of Glasgow. He became a soldier in the wagon-train commanded by Colonel Hamilton and served under the Duke of York in Holland [*a disastrous action against the French*], where on the 6th of October 1799 he lost his right arm and left leg, and his place in the army.

His misfortunes thrust distinction upon him. From having been a private in the ranks, where he would have remained a single undistinguishable cipher 0 amongst a row of ciphers 000000000, he now makes a figure in the world, and is perhaps better known throughout England than any other individual of his order in society, for he has visited almost every town with 'young lambs to sell'.

He has a wife and four children. The latter are constantly employed in making the 'young lambs', with white cotton-wool for fleeces, spangled with Dutch gilt, the head of flour paste, red paint on the cheeks, two jet-black spots for eyes, horns of twisted shining tin, legs to correspond, and pink tape tied round the neck for a graceful collar. A full basket of these, and his songlike cry, attract the attention of the juvenile population, and he contrives to pick up a living...

The day after last Christmas day his cry in Covent Garden allured the stage-manager to purchase four dozen of 'young lambs', and at night they were brought out at the theatre in the basket of a performer who personated their old proprietor, and cried so as to deceive the younger part of the audience into a belief that he was their real favourite of the streets.

I remember the *first* crier of 'young lambs to sell!' He was a maimed sailor, and with him originated the manufacture. If I am not mistaken, this man, many years after I had ceased to be a purchaser ... was guilty of some delinquency for which he forfeited his life. *His* cry was:

> Young lambs to sell! Young lambs to sell!
> Two for a penny young lambs to sell —
> Two for a penny young lambs to sell !
> If I'd as much money as I could tell
> I wouldn't cry young lambs to sell!
>
> Young lambs to sell! Young lambs to sell —
> Two for a penny young lambs to sell!
>   Young lambs to se–e–ll,
>   Young la–a–mbs to sell!

Though it is five-and-thirty years ago since I heard the sailor's musical cry, it still sings in my memory, It was a tenor of modulated harmonious tune, till in the last line but one it became a thorough bass and rolled off at the close with a loud swell that filled urchin listeners with awe and admiration. During this chant his head was elevated, and he gave his full voice, and apparently his looks, to the winds; but the moment he concluded, and when attention was yet riveted, his address became particular: his persuasive eye and jocular address flashed round the circle of 'my little masters and mistresses' and his hand presented a couple of his snow-white fleecy charge, dabbled in gold, 'Two for a penny!' Nor did he resume his song till ones and twos were in the possession of probably every child who had a halfpenny or penny at command...

The new lamb-seller ... declares, notwithstanding all the noise he makes, the carrying on of the lamb business is scarcely better than pig-shaving: 'Sir,' says he, 'it's great *cry* and little wool' [*proverbial: an unprofitable task was likened to shearing a pig*]...

Not having been at his native place for two-and-twenty years, the desire to see it once more is strong within him, and he purposes next Easter to turn his face northwards with his family, and 'cry' all the way from London to Glasgow. Let the little ones, therefore, in the towns of his route keep a penny or two by them to lay out in 'young lambs', and so help the poor fellow along the road in this stage of his struggle through life.

Waiting for water: a summer scene

Down in the Potteries it's 'a sight'
The whole day long, from morn till night,
To see the girls, and women grown,
The child, the damsel and old crone
By the well-sides, at work or singing,
While waiting for the water's springing;
Telling what Francis Moore presages
Or who did not bring home his wages.

266

P'raps one exclaims, 'Time runs away!'
Her neighbour cries, 'Why, what's today?'
And when she knows, feigns mighty sorrow —
She thought today would be tomorrow!
Another thinks another's daughter
Grows monstrous tall —— 'Halloo! the water!'

Up it rises, and they scurry
In a skimble-skamble hurry,
Shouting and bawling, 'Where's the pot?'
'Why, I was first' — 'No you were not.'
As quick as thought they empt' the well,
And the last-comers take a spell
At waiting, while the others go
With their full pitchers, dawdling so
You'd think they'd nothing else to do
But to keep looking round at you.
However, all are honest creatures
And some have pretty shapes and features:
So if there be an end of lotteries
You may find prizes in the Potteries.   *Hone*

Flowers 'all alive' for humble streets

'HERE THEY ARE! Blowing, growing, all alive!' This was an old London cry by little flower gardeners who brought the products of their grounds to the metropolis and wheeled them through the streets in a barrow, 'Blowing, growing, all alive!' to tempt purchasers in the humble streets and alleys of working neighbourhoods. Acts of Parliament have put down the flowerpots which were accustomed to topple on the walkers' heads from the windows of houses wherein flower-fanciers dwelt.

An act of 1817 banned flowerpots on London windowsills , unless 'perfectly secured from falling'.

Laces, pins, wigs and shoeblacking

Commenting on Marcellus Lauron's 17th-century prints, *Cries of the City of London*, Hone notes what has changed or not changed. For example:

Long thread laces, long and strong

This cry was extinct in London for a few years while the females dressed naturally [*corsetry went out in the 1790s*]. Now, when some are resuming the old fashion of stiff stays and tight-lacing, and pinching their bowels to inversion, looking unmotherly and bodiless, the cry has been partially revived.

Pretty Maids, pretty Pins, pretty Women

A man with a square box sideways under his left arm holds in his right hand a paper of pins opened. He retails ha'p'orths and pen-n'orths which he cuts off from his paper. I remember when pins were disposed of in this manner in the streets by women. Their cry was a musical distich: *Three-rows-a-penny, pins! / Short whites and middl—ings!*

Fine Tie or a fine Bob, sir?

A wig-seller stands with one on his hand, combing it, and talks to a customer... Wigs on blocks stand on a bracketed board outside his window. This was when everybody, old and young, wore wigs — when the price for a common one was a guinea, and a journeyman had a new one every year — when it was an article in every apprentice's indenture that his master should find him in 'one good and sufficient wig yearly, and every year, for and during and unto the expiration of the full end and term of his apprenticeship'.

Japan your Shoes, your honour!

I recollect shoeblacks formerly at the corner of almost every street, especially in great thoroughfares. There were several every morning on the steps of St Andrew's Church, Holborn, till late in the forenoon. But the greatest exhibition of these artists was on the site of Finsbury-square when it was an open field and a depository for the stones used in paving and street-masonry. There a whole army of shoeblacks intercepted the citizens and their clerks on their way from Islington and Hoxton to the counting-houses and shops in the city, with 'Shoe-black, your honour!' 'Black your shoes, sir!'

Each of them had a large old tin kettle containing his apparatus, viz: a capacious pipkin or other large earthen pot containing the blacking, which was made of ivory black, the coarsest moist sugar and pure water with a little vinegar — a knife — two or three brushes — and an old wig. The old wig was an indispensable requisite to a shoeblack. It whisked away the dust, or thoroughly wiped off the wet dirt which his knife and brushes could not entirely detach. A rag tied to the end of a stick smeared his viscid blacking on the shoe, and if the blacking was 'real japan' it shone. The old experienced shoe-wearers preferred an oleaginous, lustreless blacking. A more liquid blacking, which took a polish from the brush, was of later use and invention.

Nobody, at that time [*before 1810 or so*], wore boots, except on horseback, and everybody wore breeches and stockings. Pantaloons or trousers were unheard-of [*except among the lower orders*]. The old shoeblacks operated on the shoes while they were on the feet, and so dextrously so as not to soil the fine white cotton stocking which was at one time the extreme of fashion, or to smear the buckles...

Latterly you were accommodated with an old pair of shoes to stand in, and the yesterday's paper to read, while your shoes were cleaning and polishing and your buckles were whitened and brushed.

When shoestrings first came into vogue, the Prince of Wales, now the king [George IV], appeared with them in his shoes, and a deputed body of the buckle-makers of Birmingham presented a petition to his royal highness to resume the wearing of buckles, which was good-naturedly complied with. Yet in a short time shoestrings entirely superseded buckles.

The first incursion on the shoeblacks was by the makers of 'patent cake-blacking', on sticks formed with a handle, like a small battledore. They suffered a more fearful invasion from the makers of liquid blacking in bottles. Soon afterwards, when Day & Martin manufactured the *ne plus ultra* of blacking, private shoeblacking became general, public shoeblacks rapidly disappeared, and now [1827] they are extinct. The last shoeblack that I remember in London sat under the covered entrance of Red Lion-court, Fleet-street, within the last six years.

Why Johnnie did sae ill

AT A LITTLE SELECT PARTY in Edinburgh of 'bien bodies' there was an ancient couple present who had made a competency in a small shop in town and retired from business, leaving their only son as successor in the shop, with a stock free from every encumbrance [free of debt]. But John, after a few years, had failed in the world, and his misfortunes became the theme of discourse:

Mrs *A* Dear me, Mrs K, I wonder how your Johnnie did sae ill in the same shop you did sae weel in?

Mrs *K* Hoot, woman, it's nae wonder at a'.

Mrs *A* Weel, how did it happen?

Mrs *K* I'll tell you how it happened. Ye mun ken, when Tam and me began to merchandize, we took parritch night and morning, and kail to our dinner. When things grew better we took tea to our breakfast. A-weel, woman, they aye mended, and we sometimes coft [bought] a lamb-leg for a Sunday dinner, and before we gae up, we sometimes coft a chuckie [hen] — we were doing sae weel.

Noo, ye maun ken, when Johnnie began to merchandize, he began at the chuckie first.

A lover of a chirruping cup

Tommy Bell of Houghton-le-Spring

This is an eccentric, goodhumoured character — a lover of a chirruping
cup, and a favourite with the pitmen of Durham. He dresses like them,
and mixes and jokes with them; and his portrait seems an appropriate
illustration of the following paper by a gentleman of the north.

Pitmen's lives and deaths

> O the bonny pit laddie, the canny pit laddie,
> The bonny pit laddie for me, O!
> He sits in a hole as black as a coal
> And brings all the white money to me, O!

GENTLE READER, whilst thou sittest toasting thy feet at the glowing
fuel in thy grate, watching in dreaming unconsciousness the various
shapes and fantastic forms appearing and disappearing in the bright
red heat of thy fire ... dost thou ever think of that race of mortals

whose whole life is spent beyond a hundred fathoms below the surface of mother earth, plucking from its unwilling bosom the materials of thy greatest comfort...?

The pitmen ... are a race entirely distinct from the peasantry surrounding them. They are principally within a few miles of the river Wear, in the county of Durham, and the river Tyne, which traces the southern boundary of Northumberland. They reside in long rows of one-storied houses, called by themselves 'pit-rows', built near the chief entrance of the mine. To each house is attached a small garden ... wherein they pay so much attention to the cultivation of flowers that they frequently bear away prizes at floral exhibitions.

Within the memory of the writer (and his locks are not yet 'silver'd o'er with age') the pitmen were a rude, bold, savage set of beings, apparently cut off from their fellow men in their interests and feelings; often guilty of outrage in their moments of ebrious mirth, not from dishonest motives or hopes of plunder, but from recklessness and lack of that civilization which binds the wide and ramified society of a great city. From the age of five or six years their children are immersed in the dark abyss of their lower worlds, and when even they enjoy the 'light of the blessed sun', it is only in the company of their immediate relations...

The pitmen have the air of a primitive race. They marry almost constantly with their own people. Their boys follow the occupations of their sires — their daughters, at the age of blooming and modest maidenhood, linking their fate to some honest *neebor's bairn*. Thus from generation to generation family has united with family, till their population has become a dense mass of relationship, like the clans of our northern friends...

The dress of one of them is that of the whole people. Imagine a man of only middling stature (few are tall or robust), with several large blue marks, occasioned by cuts impregnated with coaldust, on a pale and swarthy countenance, a coloured handkerchief round his neck, a 'posied waistcoat' opened at the breast to display a striped shirt beneath, a short blue jacket somewhat like but rather shorter than the jackets of our seamen, velvet breeches invariably unbuttoned and untied at the knee, on the tapering calf a blue worsted stocking with white clocks, and finished downwards by a long, low-quartered shoe, and you have a pitman before you, equipped for his Saturday's cruise to 'canny Newcastle' or for his Sabbath's gayest holiday.

On a Saturday evening you will see a long line of road leading to the nearest market town grouped everywhere with pitmen and their wives or lasses, laden with large baskets of the stomach's comforts sufficient for a fortnight's consumption. They only are paid for their labour at such intervals, and their weeks are divided into what they term 'pay week' and 'bauf week' [also 'baff']. (The etymology of 'bauf' I leave thee, my kind reader, to find out.)

All merry and happy trudging home with their spoils — not unfrequently the thrifty husband is seen 'half seas over', wrestling his onward way with an obstinate little pig to whose hind leg is attached a string ... while ever and anon this third in the number of 'obstinate graces' seeks a sly opportunity of evading its unsteady guide ... and Geordie (a common name among them) attempts a masterly retrograde reel to regain his fugitive.

A long cart, lent by the owners of the colliery ... is sometimes filled with the women and their marketings, jogging homeward at a smart pace, and from these every wayfarer receives a shower of taunting coarse jokes, and the air is filled with loud, rude merriment. Pitmen do not consider it any deviation from propriety for their wives to accompany them to the alehouses of the market town and join their husbands in their glass and pint. I have been amused by peeping through the open window of a pothouse to see parties of them, men and women, sitting round a large fir table, talking, laughing, smoking and drinking con amore; and yet these women are never addicted to excessive drinking. The men, however, are not particularly abstemi–ous when their hearts are exhilarated with the bustle of a town.

When the pitman is about to descend to the caverns of his labour he is dressed in a checked flannel jacket, waistcoat and trousers, with a bottle or canteen slung across his shoulders and a satchel or haversack at his side to hold provender... At all hours, night and day, groups of men and boys are seen dressed in this fashion wending their way to their colliery, some carrying Sir Humphry Davy's (called by them 'Davys') safety-lamp, ready trimmed and brightened for use.

They descend the pit by means of a basket or 'corf', or merely by swinging themselves on to a chain suspended at the extreme end of the cordage, and are let down, with inconceivable rapidity, by a steam-engine. Clean and orderly, they coolly precipitate themselves into a black, smoking and bottomless-looking crater, where you would think it almost impossible human lungs could play, or blood dance through the heart. At nearly the same moment you see others coming up, as jetty as the object of their search, drenched and tired.

I have stood in a dark night near the mouth of a pit, lighted by a suspended grate filled with flaring coals casting an unsteady but fierce reflection on the surrounding swarthy countenances; the pit emitting a smoke as dense as the chimney of a steam-engine; the men, with their sooty and grimed faces, glancing about their sparkling eyes while the talking motion of their red lips disclosed rows of ivory; the steam-engines' clanking and crashing and the hissing from the huge boilers making a din only broken by the loud, mournful and musical cry of the man stationed at the top of the pit shaft, calling down to his companions in labour at the bottom. This altogether is a scene as wild and fearful as a painter or a poet could wish to see.

All have heard of the dreadful accidents in coalmines from explosions of fire-damp, inundations, &c, yet few have witnessed the heart-rending scenes of domestic calamity which are the consequence. Aged fathers, sons, and sons' sons ... all are sometimes swept away...

Never shall I forget one particular scene of family destruction. I was passing along a pit-row immediately after a firing, as the explosion of fire-damp is called, when I looked into one of the houses, and my attention became so riveted that I scarcely knew I had entered the room. On one bed lay the bodies of two men, burnt to a livid ash colour. The eldest was apparently sixty, the other about forty — father and son. On another bed in the same room were 'streaked' three fine boys, the oldest not more than fifteen ... all destroyed at the same instant by the same destructive blast let loose from the mysterious hand of Providence.

And I saw — oh God! I shall never forget — I saw the vacant, mad-dened countenance and quick, wild glancing eye of the fatherless, widowed, childless being who in the morning was smiling in her domestic felicity; whose heart a few hours before was exultingly beating as she looked on her *gudeman and bonny bairns*. Before the evening sun had set she was alone in the world, without a prop for her declining age, and every endearing tie woven around her heart was torn and dissevered.

I passed into the neat little garden — it was the springtime — part of the soil was fresh turned up, and some culinary plants were newly set. These had been the morning work of the younger father — his spade was standing upright in the earth at the last spot he had laboured at. He had left it there ready for the evening's employment. The garden was yet blooming with all the delightful freshness of vernal vegetation — its cultivator was withered and dead. His spade was at hand for another to dig its owner's grave.

Amidst all their dangers, the pitmen are a cheerful, industrious race of men. They were a few years ago much addicted to gambling, cockfighting, horseracing, &c. Their spare hours are diverted now to a widely different channel: they are for the most part members of the Wesleyan sects; and not unfrequently, in passing their humble but neat dwellings, instead of brawls and fights you hear a peaceful con-gregation of worshippers uttering their simple prayers, or the loud hymn of praise breaking the silence of the eventide...

Yorkshire's pace-setting omnibus

The Velocitas, or Malton, Driffield and Hull Fly Boat.

A CARRIAGE bearing this name, of which the above is a sketch, forms a neat, safe, pleasant and commodious conveyance from Malton by way of Driffield to Hull every other day, and from Hull to Malton on the intermediate days, during the summer months.

The vehicle is, in fact, a boat on wheels, driven like a stagecoach, and furnished on each side of the body with a seat extending the whole length, on which the passengers are ranged. The top is covered with a permanent awning, to which a curtain appended may be drawn up or let down at pleasure so as to enjoy a view of the country or shut out the sun and weather.

This is two years ahead of the first London omnibuses of 1829.

English coaches outshine the French

One of five contributions in 1827 from 18-year-old Mary Novello, just
before she married Charles Cowden Clarke, the early friend of John Keats.
She was to have a long literary career.

IT WAS a November morning — sullen and lowering. A dense fog left the houses but half distinguishable on either side of the way as I passed through Holborn to The Saracen's Head, Snow-hill, where I had taken my place the preceding evening in the ——— coach...

The coach, a handsome, well-built vehicle, stood on one side of the yard, in all the brilliancy of a highly varnished claret ground... The four beautiful, spirited animals belonging to it, with their glossy bright skins covered with cloths till the moment of 'putting to', were then led forth by a fellow in corduroy breeches ... terminating in a pair of dull and never-shining topboots — a waistcoat which had been of red plush spotted with black , but the glories of its gules and sable were well-nigh effaced by the long line of successive cross-quarterings of grease and mud — a face hard and liny that looked impenetrable... He came forward with that slouching gait and hoarse, rasping voice so well personified by the admirable and all-observing Charles Mathews [noted comic actor].

Then the coachman appeared — well buttoned up to the throat in an enormous box-coat of a whitish drab colour, fastened with immense mother-o'-pearl buttons — a yellow silk handkerchief round his neck, reaching just under the nether lip and covering the tips of his ears — a hat with brims like the walls of Babylon — and an air of affected nonchalance which tells you that you are expected to look upon him in a very different light from the attentive 'coachee' of some years back. He is now a complete fine gentleman; for as the gentleman affects the coachman [adopts his style], why should not the coachman affect the gentleman? They are now not to be known apart.

The luggage is then brought forth and loaded, and all the passengers installed... 'More last words', and a paper of biscuits is handed in at the coach-window to the little boy who is going to ——— under the special care of the coachman, and as his mamma delightedly observes, is already become a favourite with the 'kind-looking lady' opposite to him. The small parcel 'to be left at Mr K——'s at the small white cottage' is snugly slipped into the coach-pocket — and the final 'all right' is given from the impatient passengers 'behind'.

How different is the quiet and orderly manner in which a vehicle is thus despatched to go hundreds of miles, from the dire bustle and utter 'confusion of tongues' attendant upon the departure of a French *diligence* [stagecoach].

Imagine a spacious yard paved with stones shaped like enormous sugared almonds jutting out in all directions to the utter annoyance of the *five* poor animals, or rather skeletons, in rope harness, which are about to be yoked to an uncouth machine, looking the complete antithesis of rapidity of motion — of a colour perfectly indescribable but something approaching to a dingy red intermixed with a rusty, dusty black — straw peeping out in every direction, whether from roof or sides, or entangled among the broken, rickety steps which project in awful forewarning of grazed shins and sprained ankles.

The *conducteur* in his dark blue jacket turned up with scarlet — leather breeches shining with the perpetual friction of the saddle — boots like brewing vats — a hat very nearly a perfect cone with a rim, set in the middle of a regular copsewood of coal-black hair, surmounting a face whose dark complexion, fiercely sparkling eyes and stiff mustachios help to give force to the excessive tension of muscle in his countenance, which is actually convulsed with ire as he sends forth volleys of *sacrés* and *morbleus* at the *maudit entêté* on the roof who persists in loading the different articles in exact opposition to all the passionate remonstrances and directions of poor *monsieur le conducteur*. *Femmes de chambre* shrieking at the very top of their voices — '*garçons* of fifty' equally vociferous in bawling '*On vient! on vient!*' though no one calls — *commissionaires* insisting on the necessity of passports to incredulous Englishmen with an incessant '*Mais que diable donc, monsieur!*' — hordes of beggars shouting forth their humble petitions of '*Pour l'amour du bon dieu un petit liard, monsieur.*'

'*Ah, Seigneur! Qu'est-ce que j'ai fait de mes clefs?*' screams the landlady. '*Sacré nom de tonnerre! Tais-toi donc,*' growls the landlord in a voice like the thunder he invokes. At last the ponderous vehicle is set in motion amid the deafening clamour of the surrounding group and the hideous, unrelentingly eternal cracking of the *conducteur's* detested *fouet*.

Spit on handsel for luck

HENRI MISSON [*Memoirs and Observations in his Travels over England*, 1719] ... says ... 'A woman that goes much to market told me t'other day that the butcher-women of London, those that sell fowls, butter, eggs, &c, and in general most tradespeople, have a particular esteem for what they call handsel, that is to say the first money they receive in a morning. They kiss it, spit upon it and put it in a pocket by itself.'

The Rev George Lemon [in his *English Etymology*, 1783] explains handsel to be 'the first money received at market, which many superstitious people will spit on, either to render it tenacious that it may remain with them and not vanish away like a fairy gift; or else to render it propitious and lucky, that it may draw more money to it'. The latter is at this day [1831] the prevailing belief with lovers of handsel among the London dealers in markets and hawkers of provisions in the streets.

To him that goes to law, nine things are requisite

1 A good deal of money. 2 A good deal of patience.
3 A good cause. 4 A good attorney. 5 Good counsel.
6 Good evidence. 7 A good jury. 8 A good judge.
And lastly, good luck.

Pure water, a penny a pailful

ON THE WEST SIDE of Hampstead in the middle of one of the pleasant meadows called Shepherd's Fields, at the left hand of the footpath going from Belsize House towards the church, this arch, embedded above and around by the green turf, forms a conduit-head to a beautiful spring. The specific gravity of the fluid, which yields several tuns a day [1 tun=216 gallons], is little more than that of distilled water. Hampstead abounds in other springs but they are mostly

The Hampstead water-carriers at work

impregnated with mineral substances. The water of Shepherd's Well, therefore, is in continual request, and those who cannot otherwise conveniently obtain it are supplied through a few of the villagers, who make a scanty living by carrying it to houses for a penny a pailful... This and the ponds in the Vale of Health are the ordinary sources of public supply to Hampstead.

> A plaque, corner of Fitzjohns-avenue and Akenside-road, commemorates this spring (anciently a source of the Tyburn, one of London's lost rivers).

All Lotteries End for Ever!

In 1826, under a Tory government, it was decided that state lotteries were harmful in so many ways that they should be abolished — even though the government's cut of the takings was £250,000 a year, a great sum then.
At first the 'death of the lottery' was to be on July 18.

THE LOTTERY-OFFICE KEEPERS incessantly plied every man, woman and child in the United Kingdom and its dependencies with petitions to make a fortune in 'the last lottery that can be drawn'. Men paraded the streets with large printed placards on poles, or pasted on their backs, announcing 'All Lotteries End for Ever! 18th of July'. The walls were stuck and handbills were thrust into the hands of street passengers [passers-by] with the same heartrending intelligence, and with the solemn assurance that the demand for tickets and shares was immense! Their prices had so risen, were so rising, and would be so far beyond all calculation, that to get shares or tickets at all they must be instantly purchased!
…But on some account or other the pathetic appeal of the benevolent contractors was disregarded, and the gentlemen about to be 'turned off' were as unheeded and as unlamented as criminals who say or sing in their last moments —

> Gentlefolks all,
> Pity our fall!
> Have pity all,
> Pity our fall!

For the final draw, the lottery contractors, whom Hone calls 'speculators on public credulity', combined forces to offer the unprecedented temptation of six prizes of £30,000. One of their stunts to woo buyers was a grand procession throughout London and the suburbs:

Three men in liveries, scarlet and gold. Six men bearing boards at their backs and on their breasts with inscriptions in blue and gold, 'All lotteries end Tuesday next. Six £30,000.' Band of trumpets, clarinets, horns, &c. A large purple silk banner carried by six men, inscribed in large gold letters, 'All lotteries end Tuesday next. Six £30,000.' A painted carriage representing the lottery wheel, drawn by two dappled grey horses, tandem fashion … a boy seated in a dickey behind the machine, turning the handle… A square lottery carriage surmounted by a gilt imperial crown; the carriage covered with labels with 'All lotteries end on Tuesday next…' Twelve men in blue and gold, with boards on poles with 'Lotteries end for ever on Tuesday next…'
The event was likewise announced as certain in all the newspapers,

and by cartloads of bills showered down areas and thrust under knockers — when behold! 'The Lords of the Treasury were pleased to order' the final drawing to be postponed to Thursday the 18th of October. But all the good people so informed were wisely uninformed that this 'order' was obtained by the lottery-office folks, to give them a long day to get rid of their unsold tickets.

After this the streets were cavalcaded ... to announce the *next* 'last of the lottery'... The most pageant-like machine was an octagon

Urchins pelt the octagonal machine in slummy Monmouth-street

framework covered by printed lottery placards... It overtopped the sills of the first-floor windows... The route it chiefly took evidenced the *low* hopes of the proprietors. St Giles's and the purlieus of that neighbourhood [*noted for slums*] seem to have been selected...

Eyewitness report by an artist who saw this 'strange vehicle covered all over with lottery papers of various colours', and did the picture for Hone :

It entered Monmouth-street, that den of filth and rags, where so great a number of young urchins gathered together in a few minutes as to be astonishing. There being an empty chair behind, one of them seated himself in it and rode backwards. Another said, 'Let's have a stone through it,' and a third cried, 'Let's sludge it!' This was no sooner proposed than they threw stones, oyster shells and dirt, and burst several of the sheets. This attack brought the driver from his seat, and he was obliged to walk by the side of his machine up this foul street ... halting now and then to threaten the boys, who still followed and threw...

Hone gathers a mass of lottery material, from the 16th century on, making sixty-six close-packed pages in all. A memory from 1810:

When the tickets were publicly drawn at Guildhall ... it was a curious sight for an indifferent spectator to go and behold the visages of the anxious crowd; to mark the hopes and the fears that seemed to agitate them... It is a fact that poor medical practitioners used constantly to attend in the hall to be ready to let blood [*for a fee*] in cases where the sudden proclaiming of the fate of tickets ... was found to have an overpowering effect on their spirits.

One of various examples of unfortunate punters:

Early in the reign of George II, the footman of a lady of quality, under the absurd infatuation of a dream, disposed of the savings of the last twenty years of his life in two lottery tickets; which proving blanks, after a few melancholy days he put an end to his life. In his box was found the following plan of the manner in which he should spend the £5,000 prize, which his mistress preserved as a curiosity:

'As soon as I have received the money I will marry Grace Towers; but as she has been cross and coy, I will use her as a servant. Every morning she shall get me a mug of strong beer, with a toast, nutmeg and sugar in it. Then I will sleep till ten, after which I will have a large sack posset. My dinner shall be on table by one, and never without a good pudding. I will have a stock of wine and brandy laid in. About five in the afternoon I will have tarts and jellies, and a gallon bowl of punch; at ten, a hot supper of two dishes. If I am in good humour, and Grace *behaves herself*, she shall sit down with me. To bed about twelve.'

Among many opposers and mockers, a notable one makes a timeless point:

In 1731 Henry Fielding wrote a farce for Drury Lane Theatre called *The Lottery* ... acted with considerable success, especially about the time when the lottery was drawn at Guildhall... It opens with a lottery-office keeper, Mr Stocks [*he sings*]:

> A lottery is a taxation
> Upon all the fools in creation,
>   And heaven be prais'd,
>   It is easily rais'd:
> Credulity's always in fashion...

The promoters went on luring 'all the fools in creation' for the next 95 years with lavish advertising. In the lottery's final decades they issued innumerable handbills with puffing verses and woodblock illustrations. Here are two examples given by Hone (no doubt unaware that the milkmaid was one of hundreds of lottery-puff designs done for odd guineas by his friend George Cruikshank).

> Though the lotteries soon will be over, I'm told
> That now is the time to get pailsful of gold,
> And if there is any real truth in a dream
> I myself shall come in for a share of the cream.
> We hail, ere the sun, the first breath of the morn,
> And 'tis said, 'Early birds get the best of the corn.'
> Of the *Four Twenty-Thousands*, perhaps fortune may
> Have in store one for me, as they're drawn in *one day!*

For the gay fruits of nature what wish can you feel
When compared with the *fruits* of the lottery wheel?
My basket of fruit I'd exchange with great glee
If one *golden pippin* they'd only give me.

*One of the chief lottery agents, Thomas Bish (who thrived and became an MP),
'employed the greatest number of lottery-laureates', Hone says. Here is part of a
song about Paddy from Cork, who comes to England thinking that the streets are
paved with gold and the hedges grow guineas:*

But och, blood-and-ouns! only mark my surprise
When only great stones in the *strates* met my eyes!
No guineas at all on the bushes there grew.
Not a word that they told me, I found, sirs, was true.
'Och! Why wa'n't I drowned and made food for the fish?'
Thus I growled, till I lighted on one *Master Bish*.

Master Bish had found out the philosopher's stone,
And a thousand yellow guineas he gave me for one!
...Then honeys, attend, and pursue my advice:
Och, to 9 Charing Cross be off in a trice.
Buy a lottery chance, for the drawing-day's near,
And perhaps like friend Paddy a fortune you'll clear.

*Another effort of a Bish laureate, 'The Age of Wonders' (a parody of a hit song,
'Four in Hand', dating from 1810), publicizes a tempting roll-over. A sample:*

This is a *wonder-working* age, by all it is agreed on,
And *wonders* rise up every day for public gaze to feed on.
To sketch a few 'tis my intent while now I'm in the mind, sir,
And crown them all with *one* you'll own will leave them far behind, sir.

The greatest *wonder* yet to tell, which all the world surprises,
Is BISH's *famous lottery*, and BISH's *wondrous* prizes.
Three *fifty thousands* grace the scheme which yet remain undrawn, sir.
A *wonder* which was never known since any man was born, sir.
 Then push along, to BISH's go! Of fortune he's the man, sir.
 A vote of thanks *nem con* we'll pass for such a noble plan, sir.

282

Hone contributes a dissident ballad of his own, modelled on a popular song-form going back to the 17th century. A few stanzas:

Clerks smiled, and whispered lowly,
'This is the time or never.
   There *must* be a rise —
   Buy, and be wise
Or your chance is gone forever.'

Yet of the shares and tickets,
Spite of all arts to sell 'em,
   There were more unsold
   Than dare be told,
Although if I knew I'd tell 'em...

The lottery drew the humble
Often aside from his labour
   To build in the air,
   And dwelling there
He beggared himself and his neighbour.

If the scheme-makers tumble
Down to their proper station
   They must starve, or work,
   Turn thief, or Turk,
Or hang for the good of the nation.

" The Last."

Hone's prophetic conclusion: Here at last end the notices respecting the lottery, of which much has been said because, of all depraving institutions, it had the largest share in debasing society while it existed; and because after all perhaps the monster is 'only scotched, not killed'.

Twelve days of Christmas

Came next the chill December,
Yet he, through merry feasting which he made
And great bonfires, did not the cold remember,
His Saviour's birth so much his mind did glad.
Upon a shaggy bearded goat he rode...
And in his hand a broad deepe bowle he beares,
Of which he freely drinks an health to all his peers.

Spenser, *The Faerie Queen*, VII, vii

The boar's head, the rarest dish

WITH OUR FOREFATHERS, a soused boar's head was borne to the principal table in the hall with great state and solemnity as the first dish on Christmas day. In the book of *Christmasse Carolles* printed by Wynkyn de Worde in 1521 are the words sung at this 'chefe servyce'...

Caput apri defero
Reddens laudes Domino.

The bore's head in hande bring I,
With garlandes gay and rosemary,
I pray you all synge merely,   *merrily*
Qui estis in convivio.

The bore's head, I understande,
Is the chefe servyce in this lande.
Loke wherever it be fande
Servite cum Cantico.

Be gladde, lords, more and lasse,
For this hath ordayned our stewàrde
To chere you all this Christmasse,
The bore's head with mustàrde.

This survives on a single leaf of *Christmasse Carolles* in the Bodleian Library, Oxford — all that is left of Wynkyn de Worde's book.

A variant of the 1521 carol is still in use at Queen's College, Oxford —

A boar's head in hand bear I
Bedecked with bays and rosemary,
And I pray you my masters, be merry
Quod estis in convivio —
   Caput apri defero
   Reddens laudes Domino.

The boar's head, as I understand,
Is the rarest dish in all this land,
And when bedecked with a gay garlànd
Let us *servire cantico —*
   Caput apri defero
   Reddens laudes Domino.

Our steward hath provided this
In honour of the King of bliss,
Which on this day to be served is
In reginensi atrio —
   Caput apri, &c.

The annual feast itself has changed a little. To allow the college staff to
have Christmas day off, the Boar's-Head Gaudy is now some days earlier;
and the head 'bedecked with bays and rosemary' is a plaster replica.

For anyone who wishes to revive the real thing, here is a recipe,
courtesy of the Queen's College archivist: Cover the head with salt, leave
it for several days, plunge it into water, then salt it again. Repeat until salt
permeates the whole head. Clean it thoroughly, tie it up in a stout cloth,
suspend it in a large copper and simmer for many hours. Then plunge it
into clean cold water. Next day, glaze it, put an orange in its mouth and a
crown on its forehead, and decorate with bays and rosemary.

Heathenish and profane mistletoe

THE REV JOHN BRAND is of opinion that 'although Gay mentions
the mistletoe among those evergreens that were put up in churches, it
never entered those sacred edifices but by mistake, or ignorance of the
sextons, for it was the heathenish and profane plant, as having been of
such distinction in the pagan rites of druidism. And it therefore had its
place assigned it in kitchens, where it was hung up in great state with
its white berries, and whatever female chanced to stand under it, the
young man present either had a right or claimed one of saluting
[kissing] her, and of plucking off a berry at each kiss'.

He adds, 'I have made many diligent inquiries after the truth of
this. I learnt at Bath that it never came into churches there. An old
sexton at Teddington in Middlesex informed me that some mistletoe
was once put up in the church there, but was by the clergyman
immediately ordered to be taken away.'

He quotes from *The Medallic History of Carausius* [1757–9] by William Stukeley, who speaking of the winter solstice, our Christmas,
says: 'This was the most respectable festival of our druids, called
yuletide, when mistletoe, which they called *all-heal*, was carried in
their hands and laid on their altars... The custom is still preserved in

the north, and was lately at York: on the eve of Christmas day they carry mistletoe to the high altar of the cathedral and proclaim a public and universal liberty, pardon and freedom to all sorts of inferior and even wicked people at the gates of the city towards the four quarters of heaven.' This is only a century ago.

The cutting of the mistletoe was a ceremony of great solemnity with our ancient ancestors. The people went in procession. The bards walked first singing canticles and hymns; a herald preceded three druids with implements for the purpose. Then followed the prince of the druids accompanied by all the people. He mounted the oak, and cutting the mistletoe with a golden sickle, presented it to the other druids, who received it with great respect, and on the first day of the year distributed it among the people as a sacred and holy plant, crying, 'The mistletoe for the new year.'

John Gay, in *Trivia, or the Art of Walking the Streets of London*, 1716, has this:

> Christmas, the joyous period of the year!
> Now with bright holly all the temples strow,
> With laurel green and sacred mistletoe.

We'll sing and delight ye

In *A Select Collection of* Poems (5 vol, 1780–82) published by the eminent printer, poet, antiquary and editor John Nichols (1745–1826), Hone finds some verses 'which seem to have proceeded from his own pen' in 1780:

To H——y M———n, Esq
On his refusing a CHRISTMAS DINNER *with a Friend on pretence of gallanting some Ladies to Leicester*

> When you talk about Leicester
> I hope you're a jester.
> Why desert an old friend
> For no purpose or end?
> But to play the gallant
> With ladies who'll flaunt,
> And who, cruel as vain,
> Will rejoice in your pain!
> No — come to our pudding.
> We'll put all things good in.
> Give you beef, the sirloin,
> If with us you'll dine;
> Perhaps too a capon
> With greens and with bacon.
> Give you port and good sherry
> To make your heart merry.

Then sit down to a pool   *card game*
'Stead of playing the fool,
Or a rubber at whist;
But for this, as you list.
Next, give muffins and tea,
As you sometimes give me.
As for supper, you know,
A potato, or so,
Or a bit of cold ham,
As at night we ne'er cram;
Or a tart, if you please,
With a slice of mild cheese.
Then we'll sing — sing, did I say?
Yes, 'The Vicar of Bray';
And what I know you don't hate,
'My fond shepherds of late'.
Nor think me a joker
If I add 'Ally Croaker'.
In fine, we'll sing and delight ye
Till ye say, 'Friends, good night t' ye.'

Hone learns that Nichols has just died. In a footnote he records his warm gratitude to him: because *The Gentleman's Magazine*, which Nichols edited from 1792, gave *The Every-Day Book* 'much assistance' (as a source) and a helpful notice; but above all because when Hone's name 'appeared a few years ago in the Domestic Occurrences' (over his blasphemy trials) the magazine's reports were 'unaccompanied by remarks which some of its admirers might perhaps at that time have admired'.

House to house with the hoden

AT RAMSGATE in Kent, they begin the festivities of Christmas by a curious musical procession. A party of young people procure the head of a dead horse, which is affixed to a pole about four feet in length. A string is tied to the lower jaw. A horse-cloth is then attached to the whole, under which one of the party gets, and by frequently pulling the string keeps up a loud snapping noise, and is accompanied by the rest of the party grotesquely habited and ringing handbells.

They thus proceed from house to house, sounding their bells and singing their carols and songs. They are commonly gratified with beer and cake, or perhaps with money. This is provincially called a *hodening*; and the figure above described a 'hoden' or wooden horse. This curious ceremony is also observed in the Isle of Thanet on Christmas eve, and is supposed to be an ancient relic of a festival ordained to commemorate our Saxon ancestors' landing.

Bring out the cup of kindness

Hoary and dim and bare and shivering,
Like a poor almsman comes the aged year,
With kind 'God save you all, good gentlefolks!'
Heap on fresh fuel, make a blazing fire,
Bring out the cup of kindness, spread the board,
And gladden winter with our cheerfulness.
Wassail! To you and yours and all! — All health!   *Hone*

Christmas hospitality declines

IT IS REMARKED in the *Literary Pocket Book* that now Christmas day
only or at most a day or two are kept by people in general; the rest are
school holidays. 'But formerly there was nothing but a run of merry
days from Christmas eve to Candlemas [February 2], and the first
twelve in particular were full of triumph and hospitality. We have
seen but too well the cause of this degeneracy. What has saddened our
summer-time has saddened our winter. What has taken us from our

fields and may-flowers, and suffered them to smile and die alone as if they were made for nothing else, has contradicted our flowing cups at Christmas. The middle classes make it a sorry business of a pudding or so extra, and a game at cards. The rich invite their friends to their country houses, but do little there but gossip and gamble; and the poor are either left out entirely or presented with a few clothes and eatables that make up a wretched substitute for the long and hospitable intercourse of old.

'All this is so much the worse, inasmuch as Christianity had a special eye to those feelings which should remind us of the equal rights of all; and the greatest beauty in it is not merely its charity ... but its being alive to the *sentiment* of charity, which is still more opposed to these proud distances and formal dolings-out...'

And carols go out of fashion

CAROLS begin to be spoken of as not belonging to this century, and few perhaps are aware of the number of these compositions now printed. The editor of *The Every-Day Book* has upwards of ninety, all at this time published annually. This collection he has had little opportunity of increasing except when in the country he has heard an old woman singing an old carol, and brought back the carol in his pocket... These ditties, which now exclusively enliven the industrious servant-maid and the humble labourer, gladdened the festivity of royalty in ancient times...

The custom of singing carols at Christmas prevails in Ireland to the present day. In Scotland, where no church feasts have been kept since the days of John Knox, the custom is unknown. In Wales it is still preserved to a greater extent, perhaps, than in England. At a former period the Welsh had carols adapted to most of the ecclesiastical festivals, and the four seasons of the year... After the turn of midnight at Christmas eve, service is performed in the churches, followed by the singing of carols to the harp... They are sung in like manner in the houses... *Blodeugerdd Cymri*, or the 'anthology of Wales', contains forty-eight Christmas carols, nine summer carols, three May carols, one winter carol, one nightingale carol and a carol to Cupid...

In the rage for 'collecting' almost everything, it is surprising that collectors have almost overlooked carols as a class of popular poetry... The woodcuts round the annual sheets, and the melody of 'God rest you merry gentlemen', delighted my childhood; and I still listen with pleasure to the shivering carolist's evening chant towards the clean kitchen window decked with holly, the flaring fire showing the whitened hearth and reflecting gleams of light from the dresser...

In *Poor Robin's Almanac* for 1695 there is a Christmas carol., which is there called 'A Christmas Song', beginning thus:

> Now thrice welcome, Christmas,
> Which brings us good cheer,
> Minced-pies and plum-porridge,
> Good ale and strong beer,
> With pig, goose and capon,
> The best that may be,
> So well doth the weather
> And our stomachs agree...

More shall be said [on carols] in the year 1826 if the editor of *The Every-Day Book* live and retain his faculties to that time. He now, however, earnestly requests of every one of its readers in every part of England to collect every carol that may be singing at Christmas-time in the year 1825, and convey these carols to him ... with accounts of manners and customs peculiar to their neighbourhood...

In praise of card-playing

In this item and the next, Hone gives us glimpses of his family. The nine children round the table, and the baby, are his. Card-playing, he says, is 'resorted to during the twelve days of Christmas as of ancient custom'.

PERSONS who are opposed to this recreation from religious scruples do not seem to distinguish between its use and its abuse... Cards are not here introduced with a view of seducing parents to rear their sons as gamblers and blacklegs, or their daughters to 'a life of scandal, an old age of cards'... Persons who are wholly debarred from such amusements in their infancy frequently abuse a pleasure they have been wholly restrained from...

Imagine a juvenile party closely seated round a large table with a Pope Joan board in the middle, each well supplied with mother-o'-pearl fish and counters in little Chinese ornamented red and gold trays; their faces and the candles lighting up the room; their bright eyes sparkling after the cards, watching the turn-up, or peeping into the pool to see how rich it is; their growing anxiety to the rounds, till the lucky card decides the richest stake. Then the shout out of 'Rose has got it!' 'It's Rose's!'

'Here, Rose, here they are — take 'em all. Here's a *lot!*'

Emma and John and Alfred and William's hands thrust forth to help her to the prize; Sarah and Fanny, the elders of the party, laughing at their eagerness; the more sage Matilda checking it, and counting how many fish Rose has won. Rose, amazed at her sudden wealth, talks the least. Little Samuel, who is too young to play but has been allowed a place with some of the 'pretty fish' before him, claps his hands and halloos, and throws his playthings to increase Rose's treasure. And baby Ellen sits in mother's lap, mute from surprise at the 'uproar wild', till a loud crow and the quick motion of her legs proclaim her delight at the general joy, which she suddenly suspends in astonishment at the many fingers pointed towards her with 'Look at baby! look at baby!' and gets smothered with kisses, from which mother vainly endeavours to protect her. And so they go on, till ... mother bids them to 'go and sit down, and be good children, and not make so much noise'... Two or three of the least help up Samuel, who is least of all, and mother desires them to 'take care, and mind he does not fall'. Matilda begins to dress the board ... and once more they are 'as merry as grigs'.   [*January 1825. A year later, note the new baby, Number Eleven:*]

The Christmas Days

A Family Sketch

Bring me a garland of holly,
    Rosemary, ivy and bays.
Gravity's nothing but folly
    Till after the Christmas days.
Fill out a glass of bucellas.   *Portuguese white wine*
    Here boys! Put the crown on my head.
Now boys — shake hands — be good fellows,
    And all be *good men* when I'm dead.

Come, girls, come! Now for your kisses.
    Hearty ones — louder — loud — louder!
How I'm surrounded with blisses!
    Proud men may here see a prouder.
Now you rogues, go kiss your mother.
    Ah! ah! — she won't let you? — pho! pho!
Gently — there, there now! — don't smother.
    Old lady! come, *now* I'll kiss *you.*

Here, take the garland, and wear it.
    'Nay, nay!' But you must and you shall,
For *here's such a kiss!* Come, don't fear it.
    If you do, turn round to the wall.
A kiss too for Number Eleven,
    The new-come — the young Christmas berry,
My Alice! who makes my girls seven,
    And makes merry Christmas more merry.

Another good glass of bucellas
    While I've the crown on my head.
Laugh on, my good girls and good fellows,
    Till it's off — then off to bed.
Hey! Now for the Christmas holly,
    Rosemary, ivy and bays.
Gravity's nothing but folly
    Till after the Christmas days.   *December 1825*

And every hearth makes room

Glad Christmas comes, and every hearth
    Makes room to give him welcome now.
E'en want will dry its tears in mirth
    And crown him with a holly bough.
                    Clare, *The Shepherd's Calendar*, December

Harriet Dunn's plomb-pooding

Hone finds this in a newspaper of 1823:

THE HABITS and customs of the Parisians vary much from those of our own metropolis at all times, but at no time more than at this festive season. An Englishman in Paris who had been for some time without referring to his almanac would not know Christmas day from another by the appearance of the capital. It is indeed set down as a *jour de fête* in the calendar, but all the ordinary business of life is transacted. The streets are, as usual, crowded with wagons and coaches; the shops, with few exceptions, are open, although on other *fête* days the order for closing them is rigorously enforced, and if not attended to, a fine levied; and at the churches nothing extraordinary is going forward. All this is surprising in a catholic country...

On Christmas eve, indeed, there is some bustle for a midnight mass, to which immense numbers flock, as the priests on this occasion get up a showy spectacle which rivals the theatres. The altars are dressed with flowers and the churches decorated profusely, but there is little in all this to please men who have been accustomed to the John Bull mode of spending the evening. The good English habit of meeting together to forgive offences and injuries and to cement reconciliations is here unknown...

On Christmas day all the English cooks in Paris are in full business. The queen of cooks, however, is Harriet Dunn of the Boulevard. As Sir Astley Cooper [surgeon] among the cutters of limbs, and d'Egville [dancer] among the cutters of capers, so is Harriet Dunn among the professors of one of the most necessary, and in its results most grati-fying, professions of existence. Her services are secured beforehand by special retainers, and happy is the peer who can point to his pudding and declare that it is of the true 'Dunn' composition. Her fame has even extended to the provinces. For some time previous to Christmas day she forwards puddings in cases to all parts of the country, ready cooked and fit for the table after the necessary warming.

All this, of course, is for the English. No prejudice can be stronger than that of the French against plum-pudding. A Frenchman will dress like an Englishman, swear like an Englishman and get drunk like an Englishman, but if you would offend him forever, compel him to eat plum-pudding. A few of the leading restaurateurs, wishing to appear extraordinary, have *plomb-pooding* upon their cartes, but in no instance is it ever ordered by a Frenchman...

Louis XVIII [king of France 1814–24], either to show his contempt of the prejudices of his countrymen, or to keep up a custom which suits his palate [*he spent years in exile in England*], has always an enormous pudding on Christmas day, the remains of which ... he requires to be eaten by the servants, *bon gré, mauvais gré*; but in this instance even the commands of sovereignty are disregarded except by the numerous English in his service, consisting of several valets, grooms, coachmen, &c, besides a great number of ladies' maids...

Christmas Out of Town

For many a winter in Billiter Lane
My wife, Mrs Brown, was ne'er heard to complain.
At Christmas the family met there to dine
On beef and plum-pudding and turkey and chine.
Our bark has now taken a contrary heel:
My wife has found out that the sea is genteel.
　　To Brighton we duly go scampering down —
　　For nobody now spends his Christmas in town.

In Billiter Lane in this mirth-moving time
The lamplighter brought us his annual rhyme;
The tricks of Grimaldi were sure to be seen;
We carved a Twelfth-cake and we drew king and queen.
Now we lodge on the Steine, in a bow-windowed box
That beckons upstairs every zephyr that knocks.
　　The sun hides his head and the elements frown —
　　Still, nobody now spends his Christmas in town.

At Brighton I'm stuck up in Lucombe's Loo-shop,
Or walk upon bricks till I'm ready to drop;
Throw stones at an anchor — look out for a skiff —
Or view the chain pier from the top of the cliff,
Till winds from all quarters oblige me to halt
With sand in my eyes and my mouth full of salt.
　　Yet, still, I am suffering with folks of renown —
　　For nobody now spends his Christmas in town.

The wind gallops in at the full of the moon
And puffs up the carpet like Sadler's balloon.
My drawing-room rug is besprinkled with soot
And there is not a lock in the house that will shut.
At Mahomet's steam-bath I lean on my cane
And mutter in secret, 'Ah, Billiter Lane!'
　　But would not express what I think for a crown —
　　For nobody now spends his Christmas in town.

The duke and the earl are not cronies of mine;
His Majesty never invites me to dine;

The marquis don't speak when we meet on the pier,
Which makes me suspect that I'm NOBODY here.
If that be the case — why then, welcome again
Twelfth-cake and snap-dragon in Billiter Lane.
    Next winter I'll prove to my dear Mrs Brown
    That NOBODY now spends his Christmas in town.
                            from *The New Monthly Magazine*, Jan 1825

Boxing-day extortioners

A WRITER in 1731 describes Boxing day... 'By the time I was up, my
servants could do nothing but run to the door. Inquiring the meaning,
I was answered, the people were come for their *Christmas box*...
Because I had laid out a great deal of ready money with my brewer,
baker and other tradesmen, they kindly thought it my duty to present
their servants with some money for the favour of having their goods.

'This provoked me a little, but being told it was "the custom", I
complied. These were followed by the watch, beadles, dustmen and
an innumerable tribe; but what vexed me most was the clerk, who has
an extraordinary place and makes as good an appearance as most
tradesmen in the parish. To see him come a-boxing, alias begging, I
thought was intolerable. However, I found it was "the custom" too, so
I gave him half-a-crown; as I was likewise obliged to do to the bellman
for breaking my rest for many nights together.

'Having talked this matter over with a friend, he promised to carry
me where I might see the good effects of this giving box-money. In the
evening, away we went to a neighbouring alehouse, where abundance
of these gentry were assembled round a stately piece of roast beef and
as large a plum-pudding. When the drink and brandy began to work,
they fell to reckoning of their several gains that day. One [house-
holder] was called a stingy dog for giving but sixpence; another called
an extravagant fool for giving half-a-crown...

'Some of them were got to cards by themselves, which soon
produced a quarrel and broken heads. In the interim came in some of
their wives, who roundly abused the people for having given them
money, adding that instead of doing good it ruined their families and
set them in a road of drinking and gaming...

'My friend next carried me to the upper end of Piccadilly, where,
[up] one pair of stairs over a stable, we found near a hundred people
of both sexes, *some masked*, others not, a great part of which were
dancing to the music of two sorry fiddles... There were footmen,
servant-maids, butchers, apprentices, oyster- and orange-women, and
sharpers, which appeared to be the best of the company. This horrid

place seemed to be a complete nursery for the gallows. My friend informed me it was called a "threepenny hop". And while we were talking, to my great satisfaction, by order of the Westminster justices, *to their immortal honour*, entered the constables and their assistants, who carried off all the company that was left; and had not my friend been known to them, we might have paid dear for our curiosity.'

A fool and his money

In *A Banquet of Jests*, 1634, there is a pleasant story of Archee, the king's [James I's] jester, who, having fooled many, was fooled himself. Coming to a nobleman upon new year's day to bid him goodmorrow, Archee received twenty pieces of gold; but covetously desiring more, he shook them in his hand and said they were too light. The donor answered, 'I prithee, Archee, let me see them again, for there is one amongst them I would be loth to part with.' Archee, expecting the sum to be increased, returned the pieces to his lordship, who put them in his pocket with this remark, 'I once gave money into a fool's hand, who had not the wit to keep it.'

Theatre and oysters and keeping it up

In the Christmas season, the Covent Garden and Drury Lane Theatres are especially busy. The scene in January 1826:

WITHIN a hundred yards of either playhouse, hands are continually thrust into each coach window, with 'A bill of the play' and repeated cries of 'Only a penny!' The coach-door being opened, down fall the steps with a sharp clackity-clack-click, and the companies alight, if they can, without the supernumerary aid of attendant pliers [touting in the hope of tips], who offer their ever-ready arms to lean upon, and kindly entreat, 'Take care, sir! Mind how you step, ma'am. This way if you please, this way,' all against your will, and ending with 'I hope you'll please to remember a poor fellow,' the poor fellow having done nothing but interrupt you...

Then, when the whole is over, there is the strict blockade of coaches further than the eye can reach; servants looking out for the parties they came with, and getting up their masters' carriages; and a full cry of hackney coachmen and their representatives, vociferating, 'Want a coach, sir? Here's your coach, sir! Which is it, sir? Coach to the City, sir! West End, sir! Here, coach to the City! Coach to Whitechapel! Coach to Portman-square! Coach to Pentonville! Coach to the Regent's Park! This way, this way! Stand clear there! Chariot or a coach, sir? No chariots, sir, and all the coaches are hired! There's a coach here, sir — just below! Coachman, draw up!' And drawing up is impossible, and there is an incessant confusion of calls and complaints, and running against each other...

Pedestrians make their way home, or to the inns, as fast as possible, or turn in to sup at the fish-shops, which in five minutes are more lively than their oysters were at any time.

'Waiter! Waiter!'

'Yes sir! Attend to you directly, sir! Yours is gone for, sir!'

'Why, I've ordered nothing!'

'It's coming directly, sir'

'Ginger-beer — why, this is poison!'

'Spruce — why, this is ginger-beer!'

'Porter, sir.'

'I told you brandy and water!'

'Stewed oysters! I ordered scolloped!'

'When am I to have *my* supper?

'You've had it, sir— I beg your pardon, sir, the gentleman that sat here is gone, sir...'

And he who has patience is sure to be indulged with an opportunity of retaining it, amidst loud talking and laughter; varied views on the new pantomime; conflicting testimony as to the merits of the clown and the harlequin, the 'new scenery, dresses and ma-chinery'; likings and dislikings of certain actresses, the lovely Miss So-and-so or that detestable woman Mrs Such-an-one; that clever fellow Thing-a-Merry or that stupid dog What-d'ye-call-um.

These topics failing, and the oysters discussed, then are stated and considered the advantages of taking something 'to keep 'em down'; the comparative merits of Burton, Windsor or Edinburgh ale; the qualities of porter; the wholesomeness of smoking; the difference between a pipe and a cigar and the preference of one to the other; whether brandy or rum or the clear spirit of juniper is the best preservative of health; which of the company or their friends can drink most; whether the last fight was 'a cross' [a cheat], and who of all men in the fancy [prizefighting] is the most game; whether the magistrates dare to interfere with the ring; whether if fighting should be 'put an end to', Englishmen will have half the courage they had three hundred years ago, before prizefighting existed...

On these points, or points like these, the conversation of an oyster-room is turned by sitters after the play, till they adjourn to 'spend the evening' at the flash-and-foolish houses [the Cider Cellar, Coal Hole, Offley's, etc] which keep it up all night in the peculiar neighbourhood of the public [police] office, Bow-street...

More oyster-eating merrymakers

Capital oysters, I declare!
Excellent spruce and ginger beer!
Don't you take vinegar? There's the bread.
We'll just have a pipe — and then to bed.

WHY should not this be deemed a real scene, and as respectable as that just described? It is quite as lively and as intellectual…

Bring us a bowl of the best

A song 'sung in Gloucestershire on new year's eve':

Wassail! wassail! over the town.
Our toast is white, our ale is brown.
Our bowl is made of a maplin tree.
We be good fellows all — I drink to thee.

Here's to ——— and to his right ear.   *the name of some horse*
God send our maister a happy New Year,
A happy New Year as e'er he did see —
With my wassailing bowl I drink to thee.

Here's to ——— and to his right eye.   *the name of another horse*
God send our mistress a good Christmas pie,
A good Christmas pie as e'er I did see —
With my wassailing bowl I drink to thee.

Here's to Filpail and her long tail.   *the name of a cow*
God send our measter us never may fail
          Of a cup of good beer.
          I pray you draw near
And then you shall hear of our jolly wassail.

Be here any maids? I suppose there be some.
Sure they'll not let young men stand on the cold stone.
Sing hey, O maids, come trole back the pin,   *unbolt the door*
And the fairest maid in the house, let us all in.

Come butler, come bring us a bowl of the best.
I hope your soul in heaven may rest.
But if you do bring us a bowl of the small,   *small beer*
Then down fall butler, bowl and all.

Guisards get their hogmanay

A Falkirk man, John Wood Reddock, sends in December 1825 'the first
notice of the acting in our *Daft Days*'. An edited version:

EVERY PERSON knows the tenacious adherence of the Scottish
peasantry to the tales and observances of *auld lang syne*. Towards the
end of the year many superstitions are to this day strictly kept up
among the country people, chiefly as connected with their cattle and
crops... The *amories* [pantries] of every cottager have goodly store of
dainties, invariably including a due proportion of *Scotch drink*....

The grand affair among the boys in the town is to provide themselves with *fausse faces*, or masks; and those with crooked horns and
beards are in greatest demand. A high paper cap, with one of their
great-grandfather's antique coats, then equips them as a *guisard*. They
thus go about the shops *seeking their hogmanay* [new-year gifts].

In the carses [farmlands] and moorlands, however, parties of
guisards [mummers] have long kept up the practice in great style.
Fantastically dressed, and each having his character allotted him, they
go through the farmhouses, and unless denied entrance by being told
that the Old Style [calendar] is kept, perform what must once have
been a connected dramatic piece. We have heard various editions of
this, but the substance of it is something like the following:

One enters first to speak the prologue in the style of the [13th-
century] Chester mysteries... It is usually in these words at present —

Rise up gudewife and shake your feathers.
Dinna think that we're beggars.
We are bairns com'd to play
And for to seek our hogmanay.

Redd up stocks, redd upstools,   *set them in order*
Here comes in a pack of fools.
Muckle head and little wit stand behint the door,
But sic a set as we are ne'er were here before.

One with a sword ... now enters and says:

Here comes in the great king of Macedon
Who has conquered all the world but Scotland alone.
When I came to Scotland my heart grew so cold
To see a *little nation* so stout and so bold,
So stout and so bold, so frank and so free!
Call upon Galgacus to fight wi' me...

We think this speech points out the origin of the story to be the Roman invasion under Agricola, and the name of Galgacus ... makes the famous struggle for freedom by the Scots under that leader, in the battle fought at the foot of the Grampians, the subject of this historical drama [*Agricola eventually beat Galgacus in AD 84*].

Enter Galgacus

Here comes in Galgacus — wha doesna fear my name?
Sword and buckler by my side, I hope to win the game!

They close in a sword-fight, and in the 'hash smash' the chief is victorious. He says:

Down Jack! down to the ground you must go —
  Oh O! what's this I've done?
I've killed my brother Jack, my father's only son!
  Call upon the doctor.

Enter doctor

Here comes in the best doctor that ever Scotland bred...

The doctor then relates his skill in surgery.

Chief   What will ye tak to cure this man?
Doctor Ten pound and a bottle of wine.
Chief   Will six not do?
Doctor No, you must go higher.
Chief   Seven?
Doctor That will not put on the pot — *&c.*

A bargain however is struck, and the doctor says to Jack, 'Start to your feet and stand.'

    Jack Oh-hone! My back, I'm sairly wounded… There's a hole
        in't you may turn your tongue ten times round it.
    Doctor How did you get it?
    Jack Fighting for our land…

During the late war with France, Jack was made to say he had been 'fighting the French' and that the loon who took leg bail [ran away] was no less a personage than Nap *le grand*…

The strange eventful history is however wound up by the entrance of Judas with the [collecting] bag. He says:

    Here comes in Judas — Judas is my name.
    If ye pit nought sillar i' my bag, for gude-sake mind our wame!   *give food*
    When I gaed to the castle yett and tirl'd at the pin   *castle gate*
    They keepit the keys o' the castle wa' and wadna let me in.

    I've been i' the East Carse, I've been i' the West Carse,
        I've been i' the Carse o' Gowrie
    Where the clouds rain a' day wi' peas and wi' beans!
    And the farmers theek houses wi' needles an' pins!   *thatch*
        I've seen geese gaein' on pattens!
    And swine fleeing i' the air like peelings o' onions!

    Our hearts are made o' steel, but our body's sma' as ware.
    If you've onything to gi' us, *stap it in there*!

…One of the guisards who has the best voice generally concludes the exhibition by singing 'an auld Scottish sang'. The most ancient melodies only are considered appropriate for this occasion, and many very fine ones are often sung that have not found their way into collections. Or the group join in a reel … to the merry sound of the fiddle… They anciently however appear to have been accompanied with a musician who played the *kythels* or stock-and-horn … made of the thigh-bone of a sheep and the horn of a bullock.

The above practice, like many customs of the olden time, is now quickly falling into disuse, and the revolution of a few years may witness the total extinction of this seasonable doing…

The kirk of Scotland appears formerly to have viewed these festivities exactly as the Roman church in France did in the sixteenth century… In the parish of Falkirk … so late as the year 1702, a great number of farmers' sons and farm servants from the East Carse were publicly rebuked before the session, or ecclesiastical court, for going about in disguise upon the last night of December that year 'acting things unseemly'; and having professed their sorrow for the sinfulness of the deed, were certified if they should be found guilty of the like in time coming they would be proceeded against after another manner. Indeed, the scandalized kirk might have been compelled to put the

302

cutty stool in requisition [make them do public penance in church]...
• The observance of the old custom of *first fits* [first-footing] upon new year's day is kept up at Falkirk with as much spirit as anywhere else... Soon as the steeple clock strikes the ominous twelve, all is running and bustle and noise. *Hot-pints* in clear-scoured copper kettles are seen in all directions, and a good noggin to the well-known toast, 'A gude new year and a merry han'sel Monday' is exchanged among the people in the streets as well as friends in the houses.

On han'sel Monday the numerous colliers in the neighbourhood ... have a grand main of cocks [cockfights]...

Western mummers 'down along'

The Falkirk account brings a letter from 'J S jun.' about similar mummings. Hone takes the opportunity to say how gratified he will be to hear from readers 'acquainted with customs in their own vicinity similar to those that are informed of in other counties... By this means *The Every-Day Book* will become what it is designed to be made — *a storehouse of past and present manners and customs.*'

J S jun. says the Falkirk play is a variant of what is enacted at Christmas in the western counties of England by 'those paper-decorated, brickdust-bedaubed urchins yclept mummers'. He reports:

TO BE SURE, they do not begin, 'Here comes in the king of Macedon.' But we have instead,

> Here comes old Father Christmas.
> Christmas or Christmas not,
> I hope old Father Christmas
> Never will be forgot.

And then for the Scottish leader Galgacus we find,

> *Here comes in* St George, St George,
> That man of mighty name,
> With *sword and buckler by my side*
> *I hope to win the game.*

These 'western kerns' have it, you see, Mr Editor, 'down along', to use their own dialect, with those of the thistle. Then too we have a fight. Oh! how beautiful to my boyish eyes were their wooden swords and their bullying gait! Then we have a fight, for lo —

> Here come I, the Turkish knight,
> Come from the Soldan's land to fight,   *sultan's*
> And be the foe's blood hot and bold,
> With my sword I'll make it cold...

The cross is victorious, the crescent o'erthrown... The doctor is sent for, and he is addressed, paralleling again our players of 'Scotia's wild domain', with

> Doctor, doctor, can you tell
> What will make a sick man well?

and thereupon he enumerates cures which would have puzzled Galen and put Hippocrates to a non-plus; and he finally agrees, as in the *more classical* drama of your correspondent, to cure our unbeliever for a certain sum. The last scene ... consists in the entrance of the most diminutive of these thespians, bearing, as did Æneas of old, his parent upon his shoulders, and reciting this bit of good truth and joculation (permitting the word) by way of epilogue:

> Here comes I, little Johnny Jack,
> With my wife and family at my back,
> Yet though my body is but small,
> I'm the greatest rogue amongst ye all.
> This is my scrip — so for Christmas cheer,
> *If you've any thing to give, throw it in here...*

I dote upon old customs and I love hearty commemorations, and hence those mimics of whom I have written ... are my delight, and in the laughter and merriment they create I forget to be a critic...

This is our merry night

THE FOLLOWING pleasant old song ... from Joseph Ritson's collection of *Ancient Songs* [1790] was met with by the editor of *The Every-Day Book* in 1819 at the printing-office of Mr Rann at Dudley, printed by him for the wassailers of Staffordshire and Warwickshire. It went formerly to the tune of 'Gallants come away'.

A Carroll for a Wassel-Bowl

> A jolly wassel-bowl,
>   A wassel of good ale —
> Well fare the butler's soul
>   That setteth this to sale,
>   Our jolly wassel.
>
> Good dame, here at your door
>   Our wassel we begin.
> We are all maidens poor,
>   We pray now let us in
>   With our wassel.

Our wassel we do fill
   With apples and with spice.
Then grant us your good will
   To taste here once or twice
      Of our good wassel.

If any maidens be
   Here dwelling in this house
They kindly will agree
   To take a full carouse
      Of our wassel.

But here they let us stand
   All freezing in the cold.
Good master, give command
   To enter and be bold
      With our wassel.

Much joy into this hall
   With us is entered in.
Our master first of all
   We hope will now begin
      Of our wassel.

And after, his good wife
   Our spicèd bowl will try.
The Lord prolong your life!
   Good fortune we espy
      For our wassel.

Some bounty from your hands
   Our wassel to maintain.
We'll buy no house nor lands
   With that which we do gain
      With our wassel.

This is our merry night
   Of choosing king and queen.
Then be it your delight
   That something may be seen
      In our wassel.

It is a noble part
   To bear a liberal mind.
God bless our master's heart,
   For here we comfort find
      With our wassel.

And now we must be gone
   To seek out more good cheer,
Where bounty will be shown

As we have found it here
With our wassel.

'Much joy betide them all'
Our prayers shall be still.
We hope, and ever shall,
For this your great good will
To our wassel.

A good example of an old song being revived among country people by
a local printer. Ritson's source for the carol was *New Christmas Carrols*, a
little black-letter book of 1662, now in the Bodleian — the only known
surviving copy. The tune dates from Shakespeare's time.

Here's to thee, old apple-tree

IT WAS a practice formerly for itinerant minstrels to bear a bowl of
spiced-wine to the houses of the gentry and others from whom they
expected a hospitable reception, and calling their bowl a wassail-bowl,
to drink wassail to their entertainers… There are still places where the
wandering blower of a clarinet and the poor scraper of as poor a
fiddle will this evening [Twelfth Night, January 5] strain their instruments to charm forth the rustic from his dwelling, and drink to him
from a jug of warm ale, spiced with a race of ginger, in the hope of a
pittance for their melody and their wish of wassail…

In certain parts of Devonshire, the farmer, attended by his work-
men, with a large pitcher of cider, goes to the orchard this evening,
and there, encircling one of the best-bearing trees, they drink the
following toast three times:

Here's to thee, old apple-tree,
Whence thou mayst bud, and whence thou mayst blow!
And whence thou mayst bear apples enow!
    Hats full! Caps full!
    Bushel, bushel sacks full,
    And my pockets full too! Huzza!

This done, they return to the house, the doors of which they are sure
to find bolted by the females, who, be the weather what it may, are
inexorable to all entreaties to open them till someone has guessed at
what is on the spit, which is generally some nice little thing, difficult
to be hit on, and is the reward of him who first names it. The doors are
then thrown open and the lucky clodpole receives the titbit…

The Rev John Brand, on the authority of a Cornishman, relates it as
a custom with the Devonshire people to go after supper into the
orchard with a large milkpan full of cider, having roast apples pressed

into it. 'Out of this each person in company takes what is called a clayen cup, that is an earthen cup, full of liquor, and standing under each of the more fruitful apple-trees, passing by those that are not good bearers, he addresses it in the following words:

> Health to thee, good apple-tree,
> Well to bear, pocket-fulls, hat-fulls,
> Peck-fulls, bushel-bag-fulls!

'And then drinking up part of the contents, he throws the rest, with the fragments of the roasted apples, at the tree...'

In the 17th century, according to the poet Robert Herrick, who spent eighteen years in Devon, it was a Christmas-eve ceremony: 'Wassail the trees, that they may bear / You many a plum and many a pear.'

Twelfth Day cakes and coat-tails

IN LONDON, with every pastrycook in the City and at the west end of the town it is 'high change' on Twelfth Day ... attending to the dressing-out of the window, executing orders of the day before, receiving fresh ones... Before dusk the important arrangement of the window is completed. Then the gas is turned on, with supernumerary argand-lamps and manifold waxlights, to illuminate countless cakes of all prices and dimensions that stand in rows and piles...

The richest in flavour and heaviest in weight and price are placed on large and massy salvers ... and all are decorated with all imaginable images of things animate and inanimate. Stars, castles, kings, cottages, dragons, trees, fish, palaces, cats, dogs, churches, lions, milkmaids, knights, serpents and innumerable other forms in snow-white confectionery, painted with variegated colours, glitter by 'excess of light' from mirrors against the walls festooned with 'wonders of Flora'...

The people in the shop hear 'tapping of hammers and peals of laughter from the throng surrounding the house'. What is going on?

BOY I say, I say! Halloo! Here's a piece of work! Look at this gentle-man next to me — his coat-tail's nailed to the window! Look, *look*!
COUNTRYMAN Aye, what?
ALL THE BOYS Ah! ah! ah! Huzza!
COUNTRYMAN Who nailed my coat-tail? Constable!
BOY That's the boy that's got the hammer!
BOY What, *me*? Why, *that's* the boy — there. And there's *another* boy hammering! And there's a *man* with a hammer!
BOY Who pinned that woman to the gentleman?

Technical note: the mis-spelling of 'pastry' in this proof version
of the block was corrected before publication

COUNTRYMAN Constable! constable!

BOY Here comes the constable. *Hark* at him!

CONSTABLE Clear away from the doors! Let the customers go in. Make
way! Let the cakes come out…

ALL THE BOYS Huzza! huzza! *More* people pinned and *plenty* nailed up!

To explain to those who may be ignorant of the practice. On
Twelfth Night in London, boys assemble round the inviting shops and
dextrously nail the coat-tails of spectators who venture near enough to
the bottoms of the window-frames, or pin them together strongly by
their clothes. Sometimes eight or ten persons find themselves thus
connected. The dexterity and force of the nail-driving is so quick and
sure that a single blow seldom fails of doing the business effectually.
Withdrawal of the nail without a proper instrument is out of the
question, and consequently the person nailed must either leave part of
his coat … or quit the spot with a hole in it…

Scarcely a shop in London that offers a halfpenny plain bun to the
purchase of a hungry boy is without Twelfth-cakes and finery. The

gingerbread-makers ... periwig a few plum-buns with sugar frost, and coaxingly interpolate them among their newmade sixes, bath-cakes, parliament [crisp gingerbread] and ladies' fingers. Their staple ware has leaves of untarnished dutch-gilt [tinsel] stuck on. Their upright cylinder-shaped show-glasses, containing peppermint-drops, elecampane [a sweet flavoured with this plant's root], sugarsticks, hardbake [toffee], brandyballs and bull's-eyes, are carefully polished...

What a roar of mirth!

At Twelfth Night parties the custom was to have everyone draw for
'characters ' — printed sheets with grotesque figures and comic verses.

YOUNG FOLKS anticipate Twelfth Night as a full source of innocent glee to their light little hearts. Where and what is he who would negative hopes of happiness for a few short hours in the day-spring of life? A gentle spirit in the *London Magazine* beautifully sketches a scene of juvenile enjoyment this evening:

'I love to see an acre of cake spread out — the sweet frost covering the rich earth below — studded all over with glittering flowers, like ice-plants, and red and green knots of sweetmeat, and hollow yellow-crusted crowns, and kings and queens and their paraphernalia. I delight to see a score of happy children sitting huddled all round the dainty fare, eyeing the cake and each other, with faces sunny enough to thaw the winter snow. I like to see the gazing silence which is kept so religiously while the large knife goes its round, and the glistening eyes which feed beforehand on the huge slices, dark with citron and plums, and heavy as gold.

'And then, when the characters are drawn, is it nothing to watch the peeping delight which escapes from their little eyes? One is proud, as king; another stately, as queen. Then there are two whispering grotesque secrets which they cannot contain (those are Sir Gregory Goose and Sir Tunbelly Clumsy). The boys laugh out at their own misfortunes; but the little girls (almost ashamed of their prizes) sit blushing and silent. It is not until the lady of the house goes round that some of the more extravagant fictions are revealed. And then what a roar of mirth! Ha ha! The ceiling shakes, and the air is torn. They bound from their seats like kids, and insist on seeing Miss Thompson's card. Ah! what merry spite is proclaimed — what ostentatious pity! The little girl is almost in tears, but the large lump of allotted cake is placed seasonably in her hands, and the glass of sweet wine "all round" drowns the shrill urchin laughter, and a gentler delight prevails.' Does not this make a charming picture?

Hone quotes John Brand : The practice of choosing 'king' on Twelfth Day is similar to a custom that existed among the ancient Greeks and Romans, who on the festival days of Saturn [the Saturnalia], about this season of the year, drew lots for kingdoms, and like kings exercised their temporary authority.

And Thomas Fosbroke on 16th-century ways: The cake was full of plums, with a bean in it for the king and a pea for the queen, so as to determine them by their slices. Sometimes a penny was put in the cake, and the person who obtained it, becoming king, crossed all the beams and rafters of the house against devils. A chafing-dish with burning frankincense was also lit, and the odour snuffed up by the whole family to keep off disease for the year. After this, the master and mistress went round the house with the pan, a taper and a loaf, against witchcraft.

Night parade of the flaming tree

Hone's correspondent in Westmorland (see his account of Brough fair, pages 246–7), tells of the town's Twelfth Night parading of the 'holly tree':

FORMERLY the 'holly tree' at Brough was really holly, but ash being abundant, the latter is now substituted.

There are two head inns in the town which provide for the cere-mony alternately, though the good townspeople mostly lend their assistance in preparing the tree, to every branch of which they fasten a torch. About eight o'clock in the evening it is taken to a convenient part of the town, where the torches are lighted, the town band accompanying ... and after divers salutes and huzzas from the spectators, is carried up and down the town in stately procession, usually by a person of renowned strength named Joseph Ling... Many of the inhabitants carry lighted branches and flambeaus, and rockets, squibs, &c, are discharged on the joyful occasion.

After the tree is thus carried and the torches are sufficiently burnt, it is placed in the middle of the town, when it is cheered by the surrounding populace and is afterwards thrown among them. They eagerly watch for this opportunity, and clinging to each end of the tree endeavour to carry it away to the inn they are contending for, where they are allowed their usual quantum of ale and spirits, and pass a 'merry night', which seldom breaks up before two in the morning.

Although the origin of this usage is lost ... yet it may not be a strained surmise to derive it from the church ceremony of the day when branches of trees were carried in procession to decorate the altars in commemoration of the offerings of the Magi...

Amid the feasting, a touch of charity

As the festive season draws to an end, Hone quotes from *The Mirror of the Month* a piece that glances at less merry matters. (The *Now … now … now* structure is borrowed from an essay by Leigh Hunt.)

NOW, the cloudy canopy of seacoal smoke that hangs over London, and crowns her queen of capitals, floats thick and threefold, for fires and feastings are rife and everybody is either 'out' or 'at home' every night.

Now, if a frosty day or two does happen to pay us a flying visit, on its way to the North Pole, the little boys make slides on the pathways, for lack of ponds; and, it may be, trip up an occasional housekeeper just as he steps out of his own door, who forthwith vows vengeance in the shape of ashes on all the slides in his neighbourhood, not, doubtless, out of vexation at his own mishap and revenge against the petty perpetrators of it, but purely to avert the like from others…

Now the labour of the husbandman is, for once in the year, at a stand, and he haunts the alehouse fire, or lolls listlessly over the half-door of the village smithy and watches the progress of the labour which he unconsciously envies, tasting for once in his life (without knowing it) the bitterness of that *ennui* which he begrudges to his betters.

Now melancholy-looking men wander by twos and threes through market-towns, with their faces as blue as the aprons that are twisted round their waists; their ineffectual rakes resting on their shoulders and a withered cabbage hoisted upon a pole; and sing out their doleful petition of 'Pray remember the poor gardeners, who can get no work!' [because everything is frozen: the phrase was often 'poor *froze-out* gardeners'].

Now, however, not to conclude mournfully, let us remember that the officers and some of the principal inhabitants of most parishes in London, preceded by their beadle in the full majesty of a full greatcoat and gold-laced hat, with his walking staff of state higher than himself, and headed by a goodly polished silver globe, go forth from the vestry room and call on every chief parishioner for a voluntary contribution towards a provision for cheering the abode of the needy at this cheerful season.

And *now* the unfeeling and mercenary urge 'false pretences' … with the vain hope of concealing their private reasons for refusing public charity. And *now* the upright and kindhearted welcome the annual call and dispense bountifully. Their prosperity is a blessing. Each scattereth and yet increaseth. Their pillows are pillows of peace…

The farmers sip their ale

JANUARY

Now, musing o'er the changing scene
Farmers behind the tavern screen
Collect; — with elbow idly press'd
On hob reclines the corner's guest,
Reading the news, to mark again
The bankrupt lists or price of grain.
Puffing the while his red-tipped pipe,
He dreams o'er troubles nearly ripe,
Yet winter's leisure to regale,
Hopes better times, and sips his ale.

John Clare, *The Shepherd's Calendar*

BIBLIOGRAPHY

ITEMS PUBLISHED BY HONE:
A SELECT LIST

Caricature prints drawn and etched by George Cruikshank

Louis XVIII Climbing the Mât de Cocagne, Fast Colours, Afterpiece to the Tragedy of Waterloo, 1815

Saluting the Regent's Bomb [pronounced 'bum'] and The Royal Shambles, 1816

Broadsides, etc, illustrated by Cruikshank

Hone's View of the Regent's Bomb, The Yacht for the R——t's B–m–, 1816

Great Gobble Gobble Gobble Gobble, 1817 (on Hone's trial victories)

Bank Restriction Barometer and Bank Restriction Note, 1819

Satirical pamphlets, unillustrated

The Late John Wilkes's Catechism of a Ministerial Member, The Political Litany, The Sinecurist's Creed, 1817

The Spirit of Despotism (by Vicesimus Knox), 1821

Pamphlets illustrated by Cruikshank

The Political House that Jack Built, 1819

The Man in the Moon (this one not written by Hone), *The Queen's Matrimonial Ladder* and *Non Mi Ricordo*, 1820

The Right Divine of Kings to Govern Wrong! Dedicated to the Holy Alliance (based on Daniel Defoe's *Jure Divino*); *The Political Showman —*

At Home!; A Slap at Slop and the Bridge-Street Gang (newspaper format, then octavo), 1821

Books

William Hazlitt's *Political Essays*, 1818

The Three Trials of William Hone for Publishing Three Parodies, 1818

The Apocryphal New Testament, 1820

Ancient Mysteries Described, Especially the English Miracle Plays, Founded on Apocryphal New Testament Story, 1823 (facsimile edition, Ward Lock, 1970)

Hone's Popular Political Tracts, 1825 (reissue of eight items)

Facetiae and Miscellanies (reissue of 12 items; 120 Cruikshank cuts), 1827

Periodicals

The Reformist's Register, weekly, 1816–17

The Every-Day Book, weekly, 1825 and 1826 (and each year as annual volumes)

The Table Book, weekly, 1827 (and as two half-year volumes)

EDITED BY HONE

New edition of Joseph Strutt's *The Sports and Pastimes of the People of England* (1801), with 136 wood-engravings and index, 1830 (four reissues, 1833–41)

The Year Book of Daily Recreation and Information, 1831, monthly and as annual volume; publisher Thomas Tegg

[Volumes of *Every-Day Book*, *Table Book* and *Year Book* were reissued from stereotype plates in 1841 and later; and in photographic facsimile by the Gale Research Company, Detroit, 1966–7, with introduction by Leslie Shepard.]

SOME SOURCES HONE USED FOR *EVERY-DAY BOOK*, ETC

Brady, John, *Clavis Calendaria ... illustrated with ecclesiastical, historical and classical anecdotes*, 1812

Brand, the Rev John, *Observations on Popular Antiquities, chiefly Illustrating the Origin of our Vulgar Customs, Ceremonies and Superstitions*, 1777; revised and enlarged by Henry Ellis, FRS, 1813

Douce, Francis, *Illustrations of Shakespeare and of Ancient Manners*, 1807

Fosbroke, the Rev Thomas, *Encylopædia of Antiquities*, 1825 (revised edition, 1840)

Googe, Barnaby, *The Popish Kingdome*, 1570, translated from Thomas Kirchmeyer, called Naogeorgus (for its section on customs and superstitions)

Hutchinson, William, *A View of Northumberland*, 1778

Misson, Henri, *M. Misson's Memoirs and Observations in his Travels over England*, 1719 (first published in French, 1698)

Polwhele, Richard, *The History of Cornwall*, 1803

Sinclair, Sir John, *The Statistical Account of Scotland*, 21 vol, Edinburgh, 1791

Stewart, William Grant, *The Popular Superstitions and Festive Amusements of the Highlanders of Scotland*, Edinburgh, 1823

Sykes, John, *Local Records, or Historical Register of Remarkable Events*, Newcastle upon Tyne, 1824

Tusser, Thomas, *Five Hundreth Pointes of Good Husbandrie ... of Good Huswiferie*, 1573; *Tusser Redivivus*, edited version with notes, etc, by Daniel Hillman, 1710 (both were often reissued)

(*Many other sources are cited in the body of the book*)

A LITTLE FURTHER BACKGROUND ON HONE

Rickword, Edgell, *Radical Squibs and Loyal Ripostes*, Bath, 1971: Hone's 1819–21 pamphlets, plus counterattacking Tory ones

Hone, J Ann, *For the Cause of Truth: Radicalism in London 1796–1821*, Oxford, 1982

Patten, Robert, *George Cruikshank's Life, Times, and Art*, Rutgers University Press and Lutterworth, Cambridge, 2 vol, 1992, 1996

(*And see the source-notes opposite*)

SOURCE-NOTES
TO PAGES 1–18

1 *Every-Day Book*, vol I, column 859

2 *Every-Day Book*, same article

3 Frederick Hackwood,*William Hone: His Life and Times*, 1912, p 34, quoting Hone's manuscript autobiography

4 Hone, *Aspersions Answered*, 1824, p 61

5 *The Late John Wilkes's Catechism of a Ministerial Member*

6 Hackwood, op cit, p 40

7 Hackwood, p 183

8 Hackwood, pp 186–7

9 *Aspersions Answered*, p 49

10 Hone, *Facetiae and Miscellanies*, introduction, written 1822

11 *Every-Day Book*, vol II, column 1021

12 Letter dated 22 November 1822 in Hone collection sold at Sotheby's, London, 1989; now in United States

13 Letter dated 31 July 1823 to John Bowring, in the same collection

14 Albert M Cohn, *George Cruikshank: A Catalogue Raisonné*, 1924, p xiii; original letter, 11 January 1821, in Berg collection, New York Public Library

15 British Library manuscript, Add 37949, folio 144, 6 October 1824

16 BL ms Add 40120, f 226v

17 BL ms Add 50746, f 13, 14 January 1825

18 *Table Book*, vol II, column 148 (July 1827)

19 BL ms Add 40856, f 19–20, 5 October 1825

20 *Every-Day Book*, II, column 73

21 *Every-Day Book*, I, columns 927–31

22 *Table Book*, I, column 111

23 Hackwood, p 286

24 Hackwood, p 195

25 BL ms Add 40856, f 25–6, 24 April 1826

26 Hackwood, p 248

27 BL ms Add 50746, f 21, 4 November 1828

28 Letter dated 7 May 1829 in Sotheby's 1989 sale

29 BL ms Add 40856, f 44, 6 January 1832

30 Add 40856, f 48, 2 February 1832

31 Bodleian Library ms Douce d.28, 4 December 1832

32 *Aspersions Answered*, 1824, p 66

33 Hackwood, p 57

34 BL ms Add 40120, f 50–51, 30 November 1840

35 *The Letters of Charles Dickens*, 1965—, edited by Madeline House and Graham Storey, vol III, p 337

36 op cit, p 453

INDEX